Analyses of Musical Classics
Book 3

By the same author

A GRADED MUSIC COURSE FOR SCHOOLS
Book One
Book Two
Book Three

SCORE READING, FORM AND HISTORY
Book Four of *A Graded Music Course for Schools*

ADDITIONAL SIGHT-SINGING EXERCISES
For use with *A Graded Music Course for Schools*

HARMONY

MELODY WRITING AND ANALYSIS

READ, SING AND PLAY
Book One   Teacher's and Pupils' Book
Book Two   Pupils' Book

BASIC MUSIC KNOWLEDGE

ANALYSES OF MUSICAL CLASSICS
Book One
Book Two

GRADED AURAL TESTS FOR ALL PURPOSES

Analyses
of Musical Classics
Book 3

Annie O. Warburton

Longman

LONGMAN GROUP LIMITED
London

*Associated companies, branches and
representatives throughout the world*

© Longman Group Ltd 1971

First published 1971
Fifth impression 1978

ISBN 0582 32487 4

ACKNOWLEDGEMENTS
The music on the cover is the original
manuscript of 'Rejoice in the Lord alway' by
Purcell, and is reproduced by courtesy of the
Trustees of the British Museum.

Printed in Hong Kong by
Commonwealth Printing Press Ltd

Preface

It is hoped that this, the third book of *Musical Analyses*, will prove as acceptable to teachers and students as the other two have been.

Like the other two, it consists of analyses of well-known works which have been or are likely to be prescribed for such examinations as O Level in the General Certificate of Education. Many of these analyses have previously appeared in the *Music Teacher*, and acknowledgment is gratefully made to Evans Brothers Ltd, who publish that magazine.

The present book consists of analyses of fifty-three works, taken chronologically in order of their composers' lives. Further general information about how to use these analyses, may be found in Book 1 of the series.

The collection includes five complete symphonies, seven complete concertos or orchestral suites, two overtures, five modern orchestral works, ten complete chamber works, ten complete keyboard sonatas or suites, and eleven complete choral works including Haydn's 'Nelson' mass and Brahms's *Requiem*.

Three works, parts of which were analysed in Book 1 or Book 2 of this series, are now completed in Book 3. They are: Part I of Bach's *Christmas Oratorio* (which is really a separate cantata); Brahms's Op 119 for piano; and Ireland's *London Pieces*.

This book can also be used for general study by those students who are not preparing for a particular examination. It should be helpful to anyone who wishes to study a work on his own; and it can also be used as a general basis for class study. It is hoped that it will lead to a greater appreciative understanding of the classics.

A.O.W.

Contents

Haydn

Mozart

Beethoven

Schubert

Mendelssohn

Schumann

Borodin

Brahms

Dvorak

Debussy

Ravel

Strauss

Vaughan Williams

1 Palestrina

Missa Aeterna Christe Munera

Palestrina wrote ninety-three settings of the mass. Some of the earliest were based on a plain song theme in long notes in the tenor part. But he soon discarded this and, after a period when he experimented with a number of contrapuntal devices, he began to write in a simpler style, though there was still a close link with plain song.

Some of his finest masses, including the one to be analysed here, are based upon an 'office' hymn. The Chester edition has a helpful preface, which quotes the hymn in its sixteenth-century version, though it is thought to date from the twelfth century or even earlier. It will be seen that it is on the plan **A B C A**. Each of the three different lines is used in some form in several sections of the mass, providing a motive that is passed from one voice to another, and interweaving to make a lovely texture of sound. **A** is used to represent God the Father, **B** God the Son and **C** God the Holy Ghost.

This mass is a comparatively simple one, both to listen to and to sing, partly because it is written in the Ionian mode, which is easy for us to apprehend as it is our modern major scale. It is, however, transposed a fourth higher, with a flat in the key-signature, so as to suit the voices. (Every mode was available in the 'open' key and also transposed a fourth higher, with a flat in the key signature.) There are a few accidentals in the music, inserted by Palestrina, in accordance with the principles of *Musica Ficta*, and they seem to us, today, to create the effect of modulation. In addition, a few have been added by the editor in the Chester edition, because they would certainly have been sung by Palestrina's singers, in accordance with *Musica Ficta*, even though they were not marked.

The Chester edition prints the music with the crotchet as the beat, rather than the minim which was used in the sixteenth century; and the editor has added marks over notes which require musical stress, to help modern singers realise that the bar line does not necessarily denote an accent, as it does in the music of today. The rhythm is very fluid, with each part carrying its own natural stresses, which are frequently different from those of the other parts.

KYRIE Theme **A**, the first line of the hymn, representing God the Father, is used imitatively for 'Kyrie eleison'; and theme **B**, God the Son, is similarly used for 'Christe eleison' (14). When 'Kyrie eleison' returns (30) a quicker variant of **A** is heard in alto and tenor against **C** in the treble; and the two motives combine to the end.

GLORIA IN EXCELSIS DEO Theme **A** starts imitatively in treble and alto, while a variant of **B** starts at 'Laudamus te' (7). Thereafter Palestrina continues with the usual imitative entries, based on new figures, though at 'tu solus Altissimus' (53) the style becomes momentarily homophonic.

CREDO IN UNUM DEUM This has a homophonic start, based on a rhythmic variant of **A**. A variant of **B** starts imitative entries at 'Visibilium omnium' (6); and at 'Filium Dei' (15), **B**, God the Son theme, appears again, as befits the words. Imitative entries on subordinate themes then continue for some time until **C**, God the Holy Ghost theme, appears at 83 to the words 'Et in Spiritum Sanctum', in homophonic style. Imitative entries return again at 'Et unam sanctam catholicam' (105), and this imitative style continues to the end.

SANCTUS The 'Sanctus' starts with imitative entries of a varied form of **A**. **B** appears at 'Dominus Deus Sabaoth' (13), and **C** at 'Pleni sunt coeli' (23). The style is imitative throughout.

BENEDICTUS The basses are silent in this number until it reaches 'Hosanna'. The 'Benedictus' section begins with imitative entries of an augmented version of **B**, and goes on to a variant of **C** at 'in nomine' (19). When the basses enter at 'Hosanna' (32), **A** is heard imitatively.

2

AGNUS DEI. I This starts with imitative entries of yet another variant of **A**, while a variant of **B** enters at 'qui tollis' (19) and a variant of **C** appears at 'miserere nobis' (22). There seems little doubt that Palestrina is representing the Holy Trinity in a mystical combination here.

AGNUS DEI. II Another variant of **A** now appears in the alto against an independent quicker-moving part in the bass, and the two parts combine for some time. At 'qui tollis' (11) another variant of **B** appears in the bass, followed by the usual imitative entries. But another variant of **A** appears at 'dona nobis pacem' (25), and imitative entries of this bring the mass to an end. Notice that in this final chorus Palestrina uses five vocal parts for the first time, thus providing a fitting climax to the work.

2 Sweelinck

Hodie Christus Natus Est

Sweelinck (1562–1621) was a Dutch organist and composer who, indirectly, had a great effect on Bach and Handel. His father was an organist in Amsterdam, and the son followed in his father's footsteps, living in Amsterdam for the whole of his life. He was organist there for forty-four years and his fame spread throughout Europe. He was a contemporary of the English John Bull, who wrote a fantasia on one of his themes.

Sweelinck was the last of the composers of the Netherlands School, but his teaching spread to other countries, so that he can be said to be the founder of seventeenth-century European organ performance and composition, with its centre in northern Germany, from which Bach and Handel sprang.

He was also known as a composer of vocal music, both sacred and secular, during a period when the old modes were dying out and the classical contrapuntal style of Bach and Handel was being born. Thirty-seven *Cantiones Sacrae* are extant, of which 'Hodie Christus Natus Est' is one of the most famous.

This is a motet in five parts, which is obviously intermediary in style between the sixteenth-century madrigal period and the later classical school. It frequently changes between C and 3/2 time, starts imitative figures and has traces of modal harmony, all features common to the earlier period. Yet it really is in B flat major, with frequent use of dominant and tonic chords; and the cadences are often reiterated, almost as if Sweelinck were underlining the new feeling of tonality. Also he frequently modulates to the dominant key, but only for a short time, without the use of the planned kind of key-scheme which would be found in later composers. In fact, he vacillates between the two keys most of the time, though G minor and C minor are also used. But again, when he moves to these keys, he usually repeats V I several times, as if to show that he really means what he has written—and perhaps also to familiarise the listener with the new tonal effect.

The motet divides into four sections, each of which begins with 'Hodie' in 3/2 time. In Section I the one-bar dotted figure which starts in the tenor (*a*) is repeated immediately by inversion; and then it is taken up in both forms by the other four parts. Then the time signature changes to C and an imitative quaver figure (*b*) starts on 'natus', being sung in all the parts except the bass. It is followed at bar 11 by another figure, (*c*), to the word 'Noe', which is used imitatively in all five parts, repeating V I in F major four times.

Section II returns to the tonic key at 15 in 3/2 time with 'Hodie'; but, although the tenor starts it again, this time the inverted form of (*a*) appears first. It continues with (*d*) to the words 'Salvatur apparuit', in which the main feature is a complete rising scale of B flat major in semibreves in the bass, over which canto firmo quicker imitative parts appear. This is followed by (*e*) 'Alleluia' treated imitatively. Notice how, here and elsewhere, the figure often appears in two-part harmony. It modulates to the dominant key twice but eventually returns to the tonic.

Section III starts with 'Hodie' in its original form at 37; and it continues with (*f*) 'in terra canunt angeli', quite a long figure which is treated imitatively. At 51 the music reverts to 3/2 time, the first time it has done this except when the singers are singing 'Hodie'. A new imitative figure (*g*) starts to the words 'laetantur archangeli', again usually sung by two voices at once. And now Sweelinck ventures away from tonic and dominant keys, writing V I V I in G minor at 58–61, followed by a modulation to C minor which speeds up to common time at 63 and has four cadential repetitions in this key, followed sequentially by four in the tonic key, all to 'Noe' (*h*).

Section IV starts with 'Hodie' at 69 in the same version as II, and is followed by a crotchet 'gloria' (*i*), again frequently sung in two parts at once. Imitative entries of 'In excelsis Deo' (*j*), start at 85, reaching C minor and ending with a tierce de Picardie at 92. The 'gloria' then returns over a dominant pedal of the tonic key at 93, followed by a tonic pedal at 99. Over the tonic pedal 'In excelsis Deo' (*j*), returns. From 105 to the end there is a *stringendo* effect caused by a short four-note figure (*k*), sung in all the parts in turn, sometimes to 'alleluia', sometimes to 'Noe'. Section IV is a longer section than we have heard before, and touches on C minor at 112–3, and F major at 114–5 before reverting to the tonic key. The figure becomes even shorter at 117, consisting of two notes to 'Noe', which build up to a climax and end with a broad plagal cadence.

3 Purcell

Fantasia No 4 in G minor in four parts for strings

(Purcell Society: edited Dent, Novello)

The nine four-part string fantasias were written between June and August 1680, and were based on the style of the old Elizabethan 'fancy', written for a consort of viols by composers such as Byrd. They had no continuo part, and were written in a very contrapuntal style. Three years later Purcell began to write in the more modern style used by contemporary composers such as Corelli, writing trio-sonatas for two violins and a bass, with a continuo part for the harpsichord. These later sonatas were in several movements, whereas all the fantasias are in one movement, though they contain changes of speed, marked by Purcell himself.

The original manuscript of this Fantasia No 4 in G minor was written with its four parts in the treble, alto, tenor and bass clefs, but the Novello edition prints it with the two middle parts using the alto clef, presumably so that they can be played on the viola. Purcell uses the C clef in the soprano, mezzo-soprano, alto and tenor positions in various numbers of these four-part fantasias; but the Novello edition rearranges five of them for violin, two violas and 'cello, and four for two violins, viola and 'cello, according to the range of their middle parts.

THE FIRST SECTION of the fourth Fantasia in G minor starts with imitative entries in 4/2 time. The same figure starts again in the treble half way through bar 7, imitated by the second alto a beat later and then by the bass and the first alto in an inverted form in bar 8.

In bar 9, the same figure appears in augmentation in the treble; and a further augmentation, in varied form, starts in the bass on the last beat of bar 11, while the other parts become more florid.

The same figure returns to its original speed at 14, with imitative entries in the first alto, the treble and the bass, followed by inverted entries in the first alto, starting in the second half of bar 15 and in the treble in 16.

Meanwhile the second alto has the figure in notes four times as long, starting at 14, and the bass has it in notes twice as long at 16 and again at 18. All the four parts come together with an imperfect cadence in the tonic key at 20–21, and this ends the first section of the fantasia.

THE SECOND SECTION, which Purcell himself marked *slow*, starts at the end of 21 and is, in effect, in 8/4 time. It is more harmonic in style, and modulates frequently to the most unexpected keys. It begins with a chord of B flat, but its first cadence is in F sharp minor at 23–4, though it ends with a tierce de Picardie.

Then [7]V I in A major is followed immediately in the treble by a C natural; and the same kind of thing happens again, [7]V I in E major followed immediately by a G natural in the treble. A modulation to C major occurs at 25–6, and this phrase ends at 26–7 in E major.

But again the G sharp in the first alto is immediately contradicted by G natural in the second alto. [7]V I in B major follows at 27–8, again followed by a D natural in the first alto. This juxtaposition of chords containing a major and a minor third is a feature of Purcell's style. The second section of the fantasia ends with a perfect cadence in D major at 28–9.

THE THIRD SECTION, marked *brisk*, starts in 29 with a return to imitative entries. But now two figures are used. The slower figure, (*a*), is heard in the treble at 29, in the bass starting at the end of 30, in the second alto after the rest in 31, and in a modified form in the first alto after the long note in 32 and the treble at the end of the same bar. The quicker figure, (*b*), occurs in the first alto at 29, the second alto at 30, the treble at 31, the bass at the end of the same bar, and several times more in all the parts before the cadence of this

7

section is reached at 35. It is in the tonic key, G minor, but again ending with a tierce de Picardie.

THE FINAL SECTION, starting at the end of 35, is in 4/4 time, though the change is not marked. It consists almost entirely of imitative entries of the figure which starts in the first alto; and ends with a final cadence in 4/2 time, on a chord without a third at all.

4 Purcell

Rejoice in the Lord Alway

Purcell was organist of Westminster Abbey and the Chapel Royal in three reigns: those of Charles II, James II, and William and Mary. 'Rejoice in the Lord Alway' was probably written between 1682 and 1685, during the reign of Charles II; and it reflected this monarch's taste for bright, cheerful music, using string instruments, even in church, that he had acquired when in exile in the court of Louis XIV. Although Purcell continued to write 'full' anthems, which were unaccompanied and followed the tradition of Byrd and Gibbons, the 'verse' anthems, of which this is an example, made use of the new violin family of string instruments, rather than the pre-commonwealth viol. They were used for the first time in 1662. It will be seen that in this anthem they play a very important part, their function being, at least partly, to provide entertainment in church.

This anthem was nicknamed 'the Bell Anthem', even in Purcell's day, because of the bell-like effect of the scale passages in the opening orchestral 'symphony'. The scale in the bass is repeated five times as a ground; and by bar 7 it is being used, in similar or contrary motion, by all the instruments. The passage is then repeated in full, thus making a grand introduction, before the first 'verse', for alto, tenor and bass soloists appears.

A 'verse', in church music of this period, meant a passage for solo singers. This particular passage, **A**, 17–28, is used repeatedly, thus producing the form of a rondo; and it has two variants, one played by the orchestra, the other sung by the full choir.

Notice the syncopated crotchet-minim effect in bar 18, which is typical of Purcell. He was also very fond of dotted notes; and even more of them were performed than were written in the original printed copy, as the comments by Watkins Shaw in the Oxford University Press edition indicate.

The verse, **A**, is in binary form, with the first half reaching the dominant key, G major, by way of D minor; and the second half returning to the tonic, with another touch of D minor at 23–4.

At bar 29 this passage is repeated by the orchestra, with more dotted figures added (the orchestral variant of **A**).

Then the orchestra continues with another strain, **B**, at 41, longer than the first, with the first phrase ending in A minor at 46, the second returning to the tonic but ending in G major at 52, and the third and fourth phrases, although they contain subsidiary modulations, each ending in the tonic. The dotted figures are even more in evidence, so much so that, to some modern ears, they become monotonous.

The original verse, **A**, is then repeated by the three soloists at 65–76. The final phrase is repeated in soft imitation by the strings.

The tenor soloist starts **C** at 79, with imitative entries by the other two soloists. It is quite short, the first phrase ending in A minor and the second in the tonic key, C major; and it is very similar in style to **A** and **B**.

The chorus starts its variant of **A** at 90. Twice the soloists interrupt for one bar (marked verse). The last phrase is sung twice with an unexpected discord the second time at 109, the B flat in the tenor being followed by B natural in the trebles in the same bar. Purcell is very fond of this kind of 'false relation'.

The orchestra then plays an exact repetition of its variant of **A**. At 123 it continues with **B**, also exactly as before.

The bass soloist starts **D** at 147 and continues alone up to 155, when the tenor enters in imitation, being followed by the alto two bars later. The whole of this passage contains frequent short modulations; and it ends in E minor with a tierce de Picardie at 168, G natural being followed by G sharp, another example of Purcell's 'false relations'.

Then the three soloists change to 2/2 time and sing a solemn section, **E**, starting with the words 'And the peace of God'. They repeat their last phrase, as a soft echo, at 183–4.

The orchestra then plays its variant of **E**, starting in C major instead of A, and copying the singers in playing a soft echo at the end of its last phrase.

At 200 the three soloists sing **A** again; and this is followed by the orchestral variant at 213, as at 29–40. The chorus follows at 224 with its variant of **A**, an exact repetition of 90–110; and this brings the joyous anthem to an end.

5 Bach

Brandenburg Concerto No 1 in F

This analysis refers to the Boosey and Hawkes edition. There may be differences in the bar numbering of other editions, particularly in the menuetto, trio I, polacca and trio II.

There are general comments about the Brandenburg concertos in the first book of *Analyses of Musical Classics*, so they are not repeated here.

The first concerto is scored for a small violin (kit violin or violino piccolo), 2 horns, 3 oboes and bassoon, plus the usual strings and continuo. In this concerto Bach treats the concertante instruments much more as a part of the general orchestra than as a separate solo group, so the work is more like a symphony than a concerto. But, as always, he writes a series of contrapuntal lines in which one set of instruments frequently doubles another with the same line, so that there is little contrast of orchestral tone-colour, such as one finds in the work of later composers. Rarely do any of the instruments have a rest for more than a few bars, except in the slow movement which does not use horns, the trios at the end which are for wood alone, and the polacca which is for strings alone.

First Movement, *Allegro*

The opening ritornello, in which all the instruments participate, consists of a number of figures which are used almost continuously throughout the movement. The first figure to attract notice is that played in semiquavers in the oboes in bar 1, (*a*); while (*b*), which consists of quavers in arpeggio in violin and second horn at the same time, is imitated a bar later by viola and first horn. The semiquaver figure continues in oboes and violins up to the first cadence in the dominant major at 5–6.

Then two new figures appear: (*c*), rising quavers in the oboes at the beginning of bar 6; and (*d*), which first appears in the bassoon at the beginning of bar 6 and is then transferred to oboe and violin, while (*c*) is transferred to second oboe, second violin and the bass parts at the end of bar 6. Thereafter (*c*) and (*d*) continue through bars 7 and 8 in various instruments, passing through G minor on the way back to the tonic key; while (*a*) and (*b*) reappear in oboes and upper strings at the end of bar 8. Figure (*a*) is combined with (*d*) in bar 9 and passes sequentially through B flat major in bar 10, returning to the tonic key in bar 11. The cadence of this first ritornello is reached at 12–13.

But the next section, though a little more lightly scored, does not seem so very different from the ritornello. It is based on the same figures, though they are treated more imitatively. In bar 13 the horns have (*a*) while the oboes have (*b*); in 14 the oboes and upper strings have (*a*) while the bass parts have (*b*); in 15 the oboes have (*b*) while the upper strings have (*a*), and they begin to modulate to C major. Figures (*c*) and (*d*) reappear in the violins at 18, modulating to G minor, and are imitated by the oboes at 19, modulating sequentially to D minor, and then by the horns at 20. Then (*a*) reappears in oboes and violins at 21 and they reach a cadence in B flat at 23–4. Figure (*a*) returns to the horns at 24 accompnied by (*c*) in the bass; then (*a*) is transferred by imitation to oboes and then to violins, reaching D minor at 26–7.

The ritornello returns at 27 in D minor, though it is modified, and it changes at 29, (*a*) in the oboes and (*b*) in the upper strings being treated sequentially. It ends in D minor at 32–3.

Then, at 33, (*a*) is played by the horns, accompanied by a descending scale in the oboes, (*e*), which is, in effect, an inversion of (*c*) but continuing for longer. In the next bar (*a*) is transferred to oboes while the descending scale, (*e*), is heard in violins and violas. The following bar again, 35, (*a*) is played by violins while (*e*) is heard in the bass parts, and they reach F major at 35–6.

Two new figures then appear: (*f*) which consists of three quavers in arpeggio in oboes, and is really an incomplete form of (*b*); and (*g*) in the horns, which consists of minims moving against each other in syncopated suspensions. Figure (*a*) continues in the bass and is transferred to the horns a bar later while, in 38, (*f*) continues for an extra note in the oboes, so that it approximates even more to (*b*) than before. It continues in rising sequences, while (*a*) continues in horns and bass in imitation. By 40 (*a*) is heard in alternate beats in horns and oboes while (*b*) is heard in all the strings in its original form or inverted. This reaches another cadence in C major at 42–3.

The ritornello now starts in C major but changes two bars later and has rising, modulatory sequences until it reaches A minor at 47–8.

Quieter imitations then again take over as contrast, starting with (*a*) in horns against (*c*) in the bass. Figure (*c*) is transferred to the oboes a bar later and to the violins a bar later again, at which moment (*c*) becomes (*e*) in the bass.

G minor is reached at 51–2, when (*a*) is heard in the oboes against (*b*) in the violins. Then (*a*) passes from horns to an oboe and on to the violino piccolo, against (*c*) in the bass, at 53–4; and the same occurs again at 55–6.

Another ritornello in the tonic key starts at 57. Figure (*a*) passes to the horns at 58, and the ritornello ends at 62–3 in C major.

At 63, (*a*) passes to the first and second oboes while (*e*) is heard in the third oboe. A bar later (*a*) is heard in the violins against (*e*) in the viola. Figure (*b*) is then heard in stretto between violins and oboes, while the syncopated figure, (*g*), reappears in the horns, and (*a*) is in the bass. Figures (*a*) and (*b*) are heard in rising sequences leading to a cadence in the tonic key at 71–2.

At 73 the opening ritornello is heard again in its entirety, finishing with a prolonged cadence in the final bar.

Second Movement, *Adagio*

No horns are used in the second movement, which is in D minor. It starts with a slow-moving melody in the first oboe against quiet repeated chords in the rest of the orchestra.

The melody is transferred to violino piccolo at bar 5, while the repeated chords continue in the oboes. Then it is transferred to the 'cello at 9, starting in G minor, while an imitative mordant-like figure is used in imitation between wind and strings.

At 12 the melody is heard in imitation between first oboe and violino piccolo, and they modulate to A minor, playing together for a bar at 15; and the violin carries on alone at 16. They return to imitations of each other at 18, modulating to D minor, while the 'cello takes over again at 20, starting in A minor, and modulating to D minor.

At 23 violino piccolo and oboe imitate each other again though, once more, they join together at 26. The first oboe continues alone for two bars, modulating to G minor, then the violino piccolo is alone for two bars, modulating to D minor, then the 'cello has the theme for three bars, leaving the first oboe to bring the tune to an end at 35. Four bars then lead to an imperfect cadence and a pause, which marks the end of the movement.

This movement has been much more in concertante style than the first movement, and consists of one slow-moving melody divided between first oboe, violino piccolo and 'cello, with the rest of the orchestra acting as ripieno and playing a simple accompaniment.

Third Movement, *Allegro*

This movement brings in the horns again, but has more contrast between concertante and ripieno than has the first movement.

The ritornello starts with the main theme, (*a*), in all the oboes and upper strings while the horns have a little subsidiary figure, (*b*). The main theme moves on to another figure, (*c*) at 5 in the first oboe and first violin, while the horns temporarily have a rest. But they start again with their (*b*) figure at 8, while the rest of the orchestra reverts to (*a*). It moves to another figure, (*d*), at 12 in first oboe and first violin; and the first ritornello ends at 17 in the tonic key.

Then the violino piccolo has a short solo based on (*a*), accompanied only by the bass continuo.

The ritornello returns at 21, starting as at bar 1 but moving to C major at 25, when figures (*c*) and (*a*) are combined in oboe and violin; and this ritornello ends in key G at 30.

There is then a short concertante passage for horn and violino piccolo with continuo, in which (*c*) and (*a*) are combined in imitation so that the repeated notes of (*a*) alternate between horn and violin.

This lasts up to 35, when a shortened ritornello begins again, this time starting in C major and ending on V of that key.

The concertante section which follows starts with violino piccolo and continuo using figure (*c*), which is taken up by all the first violins two bars later. By 44 everyone is playing except the horns; and oboes and violins play half-a-bar of (*b*) and half-a-bar of (*a*) in alternation. But the violins revert to (*d*) at 48 and reach a cadence in C major at 50–1. There is a short extension for two bars, with the violins playing (*d*).

Then follows a contrasting, modulatory section, which starts with the violino piccolo and oboe alternating, the violin playing (*e*) and modulating to D minor at 54, then the oboe playing (*f*) against (*g*) in the violino piccolo. They reach A minor at 58 and continue in a similar style, though with the horns joining in, until they reach E minor at 63.

Bar 64 starts a rather similar section to that starting at 44, but with the oboe and violin parts changed round, using (*a*) with the repeated notes alternating with the semiquavers in different halves of the bar. And now the oboes, instead of the violins, are left to themselves at 68, playing (*d*) and reaching a cadence in A minor at 70.

Next the violino piccolo and the first horn alternate with a figure based on (*a*). But at 75 the violino piccolo reverts to (*g*); and this section ends with a cadence in B flat major at 81.

Two bars of *adagio* repeat the cadence; and then the music reverts to *allegro* and to an introduction played by violino piccolo based on (*a*) which leads to a repetition of the opening ritornello. It is modified at 92, though still based on the same figures, and drops down in a series of sequences ending on V in the tonic key at 97.

Four bars of violino piccolo and horn in imitation lead to another short ritornello, similar to bars 1–4.

But again it breaks off; and violino piccolo with only the continuo accompaniment has two bars alone before the ritornello returns once more. This time it continues to the end of the movement, so that 108–24 is identical with bars 1–17.

Fourth Movement, *Menuetto, with two trios and a polacca*

In the menuetto the three oboe parts are almost identical with the two violins and the viola part throughout, while the horns play little more than a fanfare. So far as the scoring is concerned, it is sufficient to follow the string parts.

The style is harmonic, with the first violin and the oboes having the melody throughout, though the continuo imitates the first two bars of the melody at the beginning of each half of the binary movement. The opening is peculiar, as the repeated E flat gives the impression of the key of B flat for the first four bars. But the prevailing key is F, the tonic key; and the first half ends in the dominant key and is repeated, as is usual, while the second half finally returns to the tonic.

The menuetto was scored for full orchestra but trio I is for two oboes and bassoon alone. It is in simple three-part harmony, and is in D minor, the relative minor. The first section ends in V in that key. The second section is longer, as is customary, and modulates to C major (35–6), G minor (39–40), F major (41–2), D minor (44–5) and F major again (46–8) before returning to the tonic key, D minor.

Then the menuetto is repeated, followed by the polacca (which is numbered from bar 1 in the Boosey and Hawkes edition).

This is for string orchestra alone, without the violino piccolo. It is again in binary form and is in F major. The first violin has the melody throughout, while the rest of the strings have continuous accompanying quavers until the last three bars. The first half modulates to the dominant major, while the second half, which is the same length, modulates to D minor (20–4), B flat major (25–7) and C major (28) before returning to the tonic key.

The menuetto is then repeated once more and is followed by trio II which is for horns and oboes alone. Once more it is in simple three-part harmony, with all the oboes playing in unison and, rather surprisingly, providing the bass part. It is in F major throughout, with an imperfect cadence half-way through.

Finally the menuetto is repeated once again, which means it is heard four times with a contrasting movement in between each repetition. It will be realised that this movement is much simpler in style than the first three movements.

6 Bach

Orchestral Suite No 3 in D

Of the four orchestral suites by Bach perhaps No 2 for flute and strings is the most popular. But No 3 is particularly famous for its 'air', which was arranged by Wilhemj in 1871 as 'Air on the G string', transposed a ninth lower into the key of C, and which is in the repertoire of every concert violinist in this form.

It is probable that these suites date from the Cöthen period (1717–23), when Bach conducted the court orchestra and therefore had opportunities of having his orchestral works performed. The last two are composed for the largest orchestra and for the same combination, consisting of 2 oboes, 3 trumpets, 2 drums, strings and continuo. The first two make no use of brass or percussion.

Bach called the works 'overtures' as was customary in those days when a suite or partita was written for orchestra; and they all consist of a long and important movement called an overture followed by a string of much shorter and slighter dances (the 'French' overture, in fact, invented by Lully).

I The Overture

The overture starts with a preliminary *grave* introduction, containing many dotted figures, as was common in this type of overture. It lasts for twenty-four bars and is repeated, as is usual.

The first violins and the oboes begin with figure (*a*), a crotchet tied to a group of semiquavers, inverted in bar 2; and they change to (*b*), the dotted figure, in bar 3. The second violins, violas and continuo use (*b*) most of the time, often in imitation; and the trumpets mark the accents for two bars until they join all the other instruments, including the timpani, with (*b*) in bar 3. Trumpets and drums cease in bar 5 and do not enter again until the coda at 18, when they can play in the tonic key again and add to the climax with

17

the dotted figure, which they continue up to the end of the introduction.

The theme is mainly in the first violins and oboes, in unison, and it alternates with (a) and (b). Otherwise the chief interest lies in the modulations. The first half ends in A major in bar 8. The second half passes through E minor at 10, B minor at 12, E major at 14 and returns to A major at 17. Bars 18–24 form a short coda starting in the tonic key at 22, in which key the introduction ends on the dominant chord.

The *vivace* is a four-part fugue in which the first oboe plays in unison with the first violins and the second oboe plays with the second violins most of the time. Trumpets and drums enter at the climaxes, but mainly with repeated quavers, though the first trumpet does manage to play the subject in unison with the first violins and first oboe at 35–6. There are also three passages, between 50 and 56, 76 and 80, and 81–7, when the oboes are independent. In the first and last they play slow suspensions, while between 76 and 80 they play independent quavers.

The subject enters in first violins and first oboe at 24(b), the answer enters in second violins and second oboe at 25, the subject re-enters in the violas at 28 followed by the answer in 'cellos and continuo at 29. There are no fewer than three counter-subjects used at varying times in the fugue. The first one, in quavers, enters in the first violins and oboe against the answer at 25; the second one, in semiquavers, is played by the same instruments at 28, while second violins and second oboe play the first one; and the third one is played by them at 30 and consists of bright repeated notes which sometimes appear later in the trumpets, as at 50.

After the four voice parts have entered there are further entries of the subject in the bass at 31, the first violins at 32, the first violins again at 35 (when the trumpet joins in), and the bass again at 38, before the exposition comes to an end at 42.

The middle section starts with an episode in strings alone, in which the first violin plays continuous semiquavers, rather like the second counter-subject up to 57, in a virtuosic passage perhaps intended for a solo violin in the concertino. During this time there are middle entries in the second violins in B major at 50, in violas in E major at 51, in second violins again in A major at 53 and in violas again in D major at 54. This part ends in A major at 58.

The next part starts with an entry in the bass in the tonic key, while all three counter-subjects are heard above it. Another entry starts in the bass in E major at 59 and is followed by an entry in the first violins in A major at 61.

A short episode leads to another entry in the bass in B minor at 66, again with the three counter-subjects above it.

Bars 71–84 are very similar to 42–58, with the first violins having continuous semiquavers, now starting in B minor instead of D major, and entries of the subject occurring in E major in the violas at 81, in A major in the second violins at 82 and in D major, the tonic key, in the violas at 84.

This last entry marks the beginning of the final section in the tonic key. Bars 84–99 are similar to the exposition, 24–42, but with different orchestration. The entries occur in the violas at 84, the second violins at 85, the first violins at 89, the second violins at 90 and again at 92, the bass at 94, and the first violins at 97. All three counter-subjects are present at various times. This section ends with a perfect cadence in the tonic key at 98–9.

A coda starts at 99 in which occur entries of the subject in the first violins at 100 and in the bass at 103, with all three counter-subjects above it.

This leads to a return of the *grave* section at 107. It contains the (a) and (b) figures as before, but now differently treated and with the trumpets and drums coming in with the dotted figure at the beginning and the end, when they are able to do so.

The whole of the fugue and the final *grave* section are then meant to be repeated, though this rarely occurs in modern performances.

The Dances

The dances in Bach's orchestral suites do not follow the plan which he consistently used in his clavier suites. In the third suite, for example, only the gigue of the four standard movements—allemande, courante, sarabande and gigue—is used, the other dances coming under the heading of Galanterien, the optional dances that usually came between the sarabande and the gigue.

II Air

The Air is written for strings and continuo only. In this original form, in D major, the first violin soars serenely along: 'an angelic soprano strain' as Tovey calls it. Certainly it is one of the loveliest melodies ever written. It moves slowly, in spite of the 'black' look on the page; and there are frequent long notes which act as a prelude to further arabesques.

It is in binary form, with the first part modulating to the dominant and the second part moving frequently to related keys before returning to D major. The accompaniment is very simple, with most effective quaver octave leaps in the bass almost throughout.

III Gavotte

This is nearly as well known as the Air, and is heard in many different arrangements. In the original, Bach returns to his full orchestra, though the two oboes double the first violin part throughout, and the first and second trumpets also double the violin parts, though they only play occasionally. The third trumpet and the drum play at the same places and merely mark the tonic and dominant notes. In other words the music consists of little besides an independent melody and an almost equally melodic and independent bass.

It is again in binary form, with a modulation to the dominant at the end of the first part, and modulations to other related keys in the second half on the way back to the tonic. The second half starts with an inversion of the opening figure.

There is a second gavotte in which the two oboe parts double the two violin parts with occasional touches of imitation; the trumpets play the notes of the tonic chord, apart from a touch of melody at the beginning of the second half; and the drums are silent. The continuo plays the opening figure several times in different keys, otherwise it, too, is silent. The key scheme is similar to that of the first gavotte.

Then the first gavotte is repeated, the result being what we now call minuet and trio form.

IV Bourrée

Apart from the fact that the bourrée, like all bourrées, starts all its phrases on the fourth crotchet of the bar, instead of the third as in gavottes, the two dances are so much alike that one begins to get a little tired of the same style and speed, as well as the same key.

The oboes again double the first violin part throughout, and the trumpets occasionally have a touch of the tune but for the most part join the timpani in punctuating chords, though there is a welcome pause in their use for eight bars from 13–20 and again from 24–8. Bach rarely writes contrasting, imitative parts for the various instruments, as do later composers: if he starts with the oboes they play continuously throughout a given number, and they frequently double the violins.

The dance is again in binary form with the usual key plan; and the style is harmonic, with the first violin part having the melody continuously. The second part is, as usual, very much longer than the first.

V Gigue

In this dance the first trumpet plays the oboe and violin part an octave higher in the first phrase, which makes the sound very brilliant. However, after four bars rest, it joins in again at the same octave. Then follow nine bars rest for the trumpets, after which the first trumpet enters above the violins again. The same style con-

B

tinues to the end of the movement, the trumpets having frequent rests but, when they do come in, often being at the top octave and sounding very brilliant.

The oboes play continuously in unison with the first violins, as before. But, like the first gavotte, the continuo part is as tuneful and independent as is the violin part; and it often has passages of continuous triplets, usually when the violin part is temporarily slow-moving.

The form is binary once more, with the usual kind of key scheme, and with the second part longer than the first. Sequences near the end build up to a climax in which all the instruments join with a final flourish.

7 Bach

Organ Sonata No 6 in G

Bach's six organ sonatas are sometimes called trio sonatas because they are written in three contrapuntal parts, two for manuals and the third for pedals. They are part of a very large collection of works Bach wrote for the organ, including preludes, toccatas, fantasias and fugues, and many choral preludes. Grove states that these sonatas were written between 1727 and 1733, but the Lea pocket score gives an earlier date, 1722–27. In either case they belong to the early years at Leipzig.

First Movement

This movement, which is full of interesting, contrapuntal devices, is certainly not formless, but it is rather difficult to give it a label. It might be considered to be in a free kind of ritornello form, because the material heard in bars 1–20 recurs several times. But the other figures used recur also, and the movement is completely built up of these figures. The figure development mainly occurs in the manuals, the pedals doing little more than supplying a supporting bass.

Figure (a) starts in the manuals in G major, and is repeated in modified sequence, starting at bar 5 in D major.

Figure (b) starts at the end of bar 8 in the right hand and is imitated on the same notes one beat later by the left hand. A cadence in the tonic key is reached at 19–20, and could be said to mark the end of the ritornello.

This is followed by (c) in the right hand and (d) a bar later in the left hand; and the two continue in falling, modified sequences up to 28. Then the two parts change round, thus producing invertible counterpoint, starting in D major instead of G, and otherwise being reproduced exactly.

At bar 37 two more figures appear: (e) in the right hand in semi-quavers and (f) in the left hand in quavers, each playing broken chords.

A modified form of (a) appears in the right hand in E minor at 53; and (b) recurs, in imitation as before, at the end of 61 in D major.

Then (a) returns at 73, starting in D major; but this time there are a series of imitations between the two hands, at two bar's distance, passing through A minor at 76 and reaching E minor at 78.

Figures (e) and (f) recur at 84 but now (f) is in the right hand and (e) in the left; and each moves in inverse movement, as compared with 37. They start in E minor and pass through D major at 88 on the way to B minor at 96, reaching a cadence in that key at 103.

Then (a) reappears in yet another modified form in D major in the right hand. At 108 (b) recurs in G major in the right hand against a new figure (g) in the left, starting in the pedals (which momentarily become more interesting) and being imitated a bar later by the left hand. Bars 116–21 are an invertible counterpoint of 108–14, the two manual parts interchanging and starting in C major.

Then (a) returns in G major, the tonic key, in the left hand at 124, being imitated two bars later by the right hand in D minor. It also appears in A minor at 128, with further imitations at 130 and 132.

Figure (*e*) then appears at 136 in both manuals, moving in contrary motion with each other. It begins in E minor and passes through G major (140) and E minor (148), reaching D major at 152.

At this point a dominant pedal of the tonic key appears, over which is heard (*c*) in the right hand and (*d*) in the left.

It leads to a complete and exact repetition of bars 1–20 at 159–79, a very usual way of finishing a movement in ritornello form.

Second Movement

The *lento* second movement is in three parts. The first part, 1–16, beginning in E minor and ending in the dominant, B minor, consists of imitative entries in the manuals over a continuous quaver stepwise bass. The right hand enters first, and the left hand enters at the end of bar 4 with an exact imitation of the first four bars of the right hand, now in B minor. From bar 9 the imitations between the two hands are at half-a-bar's distance, and modulate through A minor (9), G major (10) and E minor (12). From 12–16 there is a series of falling sequences in the right hand, modulating every half-bar until the cadence in B minor at 16 is reached.

The second section, 17–24, starts a new figure in the left hand in E minor, imitated exactly two bars later, a fourth higher, by the right hand in A minor. Then, as in the first part, another figure enters at 21 with imitations between the hands at half-a-bar's distance. It passes through D minor (21) and E minor (22) and reaches a dominant pedal of A minor at 23, which leads to the return of the opening theme at 25.

But this third section has interesting differences, as compared with the first section. It begins in A minor, the subdominant key, and ends in E minor, the tonic; and it starts with the left hand instead of the right. Otherwise it is exactly the same, which means that the two upper parts are in invertible counterpoint as compared with 1–16.

There is a precedent here for Mozart, who occasionally started a recapitulation with the first subject in the subdominant, so that the relationship between the two subjects was the same in exposition and recapitulation: tonic–dominant: subdominant—tonic.

Third Movement

The final *allegro* is in a loose kind of ternary form in which the middle section, 19–53, contains a repetition and development of the first figure (*a*) of the first section; and the repetition of the first section 54–end, contains a number of modifications.

Figure (*a*) starts in the left hand in G major, the tonic key, and is imitated in bar 2 by the right hand in D major. Figure (*b*), which starts with a semiquaver arpeggio, appears in imitation between the two hands in bar 2, overlapping at one beat's distance. It begins in key D but returns to G. Figure (*c*) starts in the right hand in bar 8 in key G, being imitated by the left hand in bar 9. It is then repeated sequentially in E minor and C major, with the two hands changing round each time. This leads to a return of (*a*) in G major at 14, but this time the right hand starts first and the left imitates one bar later, remaining in the tonic key. The first section of the movement ends in the tonic key at 18^3.

The middle section starts with (*d*) in the left hand in E minor and it is imitated by the right hand at 23 in B minor. A new figure, (*e*), appears in the left hand at 26, and sequential imitations of it occur between the two hands, passing from B minor, through E minor, A minor and D major to G major.

This leads to a repetition of (*a*) in the tonic key in the right hand at 32, imitated by the left hand in the dominant key at 33, and then by the right hand again, half-a-bar later. Then the second half of the figure, played by the right hand in 34^3–35^1, is developed by itself, with imitations between the two hands at half-a-bar's distance, passing rapidly through a number of related keys.

Figure (*d*) appears again at 42 in the right hand in B minor. Bars 42–5 are similar to 23–6 and pass through the same keys (B minor, A major and E minor). But figure (*e*) does not reappear: (*d*) continues instead, at first in imitation between the two hands. Then, at 49, both hands have the semiquaver part of it together in contrary motion, and this has the effect of working up to a climax.

The first section returns with modifications at 54. Figure (*a*) appears in the left hand in the tonic key, and it is followed immediately by close imitations of (*b*) in the two hands, which reach the dominant key at 60. Bars 60–62 are similar to 4–6 with the two hands changed round; but this is followed by an extension in E minor, 62–4. The music then returns to the tonic key; and bars 67 to the end of the movement are almost identical with 8–18.

8 Bach

Partita No 2 in C minor

'Partita' is the Italian word for 'suite'. In his earliest set of suites Bach used the word 'partita', while the later sets are now known as the English and French suites. The six partitas were written between 1726 and 1731, after Bach had settled in Leipzig, and were published as a set in 1731.

Sinfonie

All the partitas, like the English suites, start with some kind of a prelude but, whereas it is called 'prelude' in the English suites, it goes under six different names in the partitas. In the second partita it is called a 'sinfonie'.

The sinfonie is in three distinct sections. It starts with a seven-bar *grave adagio*, which consists of a series of solemn chords, over a tonic pedal for the first four bars, with a dotted figure, usually in thirds, over the top. The last two bars are over a dominant pedal; and it ends with a dominant chord.

The *andante* starts at 8. It is a rhapsodic section with a decorative, arabesque-like, continuous melody over quaver broken chords in the left hand. There are many little sequences in the melody but no real repetition of idea, except perhaps for the frequent use of tied notes. The first part ends in the tonic key, C minor, at 15; 16–20 are mainly in the relative major; and 21–30 are mainly in the dominant minor, ending in this key with a tierce de Picardie.

Then follows an *allegro* section. This is a free fugato for two voices. The subject enters at 30 and is answered a *fifth* lower at 33, ending in F minor. Another entry in C minor appears at 39, and this is followed by an episode which leads to an entry in G minor at 46. Another quite long, sequential episode leads to an entry in F minor at 64, followed by yet another episode. A series of partial entries from 72–80, followed by another episode, leads to an entry in F minor at 84; and an entry of the second half of the subject in the tonic key at 89 brings the movement to an end.

Allemande

This is in the usual binary form and, as always in classical suites, is in the same key as all the other movements. It consists of the usual continuous semiquavers in a moderate quadruple time, and the first part ends in the dominant minor, with a tierce de Picardie. When in a minor key Bach, in his binary form movements, modulates to the dominant much more often than he does to the relative major.

The second half is exactly the same length as the first and starts with the opening figure in G. But after two beats it modulates back to C minor. However, by the next bar, it is in F minor (a very usual modulation in the second half of a piece in binary form) and stays in that key until 22. Then it returns to the tonic key at 26, by way of E flat major at 24, and stays in the tonic key to the end.

The last four bars are the same as the last four bars of the first half, except that they are now in the tonic instead of the dominant key, and the voice parts are changed round until the final bar. This similarity between the two ends of each half is again a usual procedure.

Courante

This is the French type, in 3/2 time, with a 6/4 cadence at the end of each half. It is in three-part counterpoint, with imitative entries at the beginning of each half, and with the treble part at the beginning of the second half consisting of an inversion of that of the opening bar. As in the allemande, the last four bars of each half are identical, except that the first half ends in the dominant key and the second half ends in the tonic.

Sarabande

This Spanish dance is quicker than many of Bach's sarabandes (*andante con moto*), and more contrapuntal and less harmonic than most. It is in two-part counterpoint throughout, except for the cadences. For the first time in this suite the second part of the binary-form movement is much longer than the first, being sixteen bars long instead of eight.

An accent tends to occur on the second beat, as in all sarabandes, and the opening figure in the treble, which comes to rest on the second beat, is a characteristic feature in this particular sarabande. It is used again in the bass at the beginning of the second part, in sequence. But there is no imitation, inversion or other similar contrapuntal device in this movement, and no similarity between the endings of the two halves. Rather it is a gently meandering two-part invention, using plenty of sequences and much more modulation than in the previous movements. The first part ends in the relative major; and the second part modulates to B flat at 10, F minor at 13, B flat at 14, F minor at 16, and returns via E flat at 17 to the tonic key at 19. The last few bars are very chromatic.

Rondeau

From here to the end of the suite Bach's plan is irregular. In place of the usual series of galanteries, such as minuets and gavottes, he writes a rondeau; and in place of the final gigue he writes a caprice.

It was customary to write one or more lighter dances after the slow sarabande. The sarabande was, in a sense, the central movement of the suite, and it fulfilled a similar function to that of the slow movement of the sonata-type work which was to develop later. The rondeau which follows in this suite, is quite dance-like, and forms a suitable contrast to the sarabande.

It is in rondo form. **A** (1–16) consists of two identical eight-bar phrases, except that the first one ends with an imperfect and the second with a perfect cadence. It has a feature of sequential falling sevenths.

B (17–32) vacillates between E flat major and F minor, but returns to C minor in its last two bars, ready for the return of **A**.

A² (33–48) is identical with **A¹** except for modifications in its first and last bars, which provide a link with the preceding and succeeding sections.

C (49–64) contains two lots of falling sequences and modulates through F minor to E flat major.

Bars 65–72 form a link based on **A** in the bass. They return to the tonic key and to **A³** (73–80) at 73, but this time only its second phrase is used.

D (81–96) is in G minor and its second half makes use of the leaping sevenths from **A** in the bass.

A⁴ (97–end) repeats the whole of **A** for the last time, but now in a decorative form.

Caprice

This final movement is in fugal style, even though it is also in the two repeated sections of binary form. It is written for three voice-parts, and the subject appears in the treble voice from bars 1–4. The answer starts in the alto in bar 5 in G minor, and appears again in the bass at 8.

An episode, which starts with the leaping tenths of the subject in the bass, begins at 11 and leads to another entry of the subject in the bass at 19. This is followed by a sequential episode for two voices only, starting at 22 which, in turn, leads to another entry of the answer in the treble at 28.

Another short episode, starting at 30, leads to a partial entry in the alto in E flat at 35, followed by the subject in the tonic again in the treble at 37. And a final episode, starting at 40, leads to an imperfect cadence in the tonic key at 48, which marks the end of the first section of the binary-form movement.

The second section starts with the subject inverted in the treble, answered by an inversion in F minor at 52. Further inversions of the subject appear in the bass in C minor at 60 and in the alto in G minor at 70, separated by episodes as before. Partial inverted entries appear at 77 and 79, followed by another episode with the leaping tenths in the bass.

Finally, three partial entries of the subject in its original form at 87, 89 and 91 bring the movement to an end.

9 Bach

Christmas Oratorio, Part I, Nos 2, 3, 5, 6, 7, and 9

In the first volume of Analyses of Musical Classics there were general comments on the Christmas Oratorio and an analysis of Nos 1, 4 and 8. The analyses given here complete the analysis of Part I.

No 2 'Now it came to pass in those days'

The evangelist now sings the words from St Luke 2: 1–6, in recitativo secco, telling how Mary and Joseph went to Nazareth to be taxed. The part is for a tenor singer, and it is often very high, though it is easier to sing in the German original than in the English translation.

No 3 'See how the Bridegroom'

This is again recitative, but now it is accompanied, and is sung by the alto soloist to words written by a contemporary of Bach's. The accompaniment consists largely of swaying pairs of crotchets.

No 5 'How shall I fitly meet Thee?'

This is a setting of the well-known *Passion Choral*. It occurs five times in the St Matthew Passion and twice in this work, the second time being No 65, the last number of the work. Each of these seven versions are differently treated: Bach's powers of varied harmonisation seem to be inexhaustible. The student should compare these seven settings. The treatments in the St Matthew Passion are sad. This setting (No 5) is tranquil, and ends questioningly with an imperfect cadence, as befits the question mark in the title, while No 65 is a song of triumph, making a fitting end to the whole work.

No 6 'And she brought forth her first-born Son'

The Evangelist now sings St Luke 2 : 7, in *recitativo secco*. The setting is very short and simple.

No 7 'For us to Earth He cometh poor'

This is a combination of a choral with recitative, to contemporary words. The choral is sung by the trebles of the chorus only, and the bass soloist interpolates comments in recitative between each line. The orchestra has a florid, independent accompaniment which starts with a lovely melodious introduction, twelve bars long. This setting of the choral should be compared with No 28, when the chorus sings it straight through in a richly harmonised version in 4/4 time, instead of the 3/2 version in which it appears here.

The first orchestral passage begins and ends in G major. After the first line of the choral and the first recitative by the bass soloist the orchestra enters again with a similar shorter passage, but now starting in the relative minor and continuing against the next line of the choral. After the next pair of lines it appears in D minor, modulating to C major and then G major with the entry of the choral melody. The next orchestral entry is in A minor, modulating to D major and then G major as the choral enters. At the end, it combines with the last line of the choral in the tonic key, and continues after the voices have stopped, making twelve bars for this last entry. The swaying figure in the orchestra, making much use of consecutive thirds and sixths, provides a beautiful setting for the choral.

No 9 'Ah! Dearest Jesus'

Part I comes to an end with another choral, which is also used for Nos 17 and 23, again treated differently on all three occasions. The melody is by Martin Luther, and its title is *Vom Himmel Hoch*.

This time the choral is sung in a harmonised version by the four-part chorus; and the orchestra, including trumpets and drums, has an independent part between each line of words, which is based on the rhythmic figure of two semiquavers and two quavers and occurs immediately after the first line of the choral. The key and the orchestration are the same as in No 1, thus rounding off Part I as a separate cantata.

10 Handel
Sixth 'Chandos' Anthem

When Handel returned to London from a visit to Hanover in 1717 he thought he would continue to write successful Italian operas for London, as he had done before. But the fashion had suddenly changed: French farce had temporarily captured the town and, for three years, opera ceased to exist in London.

So Handel, like many other musicians, found himself without

the means of livelihood and he solved his problem by becoming Musical Director to the Earl of Carnarvon. The Earl had been Paymaster-General during the Marlborough campaigns and, in the course of his duties, had managed to make himself very rich. So, in 1712, he built a large palace at Cannons near Edgware, where he entertained in great style. At first he appointed Dr Pepusch, who is famous for the later production of *The Beggar's Opera*, as his musical director; but, in 1718, he decided that Handel would be a greater asset, so he dismissed Pepusch and appointed Handel.

In 1719 the Earl was created the Duke of Chandos, and Handel wrote the eleven Chandos anthems for the chapel at Cannons, in honour of his master. These 'Chandos' anthems were modelled on the English 'verse anthems' composed by Purcell and his contemporaries. They were written for solo voices, chorus and orchestra, and all the performers were professionals, with the soprano chorus parts sung by boys and the altos by men, as always at this period. (It is said that the first time women appeared in a choir was in 1773, fourteen years after Handel's death.) And it was usual to have the orchestra larger than the choir.

No 1 'O praise the Lord with one Consent'

This chorus starts with an opening 'symphony' of 36 bars, which makes use of figures to be heard later in the first part of the chorus. The opening phrase (*a*) is the same as the first phrase of the hymn tune 'St Anne' sung to the words 'O God our help in ages past'—though this may not be immediately obvious to the student who looks at the modern piano arrangement of the orchestral score. This hymn tune is attributed to William Croft (1678–1727), but it is not known whether Handel himself knew it. However, it is at least possible that he did, and that he made it the basis of this chorus in the same way that Bach used well-known German chorales as the basis for choruses in his cantatas and passions.

After this reference to 'St Anne' in bars 1–3, the orchestra goes on to the quaver figure (*b*) that is later to provide the accompaniment to the voice parts from 39 onwards, and from 48 onwards to be used also in the voice parts; and at 11 the orchestra goes on to the semi-quaver figure (c) that is later used by the singers on the word 'magnify'. At bar 13 (a) appears in diminution followed by (b) in the bass at 14–16, against syncopation in the higher parts. Then (b) and (c) combine and continue together until the entry of the voices at 37.

The sopranos have the first phrase of 'St Anne' with the rest of the choir joining in after the first four notes. It produces a simple but grand harmonious effect that is typical of Handel. Figure (b) then appears in the orchestra and the basses start (c) at 42 in a series of sequential repetitions. Then the altos use it in imitation at 47, while the tenors and basses go on to (b). This section ends at 51 in the dominant key.

The next section starts with (a) in the dominant key but immediately returns to the tonic; and then (b) and (c) continue as before, reaching a cadence in C minor at 61. Imitative entries of (c) then appear in stretto. They pass through F minor at 67 and reach G minor at 72. Then (a) reappears in the tonic key, followed by (b) and (c); but this section again ends in the dominant key at 79.

A very free kind of double fugue starts at 81 with S^1 in the soprano and S^2 in the tenor at 82. S^2 is then heard in the bass and tenor at 84 and 5 and in the soprano at 86. S^1 appears in the tenor in the dominant key, followed by further entries of S^2. S^1 then appears at 91 in the bass an octave lower than the previous tenor entry, but it returns to the tonic key.

After further entries of S^2, S^1 appears in the alto in D flat major at 101, followed by more entries of S^2. Then S^1 appears at 112 in the tenor in C major, followed by the alto and soprano in stretto, the alto having it once more in the tonic key at 115. More entries of S^2 lead to an entry of S^1 in the bass in the tonic key at 118, followed immediately by another entry in A flat major in the same voice. Finally the bass has S^1 in the tonic key at 127, the other voices being in harmony with it; and this forms a short but grand coda.

No 2 'Praise Him, all ye that in His House attend'

This air was originally intended for a male alto, but it is usually sung by a tenor today. It is based on two themes: (a) in the bass of bars 1 and 2, and (b) the first two notes in the treble in 2–3, the themes answering each other in sequences throughout.

After the orchestra has had a complete statement of the themes, ending in the tonic key, the voice enters at 16, and the music in the next fifteen bars is almost an exact repetition of the first fifteen, with the voice mainly having figure (b). Bars 31–44 continue with the same figures but modulate to the relative major.

The next section, 45–59, passes through F minor on its way to A flat; and the following section, 60–75, returns to the tonic key and then modulates to G minor.

Bars 75–83 act as a link back to the tonic key; and 83–93 correspond roughly to 18–31, with the ending shortened and modified.

Bars 93–107 form a coda in the tonic key; and the last orchestral ritornello is a shortened form of the first.

No 3 'For this our truest Int'rest'

This is a tenor air in G minor. The opening orchestral introduction is repeated twice by the tenor before he goes on to coloratura on the word 'praise' in 16, finally reaching a cadence in the relative major at 22. This section is rounded-off by a repetition of the opening bars in the orchestra in B flat major.

The next section starts with a new figure in B flat major at 27, and this includes word painting on 'delightful' and ends in D minor.

The next section, starting at 39, returns to the tonic key, though with new material, and modulates to the relative major again at 44. The coloratura passage that was heard on the word 'praise' in 16 is now applied to 'delightful' at 49 and 55. The air ends with a repetition of the opening orchestral passage, as is usual.

No 4 'That God is great'

This air for bass makes much use of dotted figures, and also has plenty of coloratura. Yet it is in a simple harmonic style, as are most of Handel's bass airs. The first section ends in the tonic key at 55; and the second section, which continues in the same style, modulates to G minor (63), F minor (75) and D minor (79) on its way back to the tonic key.

No 5 'With cheerful Notes let all the Earth'

This chorus makes simple use of word painting. The figure (a), heard in the orchestra in bars 1 and 2 and also in the opening soprano part, represents 'cheerful notes'; and figure (b) heard in the orchestra in bars 5–9, in the voices imitatively in bars 17–20, and in the orchestra again at 21–5, 'rises to heaven' most effectively, particularly as the violins softly reach their top notes at 25; while imitative entries of 'to heaven' at 15 onwards, (c), speed the way onward.

The figure (d), which appears in the sopranos at 25 against (a) in the basses, is really derived from (a), but also has a hint of 'St Anne'. It is followed by the (b) and (c) figures, as before.

Another section starts at 43 with another form of (d), while the 'St Anne' form of it is in the bass; and, at the reference to 'godly mirth', mirthful quavers appear in the orchestra at 47. Against them are heard semibreves and minims in the voices, providing 'solemn hymns'; and the 'mirth' and the 'solemn hymns' continue to the end.

No 6 'God's tender Mercy knows no Bounds'

This is another minor air, this time for the soprano. The first section contains two figures: (a) in the opening bars of both orchestra and voice part, in which the falling sixth aptly fits 'tender mercy'; and (b) the descending scale heard in the orchestra in 5–8 and the voice at 19–22. This section ends in the relative major at 44.

The second section contains new material and modulates through F major (46), D minor (51), G minor (55) and C major (57) on its way back to the tonic key. Notice the Neapolitan sixth at 68 and the return to the descending scale, (b), in the orchestra after the voice has finished.

There have been four airs in this work, one for each voice, but none is in the aria-da-capo form, which was so much used for airs by Handel and other composers of this period. Perhaps he thought it was too long and formal for this short work.

No 7 'Ye boundless Realms of Joy'

This chorus starts with another reference to 'St Anne', now in quavers. This figure, (a), alternates with rising quavers, (b), to the word 'exalt', and they combine at 11. The music reaches G minor, the relative minor, at 20 but still continues with the same figures, and returns to the tonic key at 29.

A new section starts at 30, with imitative entries to the words 'His praise your song employ', and these are heard almost continuously to the end of the chorus.

No 8 'Your Voices raise'

The final chorus makes much use of the word 'Alleluja' as do several of the Chandos Anthems. This can be compared with its later use in 'Messiah'.

It starts with a figure, (a), in the tenors, in which 'ye cherubin' is treated sequentially at 'and seraphin'. The 'allelujahs' start at 88, there being two figures: (b) in coloratura semiquavers, and (c) in disjointed quavers, each separated by a quaver rest. Figures (a), (b) and (c) combine in 12–22, and the first section ends at 22 in C minor, the relative minor.

The next section starts in C minor with imitative entries of the 'cherubin' and 'seraphin', but the semiquaver 'allelujahs' start again at 27 and the quaver ones at 28. The latter occur in diminution (i.e.

without the intervening rests) at 30, in falling sequence, and return to the tonic key at 32.

The imitative 'cherubin' and 'seraphin' return at 35, but the 'allelujahs' take over at 40 and continue in ever-growing jubilation to the end.

11 Handel

Harpsichord Suite No 5 in E

Handel wrote about twenty-three suites for the harpsichord. The first set of eight, from which this suite in E is taken, was published in 1720. At the time Handel was music master to two daughters of George II; and the subsidiary title of 'lessons' makes one think that they may have been partly intended for them.

The second set of eight suites was published in 1733 without Handel's permission, and a few others appeared later. But many of these suites, particularly the later ones, appear in rather a sketchy form. Handel probably added improvisations to them when he played them himself, so we can only guess at what they really sounded like under his hands.

Bach's suites mostly kept to the standard order of allemande, courante, sarabande, and gigue, with additional, lighter dances between the sarabande and the gigue, and sometimes also with some kind of prelude. But Handel's suites are much more free in style. Only one of the first set of eight contains all the four standard dances; many of the movements are not dances at all, but bear such ascriptions as *adagio*, *allegro* and *largo*; and there are three variation movements and five fugues, which occur at varied places in the suite. In fact, the order of the movements appears to be quite haphazard. However, all the movements in one suite are in the same key, as was customary at this period.

Prelude

This improvisatory movement consists of a series of chords in four-part harmony, with first one part and then another adding arabesque-like decorations to the harmony. It moves between tonic and dominant keys, with a touch of A major at 18.

Allemande

This is again mostly four-part writing, but is more contrapuntal than is the prelude. The top part is decorative, largely consisting of semiquavers; and semiquaver movement is kept going in the underneath parts when the top part is not moving, often by means of little points of imitation. There are also frequent sequential patterns.

The movement is in the usual binary form, with the first part ending in the dominant key at 13, and the second part returning to the tonic and ending at 35 in the tonic. As is customary it is longer than the first part.

The opening anacrusis starts the second part by inversion. The second section modulates more freely than the first, passing through F sharp minor (18), E major (19), C sharp minor (20), G sharp minor (21–4), F sharp minor (25) and returning to the tonic at 26. Bars 28–9 are similar to 4–5, but the imitations continue into 30–31. Bars 32–5 are an extended version in the tonic key of the ending of the first part, 11–13, in the dominant key, with bar 33 interpolated.

Courante

The courante starts with imitation between right and left hands, and the shape of the opening four notes is frequently heard throughout the movement. There are four voice-parts, but the number varies from bar to bar—sometimes there are only two or three.

The first section passes through F sharp minor at 10 on its way to the dominant key. The second section starts at 21 with the same figure as at the opening, except that it is now in the dominant key.

But it returns to the tonic at 25–6, and passes through F sharp minor at 30, C sharp minor at 40, B major at 43–4 and A major at 44–5, before reaching a repetition of 17–20 at 49–52, now in the tonic key. The cadences of the two sections are therefore similar, and the second section is longer than the first, as is usually the case.

Air and Variations

This movement has become known as 'the Harmonious Blacksmith', and this title has undoubtedly helped to gain it popularity. But no one knows how it received its title, and the tales about it are fictitious.

The air is a simple theme in binary form. It contains three figures: (a) 1^2–1^3; (b) 5^1–5^2; and (c) 7^2–7^3, which has a resemblance to (a). Each of these figures is repeated twice in a decorated form, immediately after it is heard.

The first part of the air is two bars long, with a repeat which is written out, and ends in the dominant key. The second part is four bars long, with its repetition shown by repeat marks, and it ends in the tonic key.

The variations gradually become quicker and more elaborate, as was customary. They 'shadow' the tune, over the same chord scheme, so that it is possible to sing the original tune while each variation is being played.

The first variation (or 'double') has a variant of the tune in the right hand in continuous semiquavers. In the second variation the semiquavers move to the left hand, while there is a variant of the tune in the right hand.

Variation 3 speeds up by having continuous semiquaver triplets in the right hand over the chord scheme, while variation 4 transfers the triplets to the left hand.

The last variation, labelled *vivacissimo*, consists of *bravura* demi-semiquaver scales over the chord scheme, in alternating hands. Bars 9^2–13 form a coda, in which the scales continue, ending in a grand *fortissimo*.

12 Handel
Music for The Royal Fireworks

Everyone knows of the two famous works written by Handel for public, out-of-doors occasions: the *Water Music* and *Music for the Royal Fireworks*. Some of the stories printed about the former work have been proved inaccurate, but there is no doubt about the origin of the latter.

The Peace of Aix-la-Chapelle ended the war of Austrian Succession in October 1748. England had taken part in the war, and George II decided to have a celebration which was to include a display of fireworks. He commissioned Handel to write music for the occasion.

Handel's music was ready early, so he had a full rehearsal in Vauxhall Gardens six days beforehand. Twelve thousand people came to it, paying 2s 6d each, and carriages over London Bridge were held up for over three hours. Perhaps it is as well that the occasion was so triumphant, because the Fireworks Celebration night itself was less free from complications.

The joint affair of the fireworks and the music was held in Green Park on 27 April 1749. Weeks had been spent beforehand on constructing an enormous wooden building, crowned by a vast sun, which was to burst suddenly into flame. There was also an enormous bas-relief of King George, but this ignominiously fell down during the firework display and the building was set on fire, causing panic among the crowd. Fortunately the music was over before the fireworks started.

The following month the work was performed again for the benefit of the Foundling Hospital—the charity which Handel supported so warmly, and which still benefits from performances of *Messiah*. On this occasion the King subscribed £2000.

Handel originally intended the work to be played by 40 trumpets, 20 horns, 16 oboes, 16 bassoons, 8 pairs of kettle drums, 12 side drums, flutes, fifes and serpents. But he decided against using the serpent; and it is thought that it was finally played by 9 trumpets, 9 horns, 24 oboes, 12 bassoons, 3 pairs of kettle drums, and side drums.

The Lea Pocket Score keeps to this, except that it also suggests that strings can double the oboe and bassoon parts, if wished, perhaps for performance indoors. This is a far cry from the many arrangements of the music that have since been made, whether by Hamilton Harty for full orchestra including strings, or simplified arrangements for school string orchestras or brass bands.

Students should therefore study this work from an original score, such as the Lea Pocket Score, rather than in any arrangement. And, if a gramophone record is bought for purposes of study, care should be taken that the scoring is as near as possible to the original. There are at least eight different recordings available at present, and four of them are of the Harty arrangement which, not being authentic, is unsuitable for examination purposes.

One of the best records is that made by Charles Mackerras in the Pye 'Golden Guinea' series. He has added two extra oboes, two extra bassoons, four double bassoons, and two serpents. The tone is most majestic, and probably as near-authentic as can be produced.

Handel thought of his band as being in three sections: the trumpets and drums; the horns; and the oboes and bassoons. Often they play antiphonally, though they all join together for the tuttis.

The form is that of the French overture: that is, it consists of a slow, grand introduction in a harmonic style, containing dotted notes, followed by a quick movement in a more contrapuntal style, and then by a series of short dances—four, in this case.

(The Lea Pocket Score also includes two concertos, both of which use the introduction to the overture of the *Fireworks Music*, and the second of which also contains some figures from the *allegro* of the overture. They are presumably included in the same volume as an illustration of Handel's well-known habit of borrowing from his own, or other people's works.)

Overture

Dotted notes were always a feature of the opening *largo*, and it was the custom in Handel's day, to double-dot the longer dotted notes, even though they were not written thus. So a dotted crotchet followed by a quaver was played as a double-dotted crotchet followed by a semiquaver. There are plenty of examples in this introduction.

The *largo* starts with a grand tutti, **A**, at 1–7, ending with a perfect cadence. This is repeated at 7³–13, with a modification at 11–13, so as to end on the dominant.

B starts at 13³ with a four-beat figure, treated antiphonally between brass and wood-wind, ending with a tutti at 17³–19².

C starts at 19³ with a sequential figure in the wood-wind ending in the dominant key at 24–5.

Two bars of tutti lead to another figure, **D**, which is very like **B**, and is treated antiphonally in the same way.

C returns at 31³, but now tutti and in the tonic key.

It ends on the dominant chord and leads to a return of **A** at 37³–43.

Bars 44–6 are a solemn, *adagio* link ending VIIb I in the dominant key, and preparing the way for the *allegro*.

The *allegro* is in ternary form, with 187–257 being an exact repetition of 47–115. Some editions may write D.C. in place of printing the whole passage again.

The *allegro* is built up of a number of short, conventional figures. It may have nothing very original to say, but its strength lies in the grandeur of the orchestration.

It starts with a rhythmic trumpet call, (*a*), in the trumpets and drums, answered by a dotted figure, (*b*), in the wood-wind. The trumpets repeat (*a*) again, and this time they are answered by (*b*) in the horns.

The two figures continue antiphonally in the tonic key up to 74, when a new figure, (*c*), starts which consists of dotted minims and broken chords in quavers. At first it is tutti; then, at 78, it is repeated without the trumpets.

Another figure, (d), starts at 82, and is repeated at 86. It is followed by (e) at 89, a one-bar figure which is treated antiphonally.

Bars 94–9 consist of the tonic chord and scales, (f). Figure (g) is another short figure which starts at 99, rising in the trumpets and then falling in the bassoons at 103.

Figure (d) reappears at 106 in the trumpets, with the addition of excited semiquavers in the oboes; and a dominant pedal leads to the end of the first section at 117.

The middle section starts with (a) in the trumpets, as in the first section, but the answer, (b), in the wood-wind modulates to B minor.

A new figure, (h), appears at the end of 126 in the wood-wind alone, and acts as a short episode.

Then (a) reappears in trumpets and horns in B minor at 138, answered by (b) in the wood-wind modulating to A major. The two figures continue antiphonally, modulating to G major at 150 and back to the tonic key at 151. By 151 most instruments are playing (b).

The tonic chord and scale figure, (f), first heard in 94–108, returns at 156, followed by (g) at 162, and (d) at 169 which is extended up to the cadence at 175. In other words, the ending of the middle section, 156–75, corresponds to the end of the first section, 94–117. So this middle section, although it began by modulating, and introduced an episodical contrast, (h) at 127, is largely built from the same material as the first section, and ends in the same way.

A modulatory *lentement* interpolation, 176–86, connects the second section with the return to the first section. It is written for wood-wind only, and provides a welcome relief from the noisy figures in D major. It modulates to B minor (178), E minor (180), B minor (182) and ends in F sharp minor; and double dotting is a feature, as in the introduction.

The recapitulation of 47–117 brings the overture to an end.

Bourrée

The first of the subsequent dances is a bourrée, and it is played by
oboes and bassoons alone. In D minor and in binary form, the first
section ends in the relative major at 10. The second section modulates through C major (14), G minor (16) and F major (16) before
reaching an imperfect cadence in the tonic key at 18. A phrase in
D minor follows, which is recapitulatory in key though not in idea,
and an extra phrase in D minor is added, 23–6, as a kind of coda. The
second section is therefore considerably longer than the first. (In the
Mackerras recording each section is repeated by three solo instruments plus a few ornaments, followed by the complete piece without repeats.)

La Paix

This dance is a siciliana in 12/8 time, though it is also given a title 'La
Paix'. It is played tutti, with the trumpets doubling the oboe parts,
and is harmonic in style—the *largo* style that one associates with
Handel at his best.

It returns to D major and is again in binary form though, this
time, the two sections are of equal length. The first half modulates to
the dominant, and the second half continues in the same style and
returns to the tonic key. The two endings are similar, apart from
key; and the trills which first appear at bar 7 were probably played
in corresponding places in the second half of the movement.

La Réjouissance

This is a very gay movement in the tonic major. The Lea Pocket
Score says that the horn parts written in small print are not in
Handel's autograph, though they were added later. The Mackerras
recording plays each half twice, the first time without horns, the
second time without trumpets and drums, and then finally repeats
the whole, tutti, with drums very much to the fore. This probably
approximates to the way it was performed in Handel's day.

Again, the first half modulates to the dominant and the second half returns to the tonic, and the movement is full of sequences, which rise and fall most effectively.

Minuets

The work ends with two minuets, the first in the tonic minor, the second in the tonic major. The first is for wood-wind only, and keeps entirely to the one key. The second is a final tutti, though again it looks, from the Lea score as if Handel did not originally write for horns. The score suggests that it should be played three times, with horns and timpani playing the second time and side drums added for the last time.

The Mackerras recording plays the D minor minuet as a kind of trio in between two performances of the major minuet, which is again a likely reconstruction of Handel's intentions. It also turns many pairs of quavers into dotted notes, and adds a few appoggia-turas and trills, all in accordance with the practice of the time. The first performance of the major minuet does not use trumpets when each half is repeated. But the final performance is a tutti, with side drums very much to the fore, providing a fitting conclusion to the whole work.

13 Haydn

String Quartet in G, Op 54, No 1

This quartet was one of a set of three composed in 1789, the year before Prince Esterhazy died, whose death terminated Haydn's regular service with the Esterhazy family. Haydn's earlier quartets were all produced in sets of six, but Op 54 and Op 55, as well as Op 71 and Op 74 reduced the number to three. He wrote 84 quartets altogether, a prodigious number, even though the first ones were comparatively slight and simple. He was virtually the inventor of works for this combination of instruments, and he always loved it very much. As a result of these compositions, quartet playing became a regular feature of cultured homes throughout Europe. Readers who want to know more about Haydn's quartets in general should read the article on Haydn's chamber music in Tovey's *Essays and Lectures on Music* (Oxford University Press).

First Movement, *Allegro con brio*

The first movement has a brilliant effect caused by the repeated use of two figures: (*a*) busy semiquaver runs, sometimes chromatic; and (*b*) repeated-note quavers. One or both of these figures is present nearly the whole time.

The movement is in sonata form and starts *forte* with (*b*) in the three lower parts and a dotted minim followed by (*a*) and then (*b*) in the first violin. Bar 3 is a varied repetition of this on dominant instead of tonic harmony. Then a chromatic scale of quavers in sixths leads to (*a*) alternating in first and second violin above (*b*) in viola and 'cello. In bars 7–10 (*a*) is heard continuously in the first violin against (*b*) in the 'cello.

Halfway through bar 10 the parts change over, (*b*) being in the violins and (*a*) in the 'cello, rising up to the viola and then into the violins again. Figures (*a*) and (*b*) are combined in the first violin in bars 12–13, producing a rather more distinctive figure which might be labelled (*c*); and all three figures are continued until they reach a perfect cadence in the tonic key at 15–16, repeated an octave lower at 16–17.

A short transition starts at 17, in which a new figure containing syncopation appears in the upper strings against (*b*) in the 'cello; and this reaches the dominant key at 21–2. Its cadence is repeated twice, thus making its effect as the end of a section more clearly felt.

But what follows, at 24–5 is a repetition of the first subject in the tonic. However, by 26 it moves to the dominant key; and one must undoubtedly call 24 the beginning of the second subject. Haydn

47

often uses the beginning of the first subject to start the second subject, though it is more commonly in the dominant than the tonic key, as here.

The figures (a) and (b) are continued as before, but now in the dominant key; and 32 starts a series of one-bar imitations of (b) between first and second violins.

A perfect cadence in the dominant key is reached at 39–40; and 40 begins the codetta which starts with a new two-note figure, separated by rests, in a series of first inversions. However, after another perfect cadence at 43–4, (c) returns and is heard three times, the last time by inversion, over a tonic pedal of the dominant key, thus ending the exposition.

The development section begins with the first subject in the tonic minor key; but, starting at 51, the figure (c), first heard in bars 12–13, appears twice in E flat major. At 63 the transition theme appears over (b) in E flat: the repeated-note figure, (b), is heard in almost every bar in the development section.

The music returns to G minor at 60, and figure (c) is heard three times in that key in the first violin, followed by its use in the second violin at 64, leading to A minor. Then the transition figure reappears at 66 in A minor; and this leads to the first subject at 74 in C major. But at 80 (c) returns, starting in E minor in the first violin with imitations in the viola and cello. Finally, at 84, the semiquaver part of (c) is heard by itself in all the instruments in imitation, and leads to the recapitulation at 87.

The recapitulation is much shortened, as compared with the exposition. It starts the same but changes at 95, the semiquaver runs, (a) taking over completely in the tonic key, with imitations, and this sounds very exciting. They reach G minor at 101, when semi-quaver runs in the 'cello are answered by the viola at 102, and taken over by the violins at 103. This leads into a perfect cadence in the tonic key at 106–7, and the codetta follows.

This means that there has been no transition and no second subject, though 103–7 is a telescoped version of 32–40 and ends with the same cadence except for the change of key.

The first six bars of the codetta are similar to those in the exposition, but now in the tonic key. Then the codetta is extended into a coda, starting at 113 and beginning with the codetta figure from 107, rising instead of falling, and continuing at 116 with (b) and (a) up to 120, when the codetta figure appears again. Four quieter and slower bars lead to a final repetition of the first subject at 126, with (c) at 129–30 being followed by two final chords.

Second Movement, *Allegretto*

This movement is again based on repeated quavers, but now in 6/8 time. It is a quiet movement of beautiful simplicity. But it does not fit exactly into any of the textbook definitions of standard forms. We must realise that, though Haydn was the founder of many of the forms upon which the textbooks are based, he was constantly experimenting, and many of these experiments did not become standardised into textbook forms. This is a case in point.

It is nearer to sonata form than to any other form but it has many unusual features. It is in C major and the first subject starts with a single, crotchet, C in the first violin followed by rests, and then continues with a two-bar fragment followed by a semiquaver figure which completes the four-bar phrase, all over repeated-quavers making a tonic chord below it.

It is followed by two bars similar to bars 2 and 3 but over dominant and then tonic repeated chords, and then by two bars similar to bar 4, to complete the next four-bar phrase.

A second sentence starts at 9, which contains three four-bar phrases, the first growing out of bars 2 and 3, the second out of bar 4 and the third rising to a high climax before sinking down into a perfect cadence in the tonic at 19–20.

Then follows a theme which seems like a second subject, but in the relative minor instead of the dominant major—the first unusual feature. Also it is not really very new. The repeated-quaver accompaniment continues, as also the single, tonic, note followed by rests,

49

starting the first phrase. The rest of the phrase—which is *six* bars long—mostly contains new material; but the second and third, more regular four-bar phrases, really grow out of bar 4. This section ends with a perfect cadence in the usual dominant key and completes the exposition.

The development section, starting at 35, continues with the repeated quavers and modulates by rising semitones into the unusual key of B flat. Bars 38–9 contain a new ascending figure.

Another three bars of semitonal rises lead to a repetition of this figure in the even more unexpected key of D flat.

The semitonal rises continue in a fuller form and lead to a climax at 47 based on Ic in key G which finally falls to a perfect cadence in that key at 43–4. It is unusual to have such a definite cadence in the dominant key in the development section.

Then the second subject figure from 21 starts again in A minor, the original key, but changes to G minor at 59 and then rises chromatically to dominant harmony of the tonic key from 63–8, ending with an effective descending scale in thirds in the two violins and leading into the recapitulation at 69.

Bars 69–88 are identical with the first subject in the exposition. But, instead of the second subject following in the tonic key at 88 there is a repetition of 34–48 from the development section, now a fourth higher, so that 88–102 are the same as 34–48 except that they lead to key C instead of key G. This is certainly unusual—an experiment of using part of the development in the recapitulation instead of the second subject of the exposition.

Its climax at Ic in the tonic key descends in thirds in the two violins, similar to the passage at the end of the recapitulation. Then it gradually sinks chromatically to a perfect cadence in C at 106–7.

The remaining bars of the movement form a coda, with the repeated notes and the semiquaver figure over a tonic pedal.

Third Movement, *Menuetto*

There is nothing unusual about the third movement which is in minuet and trio form, and returns to the tonic key, as is customary. All the same, it is a vigorous and charming movement. **A**, 1–10, ends in the tonic key; and **B** strides upwards in E minor, leaping an eleventh downwards to its cadence in D major at 19–20. A link of four bars leads to the return of **A** at 25; and a coda, starting after four beats rest, is based on **A** and brings the minuet to an end at 44.

The trio is based on continuous quavers in the 'cello, with occasional short figures above, combined with imitations of the 'cello part. **C**, 45–52, begins in G and ends on V in E minor. **D** modulates to A minor at 53–4 and moves sequentially to G major at 55–6 before returning to **C** at 62, with the upper parts an octave higher. It now ends in the tonic key.

Fourth Movement, *Presto*

Once more we have an unusual form in the fourth movement, this time combining rondo form with variation form. But there is no real contrast, as in a normal rondo, and the variations are more free than are most of those by Haydn and his contemporaries. So a more modern term like rhapsodie might come nearer to the improvisatory nature of the movement.

It starts normally enough, with a theme on the plan **A**:‖:**B A**:‖. The movement is naturally in the tonic key, G major, and **A** modulates to the dominant. **B** returns immediately to the tonic key and ends with a typical Haydn pause before returning to **A** at 18 which, this time, ends in the tonic key.

The next section, II, 26–65, starts in G minor and might therefore have been called a *minore* section, a term Haydn frequently uses. But it moves to B flat major in the fifth bar and stays in that key up to 50, when it returns to G minor. **C**, 26–40, roughly corresponds to **A**, but is 14 instead of 8 bars long, all the semiquaver runs in B flat acting as a kind of extension. **D**, 40–56, roughly corresponds to **B**, but is 16 instead of 8 bars long, the last six bars being over a dominant pedal of G minor. Then **C** returns at 57 but changes at 60 and ends quietly over a dominant chord of G minor at 65, therefore being much shorter than the first **C**. **C** and **D** both start with the three repeated notes which also began **A** and **B** and are similar in style to **A** and **B**, yet hardly similar enough to be called a variation. It is more natural to think of this section as being an episode in rondo form.

Then **A** returns in its original form at 66 but is not repeated. Instead, 73–93 is an interpolation, 73–83 being a kind of variation of **A**, which starts in B minor and passes through D major at 80–1 before ending in F sharp minor at 83. Bars 73–83 are then repeated, and are followed by a link based on the three repeated notes, which gradually sink into a return of **A** at 93 in its original form. **A** is then repeated yet again at 102–9 with the first violin an octave higher than before and with a different accompaniment, but with the same melody of the same length.

B follows, belatedly, at 109, and is the same as 8–17. After an interpolation of four bars based on the three repeated notes, **A** returns at 123, being an octave higher and having a similar treatment to that at 102–9, but otherwise corresponding to **A** at 18–26.

The whole of 66–131 can therefore be thought of as a return of the first section, I, in terms of rondo form, with variations, extensions and interpolations.

The next section, III, 131–55, is much shorter than was II, and is perhaps more like a variation of I. It starts in G major, with **A** being played an octave lower over an ornamented dominant pedal. But it moves to C major at 137–42, and then gradually rises, the semiquaver figure in the violins at 146–7 being transferred to the 'cello at 148 and the viola at 149, and ending with a pause at 150. The three repeated notes, with pauses in between them, lead to a final return of I at 156—a return which does not contain **B**.

Bars 156–64 are the same as **A** at 18–26. From 164 to the end can be thought of as coda. Or 164–76 can be considered a cadenza-like extension with all the four instruments running excitedly up and down in semiquavers followed by a varied and extended repetition of **A** at 76–86, in which the theme is in the second violin, beginning over a dominant pedal and ending with repeated cadences at 182–6. Given the latter supposition the coda starts at 186 and consists of four repetitions of the three repeated notes, the first two being separated by semiquaver broken chords.

14 Haydn

String Quartet in C, Op 76, No 3

Haydn's six quartets comprising Op 76 were written in 1799 in Vienna, three years after his second visit to London. While there he had heard *God save the King*, our national anthem, and he returned with the desire to write a national anthem for Austria. So he wrote *Gott erhalte Franz, den Kaiser*, which was played for the first time on the Emperor's birthday in February 1797 in all the theatres of Austria, and which rapidly became the most popular of all his songs.

Haydn used the theme in one of his masses and in *The Seven Words from the Cross*. But the best known use of the theme is in the variation movement of the quartet Op 76, No 3. It is rather ironic that the national anthem of our enemy in two wars should also have become popular as an English hymn, to the words 'Praise the Lord, ye Heavens adore Him', or 'Glorious things of Thee are spoken'; and many English people know it only in this form, having no idea of its origin.

First Movement

This movement is in sonata form, but it is largely built on the first five notes, (*a*), in the first violin, which form the germ of the first subject and of the first movement.

The first subject is very short and comes to an end with the perfect cadence in C major, the tonic key, in bar 4.

The repetition of this germ theme, (*a*) in the viola, starting on the

c

last quaver of bar 4, though still in the tonic key, really begins the transition. To it is now added a dotted figure in the second violin which forms a kind of short counter-subject to (*a*) and which is imitated by the first violin at 6, by the viola at the end of the same bar and by the 'cello at 7.

At bar 8 the dotted figure continues in the first violin over a tonic pedal, and is joined later by all the instruments, leading to an imperfect cadence in the tonic key at 12, quite a common ending for a transition in Haydn's day.

The second subject starts on the last quaver of bar 12 with the first subject germ figure (*a*) in the dominant key in the viola. Haydn frequently starts his second subject with the first subject in the dominant key in this way. It is now treated imitatively, and extended until it reaches a dominant pedal of the dominant key at 18, over which (*a*) continues to develop in the first violin.

This leads to a further treatment of (*a*) in A minor, starting on the last quaver of 22 in the second violin and ending with a perfect cadence in the dominant key at 25–6.

Then a second section of the second subject starts at 26, still in the dominant key. It is almost symphonic in sound, with its double-stopping, its large leaps and its wide range. It reaches G minor at 30 and E flat major at 31.

Then the germ figure (*a*) reappears once more, now in E flat major, a most unusual key for the exposition, in three parts in imitation, using low notes in all the instruments. The chord of E flat in 35–6 becomes the triad on the flattened sixth of G major and resolves on to Ic V I in that key at 37–8.

The second section of the second subject returns again in G major at 38, becoming even more elaborate at 40, and finally ending the exposition in the dominant key at 44.

The development section starts with a combination of (*a*) and the dotted figure, in the dominant key. They continue to develop, passing through A minor at 46; and then the first two notes of (*a*) are developed in imitation, reaching D minor at 50. The whole five-note figure is used again in C major at 51. Notice (*a*) in diminution in the 'cello, starting on the last quaver of 51.

Then the second section of the second subject reappears, starting in the viola on the last quaver of 52 and being imitated by the first violin in 53. Much use is made of imitation in this section; and (*a*) reappears in the viola, starting on the last note of 56. It is developed by the violins until the dominant chord of E is reached in 63–4.

Then (*a*) is heard in E major, another remote key, starting on the last quaver of 64. It is followed by the dotted figure at 68; and the whole of this section, from 65–75, is over a double *fz* tonic and dominant pedal alternating in viola and 'cello. Again, the impression is far more sonorous and symphonic than the usual effect of a string quartet.

Theme (*a*) briefly appears in E minor in 75–8 over a tonic pedal in the viola as the music quietens down; and it makes a most unusual lead in to the recapitulation in C major.

The short first subject (last quaver of 78–82) is exactly the same as in the exposition.

The transition starts the same on the last quaver of 82 but changes at 87, touching on F major on the way to D minor at 89, though it reaches a dominant chord of C major at 90, as it did at 12.

The equivalent of bars 13–18, the beginning of the second subject, is omitted, and the second subject now starts with the decoration of the first subject over the dominant pedal of the tonic key at 90, equivalent to the same treatment in the dominant key at 18.

Bars 95–8 are equivalent to 23–6 but with the theme starting in the viola instead of the second violin, and in D minor instead of A minor.

The second section of the second subject starts at 98, as at 26 but now in the tonic key. It changes at 100 and ends with two broken chords, each finishing with a pause, at 103–4. There is no equivalent to 33–44, and the last chord, ^7Vb in C major, leads into the coda.

This starts with imitations of the first two notes of (*a*), is followed by leaping minims at 109, with the viola and 'cello in syncopated imitation of the violins; and then, at 115, by the second section of the second subject. A brief appearance of the decorated version of (a) from 18 at 119 is followed by imitations of the first two notes of (a) again at 121, and this brings the recapitulation to an end.

Development and recapitulation are then repeated, as frequently happened in Haydn's day.

Second Movement

The theme itself is beautiful in its simplicity. The first phrase is repeated, and the third phrase modulates to the dominant. The fourth phrase starts with the climax of the theme and then falls away quietly to the end, though this phrase is repeated in its entirety, so that the climax occurs twice. The whole theme is played by the first violin, with simple harmonies underneath.

In the first variation the theme is transferred to the second violin, with a counter-theme in the first violin in semiquavers above it. It is therefore a duet between the two violins.

The theme moves to the 'cello in the third variation. It reverts to four-part harmony, though the viola's part consists only of occasional interjections, as a bass below the 'cello. The second violin's part 'shadows' the 'cello's theme in a similar rhythm, while the first violin makes much use of syncopation above it.

Variation III has the theme in the viola. The first violin still makes use of syncopation, and so does the second violin when it enters in counterpoint against the first violin. The 'cello is silent until the third phrase, and is then mostly very chromatic.

In the final variation the theme returns to the first violin, but it is harmonised differently, starting in E minor instead of G major; and all the parts jump an octave higher in the second phrase. They continue over a tonic pedal in the 'cello for four bars from 88–92; and then the 'cello, too, runs higher, so that all the parts are very high when the climax is reached in the fourth phrase. The repetition of this phrase is differently harmonised again, becoming more chromatic in all the parts.

There is a short coda of five bars from 100 to the end, during which the upper parts gradually sink to rest over a tonic pedal.

Third Movement

This is a minuet and trio, with the minuet in C major, the tonic key, and the trio in A minor.

The first phrase of the minuet is five bars long and the second phrase, containing further extensions, seven bars long, reaching a perfect cadence in the dominant key at 11–12. The next phrase starts with a decorated arpeggio over a tonic pedal of key G, but is the more usual four bars in length; and the last phrase of **A**, again four bars long, transfers the decorated arpeggio to the 'cello, now rising instead of falling, against falling arpeggios in the violin. Section **A** therefore ends at 20.

B, 20–32, develops the first three or four notes of **A** in imitations, often by inversion or sequence, and ends on V of the tonic key.

A returns on the last crotchet of 32. The first phrase is the same; but the second phrase, starting with the melody in the second violin, contains further extensions, and ends at 48. The third and fourth phrases begin with a decorated arpeggio, as before, but now on the chord of C instead of G, thus making **A** end in the tonic, instead of the dominant, key.

C of the trio starts in A minor but ends in E minor at 64.

D is a development of **C**, but much longer. The first phrase ends at 68 in D minor; and the second phrase develops the figure in A minor, with imitations in the viola, and extends up to the pause at 76. The next phrase changes to A *major* (a device which Schubert was to make much use of, later) and ends with an imperfect cadence. Bars 76–84 are then repeated, starting at 85 but ending with a perfect cadence.

C returns in A minor at 93, but changes at the end, so as to remain in the tonic key at 100. The minuet is then repeated.

Fourth Movement

The finale is in sonata form, and, rather surprisingly, in C *minor*, though it does end in C major. It is a tempestuous movement which starts with three *forte* chords including plenty of double and triple stopping. The next two bars form a smooth *piano* melodic contrast. But then the chords return, followed this time by five *cantabile* bars.

Then the chords appear yet again, at 12, in the upper strings, with triplets added in the 'cello, which triplets are transformed to the first violin at 14–17 while the lower parts have the *cantabile* phrase. The chords return at 18, with the triplets now in the viola, joined by the 'cello a bar later. The first subject ends at 20 with an imperfect cadence in the tonic key.

The second subject starts immediately, with the melodic phrase from bars 3 and 4 in the relative major key, thus using the first subject theme, as happened in the first movement. This time it is treated imitatively, starting in the second violin; and the theme is continued with imitations up to 46.

The second section of the second subject begins at 46, but again it is not new. It is based on the triplets first heard in bar 12, with the chords from 1–2 underneath them.

Imitations of the triplets between the violins start at 58, with the melodic phrase over a tonic pedal, still in E flat major. At 62 the triplets move to the 'cello while the chords reappear above them. At 66 the triplets move back to the first violin and continue over quietly-moving chords up to the end of the exposition in E flat major at 72.

Haydn has been economical of ideas; the whole of the exposition is based on the chords, the triplets and the melodic phrase.

The development consists of the same ideas, but now containing a good deal of modulation, all of it to flat keys. It starts with the melodic phrase in E flat major, treated imitatively.

At 84 the melodic phrase starts in the 'cello, with the triplets in the second violin and then in the viola at 86, reaching A flat major.

The triplets pass to the first violin at 88 and reach D flat major.
B flat major is passed through at 91 on the way to C minor at 93,
F minor at 95, E flat major at 97 and A flat major at 99, the triplets
and the melodic phrase moving all the time from one instrument to
another.

From 99 the triplets grow in intensity and frequency, being
present in first or second violin all the time. At first they are over a
held A flat in the 'cello; then, at 107 over a B flat repeated in triplets,
moving to B natural at 109 and thus reaching C minor, the tonic
key at 110. The music moves momentarily to F minor at 114 and to
E flat major at 116, but returns to C minor at 117 and thus into the
recapitulation at 119.

Bars 119–30 are the same as in the exposition, but then the last two
bars are repeated; and at 134 a long extension starts, using the
melodic phrase at first and then, at 137, when the music reaches
D flat major, mainly using triplets. At 143 the second violin takes
over the triplets; and at 145 the two violins imitate each other at
half-a-bar's distance, before the triplets are taken over by the 'cello
and viola at 148–50, first in imitation, then together. Bars 149–51
are very similar to 18–20, both ending on the dominant chord of
the tonic key.

But whereas the last beat of 20 started the second subject in the
relative major, as expected, the last beat of 151 starts the second
subject in the tonic *major* instead of minor, which is quite unusual.
The music touches on D minor at 155–6, A minor at 158 and D
minor at 159, but the prevailing key is C major until the end of the
movement, thus creating a sunlit happy ending to a movement
which began so tempestuously.

Bars 162–75 correspond to 33–46 but now in C major; and the
second section of the second subject starts at 175, being the same,
apart from key, as 58, which means that its first part is omitted.

At 180 the music emerges into a coda in which the triplet figure
and the melodic phrase from 3–4 are both heard.

15 Haydn

Symphony 100 (The 'Military')

This symphony is one of Haydn's last six symphonies, commissioned by Salomon for Haydn's second visit to London in 1794–5. It gained its title from the fact that triangle, cymbals and bass drum were used in the second and fourth movements as well as timpani, producing the military effect that was popularly known as 'Turkish' at that time. The big drum was played with a big stick on the accent and a little stick marking the pattern. The cymbals were played with the big stick and the triangle with the little stick. Perhaps Haydn produced this grandiloquent effect to celebrate his hundredth symphony.

Notice the clarinets are used only in the second movement, whereas they are used freely in the rest of his last six symphonies except for number 102 in B flat. This second movement was taken from a concerto in G for two lyras composed for the King of Naples about 1786, in which clarinets in C (now obsolete) were used. Haydn never used clarinets in a symphony until this last six.

The symphony was composed in 1794 and was performed for the first time at a benefit concert in London on 12 May of that year. It was also performed at another benefit concert at the King's Theatre in the Haymarket on 4 May 1795, at which Haydn made £400. He said that it was only in England that he made such sums; and his second visit, like the first, resulted in his making £1,200, enough to preclude any pecuniary anxieties for his old age. He also said that it was only after his visits to England that he became famous in Germany. His last appearance in England was on 1 June 1795. He was asked by the King to stay for the summer at Windsor but, by then, he preferred to return to his native Austria, where the last years of his life were spent.

First Movement

Like so many of Haydn's symphonies this begins with a long introduction. The first part is played by the strings, with occasional
reinforcements from the bassoons. The first violins play a beautiful
long-drawn-out melody and the first sentence ends in the dominant
key, D major, at bar 8. The next sentence passes through A minor
at 9 on its way back to the tonic key.

At 14 the music changes to G minor, with the theme in the bass,
and the whole orchestra enters, softly at first, but making a rapid
crescendo, and passing through C minor at 16 and E flat at 17, then
reaching a dominant pedal of the tonic key at 19, which continues
up to the pause at 23.

The *allegro* is, as expected, in sonata form, but contains several
unusual features, as nearly always happens with Haydn. Its opening
is unusual in that it starts with the solo flute accompanied by two
oboes; and the first sentence ends with an imperfect cadence at 30–1.
Then the subject is transferred to the strings only, now ending with
a perfect cadence at 38–9, and marking the end of the first subject.

A *f* tutti starts at 39 over a reiterated tonic pedal and this forms the
beginning of the transition. The violins carry the melody, which
builds up until it reaches the dominant key at 56. A dominant pedal
of this key is reached at 62, and from 56 the music becomes more and
more exciting, with quaver broken thirds and scalic passages until
it reaches a trill in the flute at 73.

This leads into the first subject in the dominant key with the
same orchestration as at first, that is, for flute and two oboes. Haydn
frequently leads, by means of a transition, into the dominant (or
relative major) key, only to reintroduce the first subject in this way.
The matter is, perhaps, not sufficiently discussed in text-books, and
it leaves many students and teachers puzzled as to what to call it. Is it
the second subject because it is in the complementary key, or the
first subject because it uses the same theme? Its presence is clearly
heard, and perhaps its definition would not matter if it were not for
the fact that examination candidates have to deal with it.

Personally, I feel that this starts the second part of the exposition because of its clear establishment of the complementary key, so I prefer to think of it as a particularly Haydnesque way of starting the second subject. It is identical for only five bars, the cadence at 80–1 being different. This cadence figure is then taken up in imitation between wind and strings, appearing in diminution at 83, until it leads to a perfect cadence in the wind at 86–7. But this ending overlaps with a partial restatement of the first subject, tutti, in D minor, the violins having the melody.

It ceases abruptly at 92, and is followed by two bars of an accompaniment figure in the lower strings in D major which serves as an introduction to the second section of the second subject, a gay melody in the violins, joined by the flute at 99. One feels that only an Austrian could have written such an infectious, dance-like theme. Its second sentence begins at 103; and its third sentence starts in the lower strings at 109. This latter is extended and runs into a codetta starting at 115, based on the same theme; and it finally comes to an end with the double bar at 124.

The development section starts with two bars' silence—almost as if the dancers were exhausted after the recent exhilaration. Then— off they start again with the same melody, but now in the unexpected key of B flat. The strings have it alone at first but the bassoon joins in six bars later, and the first violins imitate the seconds at 134 as the music modulates to C minor. By 139 everyone is playing, and they move to D minor in a dramatic *ff*.

Bars 146–57 repeat 133–44 a tone higher, therefore starting in D minor and reaching E minor. But the music changes at 158, moving to F major at 159 and G minor at 161, over an ostinato bass of C B C which continues from 157 until it slips down a tone at 165 and becomes a decorative dominant pedal of E minor.

This leads to a development of the first subject in the wind at 170, with the oboe now having the melody. The strings imitate two bars later; and strings and wind alternate in this way up to 178, when the first bar of the dance theme in the oboe is imitated by a bar in the bassoon. Then the figure is taken up in continuous quavers in flute and violins at 180.

A chord of G major is reached at 183, under which is heard the first bar of the dance theme in bassoon and lower strings. It continues under changing harmonies, producing a strong syncopated effect at 188–9.

Bar 191 begins by repeating 184 on a chord of C major, but moves differently and reaches V in G major at 195. This chord is continued up to the recapitulation at 202, first in the strings and then in the solo flute. Bars 202–9 of the recapitulation are the same as at 24–31. But the repetition is played tutti.

The transition is different from that in the exposition and is much shorter. It starts with the short imitations between wind and strings at 217–21, similar to those between 82–6, and the figure continues in the strings from 222–6.

This leads into the second section of the second subject in the tonic key at 226. (There would be no point in repeating the first subject as it has just been heard in the tonic key.) The first eight bars are played by the strings alone this time. It continues in the wind alone for two bars and then in the strings alone for four bars.

But this ends with a *ff* tutti and an interrupted cadence, which starts a development of the theme in E flat major over a tonic pedal, continuing up to 248. Then the bass slides down a semitone to D, the dominant of the tonic key; and the broken thirds passage, first heard at 56–62, reappears. It continues over a tonic pedal at 251–2.

Bar 251 could well have been the end of the movement, so from here to the end can be designated coda. A modulation to C major occurs over the G pedal at 252–3 and the music continues in the same style, so there is no clear break. Much use is made of the broken thirds and scale passages. The dancing theme reappears in the bass at 274 (this is a possible alternative place for the beginning of the coda). From here the music becomes ever more gay and exciting until the end of the movement is reached.

Second Movement, *Allegretto*

This movement is rather quicker than most of Haydn's slow movements, and contains the 'Turkish' effects already mentioned. It is really based on one theme of two stanzas, with a *minore* episode based on the same theme in the middle, and an effective coda.

The movement is in C major and the theme is first played by the strings, with the flute doubling the first violin to brighten the tone. It is then repeated by the wind at bar 9. The second stanza starts at 17, and is again first played by the strings and the flute, and then repeated by the wind at 38, finishing at 56.

The *minore* episode starts at 57, with the trumpets, drums, triangles, cymbals and bass drum producing the Turkish effect. It begins in C minor and moves to E flat at 61, with one-bar imitations between wind and strings. It returns to C minor at 70 with another tutti. A few quieter bars, starting at 74, have one-bar imitations between the various wind instruments and modulate to F minor before returning to C minor at 79–80. Then 81–90 repeat 70–80.

The first section returns at 92; and 92–119 corresponds to 1–56, but without the repetition of the two stanzas, and with both stanzas containing fuller orchestration. Bars 120–34 form a link in the wood-wind and lead to a tutti repetition of 112–19 at 134–41. An extension over a tonic pedal lasts from 142–52 and ends with a very definite cadence.

The coda starts at 152 with a trumpet fanfare which ends with a drum roll at 159–60. This is followed by a *ff* unexpected chord of A flat major, descending in *tremolos* in the strings, and leading to a *p* repetition of the first bar in the violins, over a dominant pedal of the tonic key, at 167. The figure is then transferred to the wind and repeated six times over the dominant pedal.

Four bars of tutti at 174–7, with the first bar repeated in the strings, lead to a tonic pedal starting at 178, over which the first bar is imitated in alternate bars by first and second violins; and the last four bars are a *forte* tutti repetition of the cadence.

Third Movement, *Minuet and Trio*

Just as the second movement was rather quicker than most of Haydn's slow movements, so the third movement is rather slower. The minuet is a vigorous *moderato*, and it returns to the tonic key, G.

The repeat of **A**, 9–16, is written out, because its accompaniment is rather different. It ends in the tonic key.

B, 17–28, starts with the last two bars of the violin part of **A** in the viola and 'cello, and modulates to D at 20–8.

Then the opening figure of the minuet is heard in imitation in 'cellos and violins, and starts a link which continues chromatically in the strings from 36–42.

A returns at 43 and is extended at 50, ending in the tonic key at 56. **B** and **A** are then repeated.

The trio is more sprightly. **C** begins and ends in the tonic key and is repeated. **D** continues with the same figure and modulates to D at 68, when four vigorous bars lead to a return to **C**, which changes at 77, rising so as to reach a climax. **D** and **C** are then repeated, and are followed by a return to the minuet, without repeats.

Fourth Movement, *Presto*

This movement is in sonata form, but is full of irregularities. It starts like a rondo, with a theme on the plan **A**:‖**BA**:‖. **A** is a cheerful tune in the strings in 6/8 time, ending in the tonic key, G, at 8. **B** continues with the same idea but starting in E minor, tutti, and touches on D minor at 13–16 before reaching D major at 17, in which key it reaches a perfect cadence at 25–6.

A link, 27–40, starts with the theme in the violas and 'cellos, imitated a bar later by the violins, and reaches a pedal D at 32, which ends with the pause at 40.

A returns at 42, and is exactly the same as the first **A**. All this can be thought of as the first subject.

A transition, 49b–67 is based on the same theme and leads to D major, the dominant key; and the second subject starts at 67 with the first subject in the dominant key, as so often happens in works by Haydn.

At 70 it is played by the violins alone and leads, at last, to a new theme, which can be called the second section of the second subject, at 74. This consists of *staccatissimo* crotchet chords, heard first in wind and strings together and then, at 78, in strings alone. Notice the effective bar's rest at 77, 79 and 81. Two slurred notes in the 'cello at 82 are answered by the flute; and 'cello and flute repeat the imitation once more.

A third section of the second subject starts at 86, when a two-bar figure, consisting of an octave leap followed by two grace notes leading to a note a second higher, is used in overlapping imitations between 'cellos and violins. The grace note figure continues alone from 90–3 in a *diminuendo* until a *forte* tutti at 94, in which the complete figure is heard again in imitation.

A tutti codetta starts at 98 and consists of continuous quavers, containing frequent octave leaps, ending over tonic and dominant notes of the dominant key, thus bringing the exposition to an end at 116.

The development section starts at 117 with the second section of the second subject, complete with its pauses. Then the first subject starts in D minor at 124 in the strings and is repeated in F major at 129 in the first violins against dotted minims in the wind. This merges into the second section of the second subject again at 132, played by violins and 'cellos alternately.

The first subject reappears at 138 in oboes and violas and passes to the bass two bars later, to upper strings two bars later again, and finally to unison strings, reaching C major at 142–5.

The unison C at 145 then slides down into A flat, in which key the third section of the second subject is heard, followed by the second section in inversion at 150, building up in a *crescendo* to D flat major at 156. Four *forte* tutti bars lead once more into the second section of the second subject, played tutti up to 162, then by two oboes for two bars and then, after a bar's rest, by the first violins, *pp*, in C sharp minor, by means of an enharmonic change. This figure has been heard ascending and descending, and has reached the most remote keys in its course.

After four more bars in the second violin, 170–3, the figure reaches E major, when it is heard in the wind, *legato* instead of *staccato*, which provides yet another change. It transfers to the violins for four bars, 178–81, and then is interrupted by a *forte* repetition of the first subject in E major. This changes to E minor at 186 and to C major, starting in the 'cellos, at 190, imitated by the violas and bassoons in B minor at 191. This imitation recurs again at 192–3, in descending sequences, and the quavers are then transferred to the upper strings, finally reaching a *forte* tutti at 198 in E minor.

At 202 the first two notes of the second section of the second subject are heard alternately in lower strings and flute, as at 82–5, but now the alternation is continued for longer, until interrupted by the first subject in the violins at 212, followed in imitation by flutes and oboes at 214 and then by the pause which has so often occurred before. These last four bars are built on the dominant seventh of the tonic key, and lead to the recapitulation at 218.

But this time Haydn appears to have completely forgotten the rondo-like form of the first subject. **A** is played once only and is followed at 226 by a tutti development of it. This leads into the *staccato* second section of the second subject, starting at 234, with the theme sliding down in semitones and reaching the unexpected key of E flat major at 241–2.

In this key the first subject reappears in the second violins for two bars at 245, then in all the violins for two bars, with imitations a bar later in the lower strings. It continues for some time in this way, the theme sometimes being inverted, until it tumbles down in thirds at 255, then gradually rises again from 257–62 in the violins, finally running down into the third section of the second subject at 265 in the tonic key. At this moment the Turkish percussion reappears and is almost continuous to 296, against the third section of the second subject until 277, and then against continuous quavers.

This is not at all a typical recapitulation, and is more like a combination of recapitulation and coda, as is sometimes found in Haydn's other works. However it quietens down at 296, when the Turkish percussion ceases; and a few hesitant bars lead into the first subject again at 304 in the strings, as at the beginning of the movement. It is repeated in the wind at 312 and then tutti at 318 with all the percussion entering once more; and the tutti continues to form a triumphant end to the movement.

16 Haydn
'Nelson' Mass

This mass is the third of six which Haydn wrote between 1796 and 1802 after his second visit to London, and is therefore influenced by having heard Handel's choral works. Haydn wrote in this score that it was composed between 10 July and 31 August 1798, in Eisenstadt, where he still went each summer. He much admired Nelson, and it is thought that the triumphant use of trumpets in the 'Benedictus' marked the news of Nelson's victory at Aboukir. Nelson and Emma Hamilton visited Esterhaz in 1800, and they probably heard it then. But the mass also has other names: Mass in Time of Peril; Imperial Mass; Coronation Mass; and *Mehlsandmesse*.

Haydn's masses are cheerful—he once said 'At the thought of God my heart leaps for joy and I cannot help my music doing the same'. But this mass is particularly joyous and vigorous; and many people think it is his greatest.

Haydn scored it for 3 clarini (high trumpets), drums, organ and strings and no wood-wind. But the earliest printed editions re-scored the work in a more conventional way and added wood-wind. The Peter's vocal score follows them in adding marks such as: ob; hbl; fl and ob 1 to the piano arrangement of the score. The Hungarian performance on records is the same as the one in the Peter's edition; but Dr Willcock's King's College version follows Haydn's original scoring. The teacher or student should be aware of these differences, if he chooses either recording.

'Kyrie'

This number starts with a triumphant orchestral tutti in D minor. The broad melody which begins in bar 2 can be labelled (*a*), and the quieter, more *cantabile* melody which starts at 11 in the strings can be labelled (*b*).

The chorus enters at 16 with octave leaps on 'kyrie', and this can be labelled (*c*). It is heard against (*b*) in the orchestra. Figure (*b*) returns in the strings at 28 and the soprano soloist enters a bar later with (*c*). The choir enters again with (*c*) at 33 against (*a*), inverted, in the full orchestra.

Two modulatory bars lead to the key of F and a coloratura soprano solo, (*d*). As this continues the chorus has a new stepwise figure, (*e*), starting at 43 ; while at 50 they sing a falling dotted figure, (*f*), which is taken over by the soloist a bar later. This section ends at 54 in F major.

Then follows a series of imitative entries in the chorus, (*g*). This might almost be called a fugato, but the entries have only the first five beats in common. The figure is used almost continuously up to 98, passing through a number of related keys. It broadens out into a cadence in A minor at 79–80, but the figure returns at 83; and, starting at 89, the four voices enter a tone higher in each bar, finally reaching V in the tonic key at 98.

The first section then returns at 99 with (*c*) in the chorus, (*a*) in the orchestra and the soloist singing again in coloratura. At 105 the choir sing (*g*) in harmony instead of in imitation and continue in this way up to the climax on a pause at 110.

Figure (*b*) then returns in the strings at 111 and the soloist enters with (*c*) a bar later. A dominant pedal starts at 116, over which (*g*) is

69

heard in the chorus; and the music broadens out again as before until it reaches a series of perfect cadences in the tonic key at 127–32. The soloist enters with coloratura again at 132, ending with an interrupted cadence at 142–3. Some final entries of (g) follow, until a perfect cadence is reached at 152–3. And cadence repetitions continue to the end.

'Gloria'

The opening stanza consists of three short phrases in D major. Figure (a) is sung first by the soprano soloist, then repeated by the chorus. The soloist follows with (b) at 5, imitated a bar later by the choir. And then she sings (c) alone at 7. From 9–15 the whole of (a), (b) and (c) is repeated by the choir.

'Et in terra pax' is then sung by soprano, tenor and bass soloists at 16–32, with the tenor and bass singing (d) in imitation.

'Laudamus te', (e), is taken up by the choir at 33 in harmony, building up to a climax at 'glorificamus' and leading to a new figure, (f), on 'laudamus' at 42. This broadens out into a cadence in A major at 49–50.

The original stanza, (a), (b), (c), is then sung by the alto soloist, who enters for the first time at 52–60. It is repeated by the soprano soloist, with minims in place of (b). And again, at 71–7, it is repeated by the choir.

The imitative figure, (d), is then repeated by the tenor and bass soloists as before, but this time without the soprano interjection. It is taken up by the choir at 91 in a harmonic style and reaches a climax at 95 before falling to a perfect cadence in the tonic key at 96–7. A short harmonic coda for full chorus follows.

'Qui tollis'

This is a bass solo in B flat with one interjection of the soprano soloist and harmonic passages by the chorus at each cadence. It is a spacious *adagio*, accompanied mainly by the strings. At the cadence in F major at 18–19 the chorus enters quietly with 'miserere nobis'.

The bass soloist starts again at 22, as at bar 2, but is interrupted by the soprano soloist at 30, who is accompanied quietly by the choir as before, now reaching D minor at 36–7.

The bass soloist enters again at 38 in G minor, returning to the opening phrase in that key at 44–7.

After four further bars of the choir singing 'miserere nobis', he enters again for the last time, now in D minor. The chorus takes over as he finishes at 58–9 with its 'miserere nobis', ending with a dramatic imperfect cadence in D minor, followed by *attacca*. So this number begins and ends in different keys and is incomplete.

'Quoniam tu solus'

This begins in D major, and bars 1–15 are a repetition of 1–15 of the 'Gloria', but to different words.

A short harmonic choral passage starting with the words 'cum sancto spiritu', which lasts from 17–22, leads to a choral fugue in D major.

The subject starts in the bass at 22, with a tonal answer in the tenor at 24, followed by the subject in the alto at 26 and the answer in the soprano at 28. All these entries are followed by a counter subject in quavers. Two more entries of the subject in the tonic in the bass at 30 and the tenor at 32 complete the exposition.

Then follow middle entries of the subject in the soprano at 33 and the answer in the bass at 35, in B minor. An entry of the subject appears in the tenor at 37 in A major, but this merges into an episode, ending at 45.

Middle entries in E minor start with the subject in the bass at 44, and an answer in the tenor in stretto, half a bar later, and followed by an entry in the alto in G major at 46. They lead to another longer episode, briefly interrupted by an entry in the bass in B minor at 51, and ending in D major at 60–61.

The fugue has therefore ended in the tonic key but there is no final section, with entries in that key. Instead there is a coda on the word 'Amen', starting with a tonic pedal over which (*d*) from the

'Gloria' is sung in imitation by bass, tenor and also soloists, with a quaver counter theme by the soprano soloist. This alternates with a tutti at 68–71 and 77 to the end, and finishes with a glorious climax.

'Credo'

The first eight bars are played by the orchestra in unison, in D major. Then the chorus enters with the first six notes of this theme in a double canon at the fifth, starting in sopranos and tenors, with altos and basses entering a bar later.

There are two short orchestral interludes at 27–31 and 47–50, the first modulating from E major to A minor and the second in B minor. Otherwise the canon continues without a break up to the pause at 77—a veritable *tour de force*. A coda of six bars in harmonic style ends the movement.

'Et Incarnatus'

This number, a *largo* in G major, starts with a soprano solo, ending at 19 in the tonic key. The chorus then enters, *espressivo*, in harmonic style, repeating the first four bars of the soloist but then changing and modulating to D. The passage from 28–35, starting with 'crucifixus' is sung by the choir in unison, ending on one repeated note at 'sub Pontio Pilato'.

The other three soloists then enter at 36, each singing different words, but the chorus interrupts with a *forte* 'crucifixus' at 38. The three upper soloists sing 'et sepultus est' at 41–3, ending with a pause. The chorus finishes the number, *pianissimo*, and is over a tonic pedal from 47 to the end.

'Et Resurrexit'

This is a joyful *vivace*, which starts in B minor but ends in D major. It begins with a chorus in which the tenors run down the scale in quavers on 'resurrexit' in bar 1, followed by the basses a beat later, while the sopranos run up the scale in the next bar, and the orchestra skips about in semiquavers. By bar 11 the voices are moving more sedately in crotchets, but the joyful semiquavers in the orchestra continue. 'Et mortuous' moves even more slowly and reaches a cadence in D major at 18–19.

The next section starts at 19 with imitative entries on 'cujus regni', and with the trumpets much in evidence. It reaches another cadence in D major at 26–7.

Then a bold modulation to B flat on the word 'Et' slips down a semitone to A in the key of D minor and 'Et in spiritum sanctum' is sung in unison on A, continuing up to 34. A solemn passage follows from 35–41, ending in the key of F.

But the orchestra has never ceased to play semiquavers, and now it has six joyous bars to itself before the voices enter again on a repeated unison C from 47–53.

The next section returns to D minor at 53, and the chorus sings in harmonic style until it reaches another unison 'Et' at 63. The soprano soloist enters at 65 and sings a coloratura passage ending at 76. By now the music is in D major and the chorus repeats the soprano's words, ending with 'Amen'.

A coda lasts from 84–108 and is built on 'Amen', with semi-quavers most of the time in the orchestra and a good deal of synco-pation in the chorus. At the end everyone is singing *ff*; and trumpets, drums and organ add to the splendour.

'Sanctus'

This starts with a solemn *adagio* in D major, with the chorus singing in a simple, harmonic style. It ends on a pause at 12.

Then a joyous allegro breaks out with 'pleni sunt coeli' moving up and down the tonic chord in unison. Imitative entries start at 19, ending harmonically with 'gloria tua' at 29–30. More imitative entries start at 31 to the words 'Osanna in excelsis', but they again end harmonically at 38–41.

A coda starts at 42 to the same words, and ends over a tonic pedal from 49–56, with a very broad cadence.

'Benedictus'

This is the number that is supposed to have been inspired by Nelson's victory, and makes much use of trumpets. It has a long orchestral introduction in D minor, which includes six themes: (a) starting at bar 1; (b) at 7; (c) at 10, which changes its shape at various times, but always consists of continuous demisemiquavers; (d) half-way through 13; (e) half-way through 19; and (f) at 24.

The soprano soloist enters at 34 with (a); (b) appears at 37–8 in the orchestra, while the chorus has it in a simplified form; (c) appears in the orchestra at 43 against a development of (a) in the choir, and continues until a version of (d) appears at 48.

Figure (a) reappears in the soprano's part at 50; but this time it modulates to F major, and the soloist continues up to 72, when the chorus enters against (f) in the orchestra. This section ends in F at 84.

Then the alto soloist enters with (a) at 84 and modulates to G minor. The bass soloist enters in imitation four bars later, the tenor soloist two bars later again, and finally the soprano soloist enters at 92, now returning to D minor.

Bars 92–102 are the same as 34–44. The orchestra continues the same as 45–8 at 103–6, but the choir moves in quavers instead of having one long note.

Figure (d) returns at 106, but this time modulates to G minor and D minor; and figure (e) appears at 113, with rests in the orchestra and dotted notes in the soloists. They reach a cadence in the tonic key at 117.

Figure (f) returns at 117 in the orchestra, with the choir having a simplified version.

A coda starts at 122 in which the trumpet fanfare on D is much in evidence. The choir reaches a *ff* climax at 131 and then falls to a cadence at 133. Figure (f) appears for the last time at 133, and leads straight into the next number.

'Osanna'

This is a short number in D major, which begins with imitative entries in the choir. The second half starts at 11, and consists of quick orchestral cadential passages against slower-moving choral parts.

'Agnus Dei'

This is an *adagio* in G major for the four soloists. The orchestra starts with a *cantabile* theme which is taken up at 10 by the alto soloist. The soprano enters with a new theme at 18 and modulates freely, ending in E minor.

The alto takes up the same theme at 30, the bass enters a bar later again, and the four continue in harmony, ending on V in B minor at 39. The orchestra continues in the same key over a dominant pedal for another two bars; and this leads straight into the final number.

'Dona nobis'

This final chorus returns to the opening key, D, but now it is major instead of minor. The orchestral accompaniment is independent, and consists of three figures: (*a*) in bar 1; (*b*) at 16; and (*c*) at 22. One or other of these is present all the time, though (*a*) predominates.

The chorus moves more slowly, and is largely built up of imitative entries of the figure which starts in the altos in bar 1. It modulates to A major at 10, and the first part ends in that key at 25.

The next section moves to E minor, then to G major at 33, and B minor at 36 and reaches a cadence in A major at 39.

Then the first part returns in the tonic key; and 40–45 corresponds to 1–6. But it continues differently, though 49 corresponds to 16 but now in the tonic key, so that the cadence at 58 is in D instead of A, as at 25.

A coda starts at 58, and builds up to a climax at 72, ending triumphantly at 77.

17 Mozart

Symphony No 36 in C (The 'Linz')

Mozart lived for the last ten years of his life (1781–91) in Vienna, but he composed only six of his thirty-nine symphonies during the whole of that time. This was the period when he wrote most of his piano concertos; and when he gave a concert of his own music it was usual to include at least one piano concerto together with, perhaps, odd movements from some of his earlier symphonies.

The 'Haffner' symphony was the first of the Vienna symphonies, but it was, in effect, a second 'Haffner' serenade. Then followed the 'Linz' in 1783, the first of the truly Viennese symphonies. It ranks, in greatness, with the 'Prague' which followed in 1786 and the last three of the Vienna set, written in 1788 in six weeks. The 'Linz' is perhaps performed less frequently than these others today, and it is rather more uneven. It was written in Linz, in November 1783 on his way home from Salzburg to Vienna, and he says himself that he wrote it at breakneck speed, as he required it for a concert in Linz.

First Movement

This is the first of Mozart's symphonies to have an introduction (the only other two to have introductions are the 'Prague' and No 39 in E flat). The idea was probably taken from hearing Haydn's symphonies, as many of those Haydn wrote at this time had introductions. But the introduction to the 'Linz' symphony was more spacious and had more dramatic and expressive contrast than any that Haydn had written up to this time. Perhaps the variety of orchestral colour and the expressive melodic line that Mozart used in this introduction helped to produce the same qualities in the introductions to Haydn's later symphonies, such as Nos 99 in E flat and 102 in B flat. There is no doubt that each of these great composers learned much from the other.

The introduction starts with a dramatic unison tutti which is quite Haydnesque. But it changes at the fourth bar to quietly reiterated quavers, over which a typically Mozartian, expressive melody is played by the violins. A plaintive, chromatic quaver figure appears in the first bassoon at bar 8, answered by the first oboe a bar later, followed by oboes and bassoon together. The basses then take it up, spreading it over two bars; and they are answered by the violins. Wind and strings then alternate, the melody becoming ever more chromatic as it continues. The sublety of this is something which was unknown to Haydn at this time.

The *allegro* starts at 20 with a rather obvious four-bar phrase, which is answered by a less usual and more chromatic six-bar phrase. Haydn made much use of irregular phrasing of this kind, and Mozart may have taken the idea from him. Tovey speaks of the enjoyment of the sense of movement which is shown in this irregular beginning and which continues throughout the movement: it represents a ripening of Mozart's symphonic style.

The sense of movement is further shown in the giant strides the melody takes in bars 30–32, though they are followed by a rather commonplace chordal reiteration. A flowing chromatic six-bar melody then brings the first subject to an end at 42.

The transition starts in a conventional eighteenth century style and, after reiterating a cadence in the key of C, begins to modulate to the dominant at 49, reaching a cadence in that key at 52–3.

A new theme begins in the dominant at the fourth beat of 53. Although it enters rather unobtrusively, I think it must be considered to be the first section of the second subject. Notice the minim leaps with which it continues at 62.

A second section of the second subject starts in E minor at 72, which makes use of trumpets and horns, and is noisy in the Turkish style, though Mozart could not make use of drums in this key. However he repeats the figure in C major at 76 and 84, and at 84 the drums do appear—perhaps that is his reason for using that key. Contrast is provided by a string figure at 77, which returns to G major; but it leads to a repetition of the E minor theme in oboes and bassoons, followed by the modulation to C major to which reference has already been made. However, even this ends in G major, thus stressing the fact that, though Mozart may digress to E minor and C major, G major is really the main key for the second subject.

The third section of the second subject, starting at 87, consists of conventional passage-work in G major that might have been written by any eighteenth-century composer. It breaks off at 105 and leads to the fourth section, a hesitant passage of imitations, which humorously holds up the movement, and which might have been written by Haydn.

The codetta starts at 111 and is again of the conventional kind. A linking melody in the violin leads back to the beginning of the exposition or on to the development section.

The development section is quite short, as was customary in Mozart's early works, so the influence of Haydn's longer development sections is not apparent here. It begins with a reference to the end of the first section of the second subject at 66–71 (which is partly derived from the transition at 44–6). This modulates to A minor, in which key the melodious link-figure returns, with wind imitating the strings at the cadences. It passes through D minor (132) and C major (137) and leads to F major at 144, at which moment the bassoon has a few bars of solo chromatic melody, though it is soon joined by the oboes.

A dominant pedal of C major is reached at 152, and the next few bars are quite conventional; but bars 159–64 are more delicately Mozartian, and they hesitantly lead to the recapitulation.

In the recapitulation the first subject is identical with its presentation in the exposition. The transition starts the same at 185 but changes at 193 and leads to the second subject in the *subdominant* at 199. However it changes at 202 and by 204 it has become a fifth lower than in the exposition and is in the expected tonic key.

The second section of the second subject, starting at 218, is in A minor, which bears the same relationship to C major that its E minor appearance had to G major in the exposition. From here to the end of the recapitulation the changes from the exposition are only slight.

The coda starts at 265 with the violin melody that formed a link at the end of the exposition (120). It continues for some time, each phrase in the violins being answered by a little comment in the wind. But all come together for the last few bars. It will be noticed that this coda is very similar to the development section.

This first movement is in rather a mixture of styles. There is no doubt that Mozart was, at times, trying to model the symphony on those of Haydn, but at other times his own idiomatic style breaks out, while there are moments where his composing 'at breakneck speed' is evidenced by his falling back on the conventional idioms of the day.

Second Movement, *Poco adagio*

Notice that this movement makes most effective use of trumpets and drums—they were still rarely used in slow movements. Also notice that the drums are in C and G, in spite of the movement being in the key of F. This makes it possible for Mozart to use the dominant and tonic for the second subject when it appears in the key of C. This was quite uncommon. Beethoven also does it in his first symphony.

The movement is in sonata form and begins with a delightful slow-moving melody, in which four bars are answered by eight—again perhaps modelled on Haydn's use of extensions.

The transition, 13–16, is very short and leads to a second subject in the dominant key. This begins with an assertive dominant in wood-wind, brass and drum, which is repeated a bar later, with a delicate string figure in between. The second section, which begins at 22, has quietly reiterated trumpets and drums as an accompaniment to a string figure in C minor. This ends with an interrupted cadence at 27–8, and a repeated extension leads to the perfect cadence at 32. A codetta, in which trumpets and drums are still a main feature, brings the exposition to an end.

The development section starts with a reference to the first subject in C major. Then, at 41, the wood-wind, brass and drums restart their repeated notes, using a tonic pedal, while a new, delicate little figure appears in the violins.

An episode starts at 45—Mozart quite often introduces an episode into his development sections. Its main constituent is a repeated figure in the bass which sometimes has B flat, C as its last two notes, while at other times he varies it by using B natural, C. It also appears in imitation in the violins at 50–54, and there is a modification of it at 55–8 before it returns to the bass again at 59.

The recapitulation starts at 66 and the melody of the first subject is more chromatic than before. The transition (78–83) uses the same figure as in the exposition but with different harmonies; and it leads to the second subject (83–100) and the codetta (100–104), in which only slight modifications occur, apart from the obvious change of key. There is no coda.

Third Movement

The first part of the minuet is very short and ends in the tonic key. The second part starts with an inversion of the figure from bar 1 and develops it in a series of rising extensions until it reaches a cadence in the dominant key at 18. The figure from 5–8 then passes through D minor (20), C major (22) and F major (26) before returning to the tonic key at 28. A short codetta (28–32) refers to bar 1 again.

The trio is still in the tonic key, and its first part again ends in the tonic. The second part continues with the same figure and reaches a cadence in the dominant key at 78, before making a complete return of the first part. So this trio, on any method of analysis, would be said to be in ternary form.

Fourth Movement, *Presto*

The finale, which is in sonata form, is a joyful movement with a wealth of themes.

The first subject contains four four-bar phrases, each with a new figure, followed by a repetition of the last two, the final one being altered and extended to eight bars.

The transition (28–58) contains three distinct themes. The first one (28–38) is the usual eighteenth century chordal passage and remains in the tonic key; the second (39–46) is a charming three-part phrase for violins and violas, and modulates to the dominant; the third (47–58) is again chordal, but is built over a dominant pedal of the dominant key.

The second subject contains four distinct sections, in addition to a link between the third and fourth and a long codetta. The first section (58–72) is a flowing string theme in the dominant. The second (73–92) consists of a fugato which grows out of the previous bars. All the string parts have the theme in turn. The third section (93–104) continues with the fugato theme in falling sequences, plus the addition of a new figure in the violins in which a falling seventh is a feature.

Bars 104–116 can best be thought of as a link based on the fugato figure and the falling seventh in diminution, mainly over a tonic pedal. It leads to the fourth section (116–32) which consists of imitative entries of a busy string figure, with a counter-theme against it in the violins at 120 and the oboes at 125, followed by a tutti cadence.

The codetta starts at 133 with string semiquavers over dominant and tonic harmony. Bars 148–58 refer to the first subject, and a few cadential bars bring the exposition to an end. It has been an unusually spacious one, with the fugato adding to the feeling of breadth.

The development section, having a wealth of material in the exposition from which it can choose for development purposes, chooses to confine itself entirely to the transition theme starting at 28. It begins unaccompanied in the first violins and, after repeating the theme once, starts it a note higher at 180 and extends it by rising again at the end of the phrase. But before it is finished, it is imitated

81

in the bass at 184. It rises yet again in the violins at 188, imitated in the bass at 192 as before.

Then the bassoon has the theme to itself in F major at 200, accompanied by the strings; and this starts a series of imitations: oboe at 204, violas at 208, second violins at 212, first violins at 216, and 'cellos and basses at 220. A few bars of chromatic scale lead into the recapitulation at 232.

The first subject is exactly the same as in the exposition; and the transition starts the same at 259 but changes during the second section, 270–81, so that the third section, 282–93, is the same as in the exposition except that it is now in the tonic key.

Modifications of the second subject are so slight as not to be worth mentioning until 393, when the last ten bars are repeated. Bars 403–11 are a cadential interpolation, and the last five bars are the same as in the exposition.

18 Mozart

Symphony No 41 in C (The 'Jupiter')

The 'Jupiter' symphony was Mozart's last symphony and was one of the three that was composed in six weeks in the summer of 1788, three years before his death. Cramer gave it the title 'Jupiter', in reference to its strength and beauty.

Mozart used clarinets in the E flat symphony, and he wrote two versions of the G minor symphony, one without and the other with clarinets. But, for some reason, he chose not to use them in the last of these three symphonies, the 'Jupiter'. The wood-wind section consists of one flute, two oboes and two bassoons; and he uses the usual two horns, two trumpets and two drums, in addition to the strings.

First Movement

The first movement is in sonata form. It has a rather formal first subject, typical of the period, with an assertive unison tutti fanfare round C, (a), followed by an appealing contrasting phrase played by the strings alone, in which suspensions are a feature, (b). Bars 5 and 6 answer 1 and 2, now round the note G; and 7 and 8 answer 3 and 4. Then there are fifteen bars of tutti based on the primary triads, ending with a strongly reiterated G.

The transition starts at 24 and consists of (a) and (b) of the first subject combined with two little counter melodies: two minims followed by a quaver scale in the flute and oboes, (c), and a crotchet broken-chord, (d), played first by the horns and then by the bassoons. Figure (b) modulates to D minor at 30 and is further developed. At 37 the four figures combine again, and 39–46 have an upper and a lower dominant pedal in the tonic key. But a dominant pedal of the dominant key is reached at 49, while the short demisemiquaver figure first heard in bar 9 appears in the second violin and viola.

The second subject begins at 56 in the usual dominant key, and consists of four sections and a codetta. The first section starts with a graceful six-bar phrase in the strings, which is then repeated with the addition of the bassoon and extended into a ten-bar phrase. Figure (b) of the first subject appears in the bass at 71, with a lovely counter-melody in the violin. It begins a repetition at 75 but breaks off on a dominant seventh of C at 79, and bar 80 is a pause.

The second section starts unexpectedly in C minor, not C major, and is a noisy tutti which returns to G major.

The third section, starting at 89, consists of a graceful dotted figure in sixths in the violins over a tonic pedal; and it is repeated more fully at 94 with the pedal now at the top of the texture and syncopated. This ends with a quiet descending dominant seventh and another pause, 99–100.

The fourth section, 101–11, is a simple, dance-like theme in octaves in the violins over tonic and dominant harmonies. Mozart first wrote this tune as an air for an opera.

The codetta, 111–20, is typical 'passage work', establishing the cadence in the dominant key, and ending with the demisemiquaver figure from bar 9.

A three-bar link in the wood-wind leads to the development section which begins with a development of the fourth section of the second subject in E flat major. Its first phrase is stated three times. Then the second phrase is used, first in the violins at 129–31, then in the wood-wind at 131–3. Further imitations follow between upper and lower strings at one bar's distance, and then, at 139, at half-a-bar's distance. The keys change frequently. By 143 the quaver figure becomes a half-a-bar one, though it begins to run on again at 145.

The first bar of its second phrase (the dotted figure first heard in 107) returns in the bass at 147, followed by its second bar of quavers, and the whole figure is now imitated between upper and lower strings.

It quietens down at 153 over a dominant pedal of A minor, and is heard in strings and wind alternately.

Bars 123–61 have all grown out of the seemingly trivial theme which was first heard as the fourth section of the second subject.

Bar 161 begins a combination of the opening figure (a) of the first subject with the transition theme from 24, in F major. It is treated sequentially, gradually getting louder and leading to a dominant pedal of the tonic key at 179. But this quietens down again and leads into the recapitulation at 189.

In the recapitulation the first subject, 189–211, is identical with its treatment in the exposition.

The transition, starting at 211, changes to C minor and then modulates to E flat major. However by 225 it has reached G major, as at 37, and 225–35 is the same as 37–47. Then the music changes so as to reach the dominant pedal of C major at 237–43, instead of the dominant pedal of the dominant key, as at 49–55.

The second subject starts at 244, and its first section is the same as in the exposition except that it is in the tonic key. Its second section starts at 269 and is a different treatment of the second section theme in the exposition. Its third section begins at 277 and is orchestrated more fully than in the exposition. Its fourth section, starting at 289, is slightly differently orchestrated; and the codetta, starting at 299, is as before.

There is a short coda, 309–13, based on the tonic chord.

Second Movement

The second movement is also in sonata form, and is in F major, the subdominant key. Trumpets and drums are not used, as was customary with slow movements of the day.

The first subject opens on muted strings, with *forte*, tutti ejaculations. Bar 1 reappears an octave higher at 5; and Mozart then proceeds to develop the figure in a more ornamental way, with gradual additions of the wind. An interrupted cadence at 8–9 extends this second phrase to seven bars. At 11 the theme appears in the bass with decorative comments in the violins and a throbbing bassoon and horn accompaniment. There is a new answering phrase at 15; and the imperfect cadence at 17–18 ends the first subject.

The transition begins at 19 with a chord of C minor and syncopated upper strings over a throbbing dominant pedal on C in the bass.

It leads to the second subject at 28 in the dominant key, C major. This starts very simply: *d r m f r; r m f s m*; but then becomes more elaborate. A short codetta, 39–43, in which strings and wind answer each other, brings the exposition to an end. A two-bar link in the violin leads back to the repetition of the exposition or on to the development section. Bars 45–6 continue similarly, so that the development section should, perhaps, be said to start at 47.

The development section starts by developing the transition figure. Then, at 56, it develops the codetta figure, passing the little sextolet from one instrument to another. A series of fundamental sevenths leads to the recapitulation at 60.

D

The first subject uses extensively the extra decoration first heard in bar 12. The theme moves a fifth lower at 64, and the music becomes rather complicated at 67, with cross-rhythm figures which give the effect of 2/4 time.

The transition starts at 71, and is different from the transition in the exposition, though it is derived from it. It is shorter, but continuity is provided by the fact that the demisemiquavers from the previous bars continue.

The second subject, starting at 76, is in the tonic key, but is otherwise the same as in the exposition. The codetta, beginning at 87, is similar, but now the violins instead of the horns have the pedal, and there are other differences in orchestration.

A coda starts at 92. It is based on the first subject combined with the decoration first heard in bar 12. The reiterated triplet Cs in the horn in the last three bars provide an effective cadence extension.

Third Movement

The minuet and trio return to C major, the main key of the symphony.

A, 1–16, starts with a four-bar phrase in the strings which is repeated a note higher at 5–8. Then, at 9–10, the first half of the phrase is used a fourth higher again, now tutti, and is repeated immediately. The sentence ends in the dominant key.

B, 17–24, is derived from **A**, and is based on a tonic pedal in the key of G.

A four-bar link, 25–8, in which the wind imitate the strings, leads to the return of **A**. It is more fully orchestrated than before, and it changes at 30, a series of sequences extending the sentence until it reaches a perfect cadence in the tonic key at 43.

There is then a charming little codetta, which starts with imitative entries of **A** in the wood-wind alone and continues, at 52, with a tutti up to 59.

The trio starts with a plain statement of V I in C major in the wind, which sounds more like an end than a beginning of a phrase.

It continues with a little answering phrase in quavers in oboes and violins, and the whole four bars are then repeated to make **C** of the plan.

D, 68–75, is a tutti based on a rhythmic treatment of a dominant pedal in A minor.

A four-bar link, 76–9, in the strings alone consists of V I in E major, followed by V I in D major; and this leads very naturally to V I in C major which starts the return of **C**, 80–7. This is a repetition of the first **C**, with slightly fuller orchestration.

Fourth Movement

This famous finale is a most unusual combination of sonata form with all kinds of contrapuntal treatment of the themes. There are four main themes, which it will be convenient to label **A B C** and **D**.

The first subject starts with theme **A** in the violins, and consists of four semibreves, rather like an old-fashioned canto-firmo. After an answering phrase, still in the strings, **A** is repeated tutti and is extended up to 19.

Theme **B**, starting at 19, consists of a repeated note followed by a downward quaver run, and is heard three times before ending with a typical eighteenth century series of repetitions of tonic and dominant harmony, 28–35.

Then **A** is heard in fugato, entering in all five string parts in turn. (It is rather unusual for the double-bass to have an entry to itself.)

At 53 there is a tutti combination of **A** in the wood-wind and strings against the repeated-note opening of **B** in the brass. Then, at 56^2, another theme, **C**, enters in the violin. It consists of rising stepwise crotchets, and is treated sequentially and in imitation in all the string parts. By now we have left the tonic key for the first time and have reached the dominant.

At 64^3 **B** returns, now in the dominant key, with imitation at half-a-bar's distance. This ends at 73 on a dominant seventh of the dominant key, ready for the second subject.

A, **B** and **C** can all be considered parts of the first subject. This is preferable to labelling **B** or **C** as a transition: **B** appears in both tonic and dominant key and is combined with **A**; while **C** appears in the middle of the texture between two entries of **B**. Nevertheless **B** and **C** together have effected the change to the dominant key.

The second subject, starting at 74^3 in the violins, introduces theme **D** in the dominant key. This is a more melodious tune, starting with three minims before running into quavers. But, by 77, **B** and **C** are both combining with it, **B** in the flute, and **C** in the bassoons. **D** continues at 80^3 with entries of **B** and **C** again at 83.

Then, at 86–94, **C** is heard in imitation in flute and bassoon, against a diminution of the first four notes of it in quavers in the violins. Bar 94^3 starts sequential imitations of the first three notes of **D** in various instruments, while its quaver continuation is heard in imitation at 100 onwards. At 115 **B** appears again, rhythmically altered and shortened, and is also extended with sequences and imitations.

The codetta starts at 135^3 with imitations of **B** at half-a-bar's distance, thus producing effective dissonances. Bars 151–7 have **B** over a tonic pedal in the dominant key, and bring the exposition to an end.

The development starts with **A** in the dominant key in the strings over a tonic pedal, followed by **B** at 161^3 in the wind. Then **A** is heard in the second violins by inversion at 162. **A** reappears in the strings in E minor at 166 over another tonic pedal, and is followed by an inversion of **B** in the wind at 169. The first three notes of **B** are played *forte* by the brass at 172 and the figure is continued by the strings in imitation. Sequences and imitations of this figure are tossed from one instrument to another, until it reappears in its inverted form at 187. It is combined with **A** by diminution in the wind at 189^3.

A and **B** now continue antiphonally, **A** in the wood-wind, **B** in the strings up to 207, when they are heard together, a pedal being added to the texture at 210.

Bars 219^3–225 consist of the first notes of **B** combined in imitation to make extraordinary harmonies, until at last the quaver part of **B** runs into the recapitulation at 225.

In the recapitulation **A** is fuller and longer than in the exposition, being extended by rising sequences. The repeated notes of **B** appear at 253 but without being followed by the run; and **C** joins in a bar later though, as compared with the exposition, it stays in the key of C, instead of modulating to G.

However the whole of **B** reappears in close imitation, starting at 262^3, a fifth higher than in the exposition, and therefore in the key of G. The further contrapuntal treatment of **A**, **B** and **C** that occurred in the exposition is now omitted, and the music moves to the second subject, theme **D**, in the tonic at 272^3.

Apart from slight changes at 313 and 325–50 the music is now the same as in the exposition up to the end of the recapitulation, apart from the change of key. Notice the repeat marks at the end, 356, showing that Mozart thought of sonata form as an extension of binary form. This repeat of development and recapitulation was gradually to die out during the next twenty years or so, and does not often occur, even in Mozart.

The coda starts at 356(*b*) with **B** in the strings, imitated by the wind. Then, at 360, **A** appears inverted and in imitation, and is joined at 371^3 by **D** in the violas, at 375^3 by **D** in the second violins, and at 376^2 by **C** in the 'cellos. **A**, **C** and **D** continue to combine for some time in a most exciting way; and **B** is finally added to the texture at 383^3 At this moment all four themes are heard together, a technical *tour-de-force*.

D drops out first, being heard for the last time at 395^3; **C** appears for the last time at 401^2 and **A** (with its extension) at 399–408, leaving the field to **B** from 408^3 to the end.

This last movement is a highly successful combination of sonata form with contrapuntal devices, and leaves one impressed with Mozart's ingenuity and exhilarated by the excitement of the music. But the first movement is a little pedantic and square, and the second and third movements are not in any way outstanding. For sheer musical inspiration this symphony cannot compare with the eloquent beauty of the G minor or the charm of the E flat, the other two symphonies which, with the 'Jupiter', were the consummation of Mozart's symphonic writing.

19 Mozart

Clarinet Concerto, K 622

This, the last of Mozart's many concertos, was written in 1791, two months before he died. It was inspired by and written for his clarinettist friend, Anton Stadler, for whom the lovely clarinet quintet was also written. Mozart first heard the new instrument, the clarinet, in the Mannheim orchestra in his youth, and was a devoted admirer of it. He was the first famous composer to write for it, and he used it in his later works whenever a clarinettist was available. But he thought of it largely as an alternative to the oboe, as we see in his last symphonies; and this concerto does not have any oboes in the score.

Notice also that the concerto uses neither trumpets nor drums. In fact, though so late and mature a work, its texture is light, and partakes almost of the feeling of chamber music. Most of the work is written for clarinet and strings, with the tutti used quite sparingly.

The first movement was originally sketched as part of a concerto for the basset horn (an alto clarinet) for the same soloist, but was then transferred to this concerto.

The concerto is in A major, and is therefore written for the A clarinet. There is a close resemblance between the opening theme of this concerto, that of the clarinet quintet and the A major piano concerto, all of which are in the same key. One associates the sunny, serene feeling of all these themes with 'Mozart in A major'.

First Movement, *Allegro*

Mozart starts the first movement with the usual orchestral exposition, almost entirely in the tonic key, and the soloist does not enter, as a soloist, until bar 56, where the second exposition starts. But the student who begins by analysing the first exposition may get into difficulties, because its form is quite irregular. Mozart avoids the use of the transition theme and the beginning of the second subject, saving them up for the soloist in the second exposition. Also he transposes the order of entrance of the themes.

So I suggest that it is best to start the analysis at 56, comparing the second exposition with the recapitulation which starts at 251. I give the comparative bar numbers of each section:

FIRST SUBJECT, 56 and 251, identical, ending in the tonic key.

TRANSITION, 78 and 272, starting the same, but changing at 275, so that 100 lands in the dominant key while 288 lands in the tonic.

Four link bars in the solo clarinet lead to the *second subject*, which contains five sections and a codetta:

FIRST SECTION, 104, dominant; 292 tonic, changing at 294 so as to exploit the lower ranges of the clarinet—its lowest note is reached at 300.

SECOND SECTION, 116, C sharp minor; 304 F sharp minor, with the main theme starting in the violin in the recapitulation, instead of the clarinet, though it changes to the clarinet at 306.

THIRD SECTION, 128, dominant; 316, tonic. This is a development of the first subject, with imitations in three parts, starting with the violin at 128 and the clarinet at 316.

FOURTH SECTION, 134, dominant; 322, tonic. Melody in the violin, accompanying figures in the clarinet at 134 but not at 322, though they start at 324. Bravura work on the clarinet follows, and leads to the:

FIFTH SECTION at 154, dominant; and 343 tonic. The passage is a tutti, and is the same, except for key.

CODETTA, 164, ending with a tutti cadence in the dominant at 172; 352, ending with the same tutti cadence at 359, but now in the tonic. This is the end of the movement.

Having established the main outlines of these two sections we can now return to the first orchestral exposition, and we find the following: first subject, bar 1, strings only, repeated tutti at 9. Fifth section of second subject in tonic, 16, tutti. Third section of second subject, 25, tonic key, with the three-part imitations. Notice that it is only for strings and that the bass is silent—it was not often at this period that 'cellos and basses were separated. Starting softly, it goes on to *forte* imitations at 31 between lower and upper strings. Fourth section of second subject in tonic, 39. Codetta in tonic, 49.

Now it remains to look at the development section. It starts at 172 with the first subject in the dominant key. Bravura passages in the clarinet over simple string harmonies lead to a tutti at 192, starting in F sharp minor, followed by a quieter passage which leads to a development of 85 (the transition) in D major at 200. The quieter passage from 194 reappears at 216, with large semibreve leaps in the clarinet, and leads to clarinet decorations at 220. Another tutti starts in F sharp minor at 227, which modulates to E major at 223 and ends in D major at 239. The fifth section of the second subject now enters, tutti, and leads to the recapitulation at 251.

So far this analysis has been solely concerned with the form, but the texture is equally important. Notice how the first subject is so often played by two instruments in consecutive thirds or sixths— violins in bar 1, solo clarinet and violin at 57. Also notice how effectively it is treated contrapuntally at 25 between the strings, and at 128 between strings and clarinet. Notice, too, the frequent effective contrasts between strings and tutti.

When the clarinet enters at 57 it soon begins to decorate the melody. Clarinets are particularly effective at playing rapid runs, wide-ranging arpeggios, and large leaps which exploit the unusually wide range of the instrument; and all of these features are shown between 66 and 75. Yet they are more than just bravura passages: they are an integral part of the texture, and they certainly add to the beauty of the sound.

Then the transition, 78–100, gives the clarinet an opportunity to play an expressive melodic line, another feature in which the instrument excels. At bar 134 and the corresponding passage in the recapitulation at 324, the arpeggios are a foil to the violin melody. No wonder this concerto is beloved of clarinettists. But notice that there is no space for the usual cadenza in this first movement.

Second Movement, *Adagio*

This movement is very simple and straightforward as far as form is concerned, though its expressive content and its lovely melodic line make it a very popular movement.

It is in the subdominant key and in episodical form. The first stanza of the main theme is played first by the clarinet with a simple string accompaniment, ending in the dominant key. It is repeated, tutti, at 9. The second stanza starts at 17, and although the soloist again has a theme with a string accompaniment there are expressive imitations of the clarinet in the violins. It is then repeated tutti at 25, as was the first stanza.

In the episode, starting at 33, the clarinet has a much more florid melodic line, making use of arpeggios, scalic runs and wide leaps, as he did in the first movement. Rather surprisingly, this section, too starts in the tonic and ends in the dominant; and the strings accompany the clarinet throughout.

Bars 54–9 form a tutti link to the return of the first theme, and they end with a pause, which gives an opportunity for a cadenza.

The first stanza of the opening theme returns as before at 60, but there is no tutti repetition. The second, starting at 68, is also the same, but the tutti repetition is now fuller than before.

A coda starts at 83 in which the clarinet has further decorative arabesques over a simple string accompaniment.

Third Movement, *Allegro*

The third movement is in sonata-rondo form. The first section of the first subject is on the plan (*a*) (*a*) (*b*) (*a*), with the second (*a*) played by the tutti at 9 and (*b*) consisting of decorative runs in the clarinet, starting at 17. A second section starts at 31, and a third section at 43, and the first subject comes to an end with a tutti at 51-6, finishing with a perfect cadence in the tonic key.

The transition starts at 57 and is played by the clarinet accompanied by strings. It leads to the dominant major, but the second subject starts at 73 in the dominant minor. It is melodic at first, but decorative arpeggios reappear in the clarinet at 84; and a dominant pedal starts at 98 which leads to a return of the first subject at 114. But this is quite short and leads to a *forte* tutti at 121 which modulates to F sharp minor for the episode.

The episode starts at 137 and consists of a clarinet melody accompanied by strings. Notice the large leaps again at 161-2 and 165-6.

The recapitulation starts at 178. The first subject is in the subdominant key, which is quite common with Mozart, but it is much modified and is very short. The transition starts at 188 and is the same as in the exposition at first, but it changes to A minor at 196 and is much longer than before.

When the second subject starts at 214 it is in A minor and is considerably developed. Notice the two pauses at 219 and 221. It reaches E major at 226, and scalic passages in the clarinet are heard over a simple chord scheme.

The link passage from 98 is then heard at 231 and is exactly the same and in the same key. It leads to a return of the first subject, but whereas this was short at the end of the exposition it is now heard in full at the end of the recapitulation; and 247-301 corresponds entirely to 1-55.

The coda starts at 301. Clarinet arpeggios are again heard over a simple chord scheme, changing to leaps at 314. Then scalic passages lead to a perfect cadence in the tonic key and to further development of the first subject in that key, starting at 322. It starts with violin and clarinet imitations, but the clarinet soon takes over and develops the first subject until the entrance of the final tutti at 346, which is a lengthened version of the tutti at 51–6.

20 Mozart

Overture to Così fan Tutte

Così fan Tutte was composed in 1789–90 and produced in Vienna in 1790, the year before Mozart's death. After nine years of prolific activity in Vienna, Mozart produced very little in 1790, as his health was then failing, though he forced himself to work again in his final year, and wrote The Magic Flute and The Clemency of Titus in addition to the Requiem and many other works.

Così fan Tutte (So do all Women) is a comic opera with an Italian libretto by L. da Ponte (1749–1838), and is concerned with two officers who are told by Don Alfonso, an old cynic, that, like all women, their sweethearts will be unfaithful if they go away. So, to test them, the men disguise themselves and each makes love to the other's sweetheart. However, after several vicissitudes, all ends happily. This story is said to be based on an actual happening in the Viennese aristocracy.

The overture sets the mood of comedy. Just as does the better-known overture to The Marriage of Figaro. But, unlike Figaro, it starts with an andante introduction, that perhaps gives a hint that there are some tender and passionate sides to the story, too. And there is a quotation from the opera, in the violin part at 10–11 and again at 231–4 in the coda, to which the words of the title Così fan Tutte are sung in the opera.

The overture is scored for two flutes, oboes, clarinets, bassoons, horns, trumpets and drums, plus the usual strings. Being a late work it makes use of clarinets, but notice that they are in C, instead of the usual A or B flat. C clarinets are obsolete today. There are no trombones, though Mozart used them in the overture to *The Magic Flute*, written a year later.

After a tutti tonic chord of C major, oboes and bassoons play a plaintive phrase and are interrupted by a dominant chord before going on to the answering phrase. Then the 'Così fan tutte' phrase appears in the violins and bassoons, followed by five *forte* slow-moving chords leading to the *presto*.

The *presto* is in sonata form, and the first subject has two distinct sections, starting at 15 and 29, connected by a tutti link passage, 25–9. Both themes make use of imitation, the first between the violins and the second between flute, oboe and bassoon.

A transition starts at 46, based on the first section of the first subject, with violin imitations as before, but now modulating to G major (49) and D major (53). A tutti passage very similar to the link at 25 leads to the second subject at 59.

The second subject starts in the dominant minor, with a light quaver figure in the violins; but the second section, starting at 65, is in the dominant major and is a *forte*, tutti passage, similar to the links at 25 and 53.

A codetta starts at 79 and is based on the wood-wind imitations which formed the second section of the first subject, now in the dominant key. It is over a tonic pedal and it is repeated at 87. This brings the exposition to an end, and it is not repeated. The repeat was usually omitted in overtures to operas, so as not to make it too lengthy.

The development section begins at 95 with imitative entries of the first section of the first subject, starting in the dominant key. Thereafter, entries of this theme at 115, 133 and 183 alternate with entries of the first section of the second subject at 107, 125 and 143, with entries of the second section of the first subject at 149 and 175, and with one entry of the second section of the second subject at 165, frequently separated from one another by the link figure from 25. The general effect of this flitting from one theme to another is disjointed and seems, probably deliberately, to be leading nowhere, until a dominant pedal of the tonic key is reached at 175, which leads to the recapitulation at 189.

The recapitulation is considerably curtailed, as compared with the exposition, probably because the main themes have been heard so frequently in the development section. The first section of the first subject is omitted, and the recapitulation starts with the link figure from 25, which goes on to the second section of the second subject at 193, the transition and the first section of the second subject being also omitted. The second section starts at 209, now in the tonic key. This is repeated at 219. Bars 73–95 of the exposition (the end of the second section of the second subject and the codetta) are also omitted.

The coda starts at 228, and there is a reference to the 'Così fan tutte' theme first heard in the introduction at 10–15. Then the first section of the first subject reappears at 241 and is repeated up the tonic chord. The link figure from 25 ends the overture. .

21 Mozart

Les Petits Riens

This ballet consists of an overture and thirteen dances, most of which are very slight and require little to be said about them.

It was written in 1778, during Mozart's third visit to Paris. He was unhappy there, as he was lost amid the intrigues of court politics, and had few friends. The ballet was written for a famous ballet-master, Noverre; and it was included in performances of Piccini and Anfossi *buffo* operas, together with other dances. The music to the dances was considered so unimportant that no composers' names were given, even though the ballet itself was produced six times. The music is very French in style; and its story is told in the preface to the Eulenberg miniature score.

Overture

This is written for a full orchestra of 2 flutes, oboes, clarinets, bassoons, horns, trumpets and drums, together with strings. This is the same orchestration as that of the 'Paris' symphony, written in the same year. But the overture is loosely put together: an Italian overture, rather than a French one, in that it is in one movement and is an *allegro*, but bearing little evidence of the mastery of form that is shown in Mozart's greatest works. It consists largely of a number of slight figures, appearing prolifically, one after another, but with no development and little change of key.

It starts as if it is going to be in sonata form, with the first subject (*a*) in bar 1, the transition starting at 9 with (*b*) and continuing with (*c*) at 13, (*d*) at 17, and ending in the dominant key at 20.

A slight figure, (*e*), which starts over a pedal G and vacillates between the keys of G and C might be thought of as a second subject, and ends on V in key C at 26.

Bar 27 appears to start the development, but in reality consists of several new figures and is mostly still in the tonic key. The first bar (27) is an inversion of bar 1, but 28 introduces another figure, (*f*), which is used, perhaps, more than any other. It is repeated at 32 and is followed by (*g*) at 35 and (*h*) at 39. This section ends with a perfect cadence in the tonic key at 46–7.

The next section lasts from 47–76 and is still largely in the key of C, though it contains some repetition of previously-heard figures. It starts with (*b*); then 54 is a varied form of (*a*) as used at 27, and is followed by (*f*) at 28. Figure (*f*) is repeated at 59 and leads to (*g*) at 62, as at 36 but now a fourth higher; and then a new figure, (*i*), is heard at 66. This section ends with another perfect cadence in the tonic key at 73–6.

Bar 76 starts a very incomplete recapitulation, with (*a*), the first subject, at 76 and (*b*), the transition, at 82. Figure (*b*) continues up to 98, when it ends with yet another perfect cadence in the tonic key. There is no use of the other figures, and no return of the second subject, (*e*), slight though it was.

Instead a coda starts at 98 and makes use of yet another figure, (*j*), followed by (*f*) at 102; and it is over a tonic pedal to the end.

The movement is therefore a strange mixture of old and new, making use of short figures, as did earlier composers, yet also containing hints of a loosely constructed sonata form. One wonders if Mozart put it together rather hastily and carelessly, relying on his power of musical invention, and not bothering much about a good formal structure.

The Dances

These use a slighter orchestra. Five (Nos 2, 3, 10, 11 and 12) are for strings alone, while the rest are for one or two instruments and strings, except for Nos 6 and 8, which are for four instruments and strings.

Nos 3 and 4 are so short as to consist of only one sentence; Nos 2, 9 and 11 are binary; Nos 1, 5, 7, 10 and 13 are ternary; while No 12 is a rondo. No 10, *Pantomime*, is particularly French, with its piquant, *staccato* style and its sudden *rinforzandi*; and it bears a resemblance to a sextet written by Mozart for his sister, Nannerl, in 1776.

This accounts for all except the two longer and more elaborate ones, written for a fuller orchestra, Nos 6 and 8. No 6 is very French in style and rather rondo-like. Its plan is: **A**, 1–8; **B**, 9–16; **C**, 17–24; **D**, 24–32; a decorated form of **A**, 32–40; **E**, 40–48; **A**, 48–56; **B**, 56–64; coda, 64 to end.

The plan of No 8 is **A**, 1–8, ending in dominant; **B**, 9–12; **A**, 13–20, ending in tonic; **C**, 21–36; **A** repeated; **B A** repeated. In other words, this is not unlike minuet and trio form, with **C** forming a short trio.

22 Mozart

Piano and Wind Quintet, K 452

Mozart wrote a great many works in many different media. When he was only seventeen he wrote a work in concertante style, K 190, which he called a 'concertone' for two violins, oboe, 'cello and orchestra. Five years later, with his interests in wind instruments continually growing, he wrote a sinfonia concertante, K 297 B, for four wind instruments and orchestra.

He continued to use wind instruments in all sorts of chamber, concertante and orchestral combinations, including his lovely serenade for thirteen wind instruments, K 361. His compositions for wind instruments are a most useful source of material for the growing number of young wind players today.

Schobert (1720–67) was the first composer to write an obbligato piano part, as distinct from the commonly used harpsichord continuo part in earlier chamber music, and he influenced later composers, including Mozart.

Mozart wrote sonatas for violin and piano at all periods of his life, but otherwise his chamber works using piano all come towards the end of his life. He wrote eight piano trios, six of them after 1786, and his two famous piano quartets in 1785 and 1786. But this quintet for piano, oboe, clarinet, horn and bassoon, K 452, is the only chamber work combining wind and piano, and belongs to the period of his great piano concertos, with which it has much in common.

It cannot, by its very nature, be a pure example of chamber music, because all the instruments cannot be equal. The piano, in effect, balances the four wind instruments; so, to this extent, it is in concertante style, and therefore has links with the two works mentioned first in this article. But the four wind instruments are treated as equals; even the horn is not subordinated. And when Mozart tosses little figures from one instrument to another he adapts them to the particular qualities of the instrument.

The work was completed on 30 March 1784; and Mozart, writing to his father, called it 'the best work I have ever composed'. It was certainly the model for Beethoven's wind quintet, Op 16, with which it is often compared.

First Movement

The first movement starts with quite a long, *largo* introduction. A series of tutti *forte tenuto* chords punctuate a soft pathetic theme which is played by the piano in the first four bars, then by the wind for two bars, then by the piano again for one bar. At bar 8 the last three quavers of the theme in the previous bar are imitated in the clarinet and horn together, and then in the oboe and bassoon; and the horn finishes off the theme with a *dolce* decorative cadence.

Bar 10 starts a new section in which a descending semiquaver scale is imitated by all the wind instruments in turn, a note higher each time, over demisemiquaver arpeggios in the piano. The piano takes over the scales at 12, first in the right hand and then in the left, where it is joined by the bassoon and used three times in ascending sequence.

A bar of dotted figure imitations between wind and piano at 14, which has grown out of the previous bar, leads to a charmingly turned cadential figure in the oboe at 15 which is imitated by the other wind instruments over a dominant pedal in the piano. In the second half of bar 17 the parts change round, the horn having the pedal while the piano has the cadential figure. The music remains poised over the dominant chord for another three bars, and the introduction ends with a *forte* reiterated dominant seventh at 20.

The *allegro moderato* is in sonata form and starts daintily with the first subject in the piano alone for the first two bars. But two bars of vigorous tutti interrupt it. Then the wind repeats the piano's first two bars and the *forte* two bars of tutti follow as before. This completes the first subject, in which the piano and wind have, in effect, played against each other in concertante style.

The transition starts a tonic pedal at 28.[3] Quiet quaver figures in the wind are interrupted by vigorous *forte* triplet scales and arpeggios in the piano. Then, at 34, the wind instruments become vigorous too, and all reach an imperfect cadence together in grand style at 36.

But the rapidly alternating moods continue, and the piano and clarinet start a soft, graceful figure at 37, answered by a dotted figure in the horn and bassoon. The graceful figure is taken up by the horn and bassoon at 39, with the dotted figure answer in the oboe and clarinet. This leads to the dominant chord of the dominant key, which the piano now decorates with arpeggios.

The second subject starts at 43 in the dominant key. The piano has the graceful theme for the first four bars, with a *forte* comment in its second bar in the wind. Then the parts change round, the oboe having the theme accompanied by the rest of the wind, and the piano having the second bar of comment.

The second section of the second subject starts at 50,[3] when the pianist has his fling in four bars of a solo cadenza-like passage—Mozart must have enjoyed playing this! Then the wind has its turn, with a similar passage adapted to the capabilities of the particular instruments: the oboe has the melody but in quavers rather than the piano's demisemiquavers; the clarinet supports it; the horn plays a plain, chordal bass; and the bassoon has bravura, scalic runs. But this time the passage is extended, with all five instruments having different parts of the figuration in turn, in imitation, and ending with a perfect cadence in the dominant key at 60–1.

A charming little codetta lasts from 61 to 65, with a dialogue between wind and piano.

The development section is quite short and is based on the first subject, modulating freely. The last bar of the exposition is repeated twice, modulating to G minor and E flat major on the way to A flat major. In this key the first two bars of the first subject are played by the piano. The last two chords are repeated by the wind modulating to B flat minor, in which key the piano repeats the first two bars in sequence. The wind again repeats the last two bars, modulating this time to C minor, and the piano follows with the two bars in C minor, in sequence once more.

Then, at 76 the wind takes over the two bars in C major (a lovely change of mode), with the melody in the oboe. The last bar of the melody is repeated by the clarinet, then by the bassoon, followed by the horn, with modulatory chords in the piano leading to A flat major, in which key the piano takes over the melody and leads into the recapitulation in the tonic key at 82.

The first subject is the same as in the exposition up to 87, where it is extended by modulatory imitations of the figure in the wind instruments, passing through F minor at 88 and G minor at 89 and reaching the dominant key at 92. This marks the end of the first subject, though it is a little unusual in that it is modified and extended, and that it modulates, as compared with the first subject in the exposition.

The transition starts at 92. It is built entirely over a dominant pedal in the tonic key and is much shorter than in the exposition, being four bars long instead of fourteen. Bars 92–3 are exactly the same as 34–5; and 94–5 are the same as 41–2, except that they are in the tonic instead of the dominant key.

The first two bars of the second subject, 96–7, are the same as 43–4 except that they are in the tonic key, but the answering phrase in the piano, 98–9, is varied in the first bar, as compared with 45. Then, at 100, the instruments change round, as compared with 47, the horn having the tune instead of the oboe, the oboe having the clarinet's part, and the pedal bass that was in the horn now being transferred to the piano. Only the bassoon remains unchanged. Then, at 102, the clarinet takes its turn with the tune for two beats before it is taken over by the oboe. All these slight changes mean that every instrument has its turn as the soloist.

The second section starts at 103^2 with solo piano having the same cadenza-like passage as before; and this is followed by the turn of the wind as before, though again with minor modifications: the triplet runs that were in the bassoon in the exposition are now in the piano, and the syncopated imitations at 109 between oboe and clarinet extend for another bar. And so it continues, with other minor instrumental changes up to the codetta at 115.[3]

The codetta, too, has the same sort of changes: the slurred two-note figure in the wind at 61 is now played by the piano at 115–6, and the piano melody at 61[4] is now played first by the oboe and then by the clarinet and bassoon. An extension occurs from 118[3]– 21[2] and the cadence at 121[3]–22 is modified.

Second Movement

This charmingly melodious movement is also in sonata form. The announcing phrase of the first subject (*a*) is played by oboe and bassoon in thirds answered by a *forte* tutti. Then (*b*) is played by oboe and bassoon in sixths, again answered by a *forte* tutti. Bars 1–8 are then repeated with the piano having the melody and with imitative extensions of (*b*) in clarinet and oboe leading to a perfect cadence in the tonic at 17–18.

The transition, 18–32, consists of fragmentary melodic phrases in each wind instrument in turn, accompanied by arpeggios in the piano. At 27 all the wind join together in a series of quaver chromatic harmonies with a falling melodic line, which leads to the dominant key at 32.

The short second subject consists of delightful melodic phrases, starting in the piano at 32, with imitations in the clarinet at 36 and oboe at 38 and accompanied by simple reiterated chords. Finally the clarinet has the theme to itself at 41 and brings the exposition to a close.

The development section starts with chromatic quaver movement which, perhaps unconsciously, grows out of the chromatic quaver movement at 27–30. Bars of *p* and *f* alternate and lead to E flat major at 51, in which key a new and charming melody appears in the horn, continuing in the upper wind instruments at 57, with imitative figures appearing in the piano at 62–6 in a *crescendo*.

This leads to a sudden *p* and an unexpected modulation into E minor. The wind support the piano which, over agitated reiterated bass notes, has snatches of melody in rapidly changing keys, reaching a *f* dominant pedal of the tonic key at 72, then sliding gently into the recapitulation at 74.

This time the first subject starts in the piano instead of the wind, while its repetition at 82 starts in the wind. Figure (*b*) appears, *f*, at 84 against the wind melody and is later taken up by various instruments in turn, as before.

The transition, 91–113, is longer than in the exposition and, though it has the same kind of piano arpeggio accompaniment, the melodic fragments which appear in the wind instruments are different, though similar. They come together at 100; now a fifth lower as compared with 27. But this time the melody rises instead of falls, has two sequential modulatory extensions, and does not reach the second subject till 113.

And yet again there are variations in the scoring. It would have been so easy for Mozart to have produced an exact repetition, yet he continues to provide charming variants which give every instrument a turn, each appropriate to its own media. The second subject melody starts in the oboe instead of the piano, and a charming dialogue between oboe and clarinet ensues, with the piano joining in the conversation at 117 and the bassoon at 122. And finally all join together in a gentle feminine ending.

Third Movement

In this movement all the wind instruments continue to have their turns with the melody, but the piano now becomes quite virtuosic, so that the movement is almost like the finale of a piano concerto— though when the cadenza comes, towards the end of the movement, all the instruments take part in it. The movement is in sonata rondo form but with the first subject omitted at the beginning of the recapitulation.

The piano has the first eight bars of the gay first subject to itself, and then the wind repeat it with the piano joining in, in imitation at 12^3.

An equally gay and tuneful transition starts at 16^3 in the piano, accompanied by the wind. The theme is repeated by the wind at 24^3 but when the piano joins in at 28 it begins to modulate and it reaches a dominant pedal of the dominant key at 32. A hesitant three bars, 37–9, lead to the second subject in the dominant key at 40.

This is played first by the oboe and then repeated by the piano. A second section starts at 51^3 in question-and-answer form, between wind and piano.

This leads to another transition over a dominant pedal of the tonic key at 63–7 which, in turn, leads to a complete and exact repetition of the first subject, ending at 87^2.

The middle section of the movement consists of a short episode in C minor with imitative entries in the wind, followed by a long modulatory transition, 103–30, in which the piano has all the fun. It ends with a dominant pedal of the tonic key, 122–9, over which the same hesitant figure occurs at 127–9 as happened at 37–9, though this time the piano has a trill in place of the long note on the oboe.

This leads to the second subject in the tonic key at 130, the recapitulation thus beginning with the second subject, and the first subject being omitted. The piano starts the theme, followed by the oboe, (the opposite way round from their places in the exposition) and each consists of only four bars instead of eight. The second section of the second subject is omitted.

The transition which was used to connect the first and second subject at 16^3–40 is now used to connect the second subject with the cadenza. It starts at 137^3 and is the same up to 149^2 when it changes and becomes more chromatic and forceful, leading to a cadential 6/4 on a pause, the usual opening for a cadenza.

But this cadenza is unusual in that it is played by all the instruments. It starts with syncopated imitative entries, the melody rising

(159–65), then falling (165–9), then rising again, sequentially.

A new figure appears at 177 starting with a rising leap of a twelfth and this, too, is used in imitation, leading to a cadence in A flat major at 187–9. A hesitant imitative figure in contrary motion between wind and piano leads to Ic again in the tonic key at 196, over which chromatic rising thirds lead to V and a trill in the oboe at 200, the usual indication of the end of a cadenza.

The first subject reappears at 205³ for four bars in the piano, followed by four bars in the wind. Then quiet broken octaves appear in the piano at 213, with sustained chords in the wind, the piano part being repeated two octaves lower at 221. Bars 225–8 are suddenly repeated loudly at 229–32, followed equally unexpectedly by four quiet bars before two *forte* chords bring the movement to an end. These dynamic contrasts create a sense of excitement about the ending.

23 Mozart

Sonata in G for Violin and Piano, K 379

First Movement, *Adagio*

This is an unusual movement, which should perhaps be thought of as an introduction to the following *allegro*, particularly as it ends inconclusively on a dominant chord and without a thick double bar. But chamber works do not normally start with an introduction, which is primarily a call to attention, though symphonies often do; and it does not sound introductory. Compare sonata 13, which is rather similar.

The piano starts the first theme and the violin takes it up at 9, though with a new answering phrase at 13. This theme is not complete in itself, but ends in the dominant key at 19.

A second theme starts in the dominant key at 20 and is almost entirely given to the piano. It ends with a perfect cadence in the dominant key at 33. The whole of 1–33 is then repeated, giving the impression to the listener that this is probably the exposition of a movement in sonata form.

But there is no development or recapitulation, and there are only 16 more bars to the end of the *adagio* section or movement. Bars 34–47 modulate to E minor and lead one to expect a perfect cadence at 39 in E minor. But instead there is an abrupt modulation to C major, in which key the second theme (from bar 20) recurs, again given entirely to the piano. It returns to the tonic key at 43, and the violin joins in at 45 to help with the reiteration of the imperfect cadence which ends with a pause at 49. This sounds unfinished, and leads straight into the following *allegro*.

Second Movement, *Allegro*

This movement is in G minor, not G major, and is in modified sonata form. The first subject is stated first by the piano alone, then it is repeated by the violin at 13. It ends with a dominant seventh followed by a pause at 24.

The second subject starts immediately in the relative major. It consists of two figures, (a) first heard at 25, and (b), first heard in the bass at 29. The piano has the (a) figure to itself at first; then, when (b) starts at 29, the left hand part of the piano and the violin have it in imitation, with a dominant pedal in the right hand. Figure (a) returns in the violin at 34 and a perfect cadence is reached at 37. But the (b) figure then continues, starting in the violin with imitations in the piano right hand, and the pedal (now on the tonic) in the left hand. The (a) figure returns in the violin at 42 and leads to two interrupted cadences at 46 and 49 before reaching a final cadence at 52. A short codetta based on (b) lasts from 52 to 56.

The second half of the movement (which is also repeated) contains a short modulatory link passing through C minor (60),

D minor (64), G minor (66) and D major (68), followed by the recapitulation which starts at 69.

The first subject is again played by the piano alone the first time, but when the violin enters with the repetition at 81 the accompaniment is different, and it changes at 85 and is extended, though it reaches the same imperfect cadence in the tonic key at 96.

The second subject starts at 97 in the tonic key. Bars 100–04 are new, but 105 starts the imitations of (b) as before. They are considerably extended, passing through C minor (119), B♮ (120) and G minor (121); and further extensions appear before the interrupted cadence corresponding to 46 appears at 129. Thereafter the music is the same, except for the key, with the codetta starting at 135. The movement is brought to an end with a *forte* repetition of the codetta, starting at 139.

Finale, Theme and Variations

The theme is in the usual binary form, each half, eight bars in length, being repeated. It is on the plan **A A B A**, with modifications. **A** (1–4) starts with a one-bar figure repeated sequentially, followed by semiquaver movement in the piano. The second **A** (5–8) starts the same but modulates to the dominant, and the semiquaver configuration is different. **B** (9–12) provides a contrast, and consists of a two-bar figure modulating to A minor, repeated in sequence in G major. The final **A** (13–16) uses the opening-bar figure higher up, and its cadence contains no semiquavers. Notice that the violin has an independent melody, in addition to that of the piano.

VARIATION I is for piano alone. The rhythmical contrasts in the theme are smoothed out, and the piano has a decorative version of the melody and chord scheme, using semiquavers throughout.

VARIATION II has triplet semiquavers in the violin thoughout, therefore sounding quicker than the first variation. It is usual for each variation to speed up in relation to the previous one. The violin hints at the piano melody, while the piano has the melody that was in the violin.

VARIATION III quickens to demisemiquaver movement in the piano. The first of each group of demisemiquavers in the right hand is the bass line of the theme for the first few bars, while the violin quavers bear a resemblance to the opening bars of the theme in the piano.

VARIATION IV moves to the tonic minor, which therefore involves harmonic modifications. It is based on a dotted figure.

VARIATION V is *adagio*. It consists of a highly decorative, slow-moving melody in the piano, 'shadowing' the original melody, against *pizzicato* in the violin. It returns to the original chord scheme except for bars 89 and 91, which each have a minor instead of a major chord.

Bar 97 brings a complete return to the original theme, and this is followed by a coda, starting at 112(b). The first phrase touches sequentially on A minor and G major, as did the second half of the theme, and ends with the same cadence. This is repeated at 116, and four more bars lead to a tonic pedal, which lasts for six bars and brings the movement to an end.

24 Mozart

Piano Sonata in F, K 332

This sonata was written in Paris in the summer of 1778, the same year as the 'Paris' symphony and the ballet music to *Les Petits Riens*.

First Movement, *Allegro*

This is a straightforward movement in sonata form. The first subject contains two sentences, the second one starting at 12^3 and ending at 22.

The transition starts with a modulation to D minor. The chord sequence is: I in D minor, 23–4; diminished seventh, 25–6; Ib, 27–8; diminished seventh, 29–30, leading to Ib in C minor, 31–2; IVb, 33–4; an added sixth on A flat in key C, 35–6, leading to V in C major, 37–40.

The first section of the second subject starts in the dominant key at 41. Its second sentence, 49–56, is a decoration of its first, 41–8. The second section starts at 56 and modulates to C minor, 58 and E flat major, 62, ending with V in the dominant major key at 67–70. Its third section starts at 70; and 77–82 is a decorated version of 71–6 an octave higher. Two bars of extension, 82–3, are repeated decoratively at 84–5 and lead to the codetta, 86–93, which ends the exposition.

The middle section starts with new material: an episode from 94–109, in which 102–9 is a decoration, an octave lower, of 94–101. Bar 109 starts an exact repetition of the second section of the second subject which continues up to 113. The rest of the middle section consists of a series of modulations linked by diminished sevenths and augmented sixths, the chord scheme being as follows: 113, I in C minor; 114 diminished seventh; 115, Ib in G minor; 120, Vb; 121, I; 122, augmented sixth; 123–8, V; 129–30, ^{7}Vc in F; 131–2, V. This leads to the recapitulation at 132.

The first subject, with its two sentences, is exactly the same as in the exposition. The transition starts the same at 155 but changes at 163, so that it leads to V in the tonic key at 176. The second subject is the same as in the exposition except that it is in the tonic key, and that the decorated repetition of the first section at 185–92 is an octave higher than at its first appearance. Even the codetta, at 222–9, is the same except for the change of key; and there is no coda.

Second Movement, *Adagio*

This is a straightforward movement in modified sonata form, in B flat major. There is a good deal of repetition, and each repetition contains more decoration than the previous one.

The first subject consists of two stanzas. The first one ends at 4 with an imperfect cadence; the second one is a decoration of the first, but changes at 6 so as to end with a perfect cadence at 8.

The second subject starts at 9 in the dominant key, and again consists of two stanzas. The first one ends at 12 with a perfect cadence; the second one is again a decoration of the first but changes at 16, ending with V on the second beat, and then continuing with an extension which bears a resemblance to bar 1, and ends with a perfect cadence in the dominant at 18–19.

A two-bar link on a pedal F, 19–20, leads to the recapitulation.

The first subject, 21–8, is similar to its appearance in the exposition, but is even more decorated, and jumps an octave lower at 26, so as to have a longer run up to the end of the bar.

The second subject starts at 29 in the tonic key, and is again similar to its appearance in the exposition, apart from the change of key and its further use of decoration.

Bars 39–40 form a short coda on a tonic pedal, and are similar to the link at 19–20.

Third Movement, *Allegro assai*

The third movement returns to the tonic key and is in sonata form, but with a few irregularities.

The first subject contains three sections, the second one starting at 15 and the third at 22. It ends with a perfect cadence in the tonic key at 35.

There are two possible places at which the second subject can be said to start, but neither begin in the expected dominant major. They are 36, which begins in D minor, and 50, which begins in C minor. Bar 36 could be considered to be a transition; but it starts a fourth higher at the corresponding place, 170, in the recapitulation; whereas it would be more normal for the transition to start the same in both exposition and recapitulation and make a gradual change as it moved to different keys. But 36–89 is very similar to

170–226 except for the change of key, so it seems rather better to consider that 36 starts the second subject.

In that case the first section of the second subject starts with a phrase in D minor at 36, repeated sequentially with decorations a tone lower at 41, thus reaching a cadence in the dominant key at 44–5.

Another phrase, containing continuous semiquavers, still in C major, leads to the second section of the second subject starting in C minor at 50. This begins to repeat itself at 58 but changes at 62, and ends with a perfect cadence in C major at 64–5.

A codetta starts at 65 which consists mainly of repetitions of V I in C major. Bar 74 begins a repetition of 65–73, but is extended from 83–90 with further repetitions.

The development section begins like bars 1–5 in C minor; but 96 starts a series of decorative four-bar sequences, passing through G minor, 94–9; C minor, 100–03; F minor, 104–07; and B flat minor, 108–11.

Bar 112 starts another new figure, now in B flat major. Bars 120–3 repeat 112–15 with decorations, but the music changes at 124, when semiquaver arpeggios begin, and lead up to a cadence in B flat major at 126–7. A further series of quaver arpeggios and broken chord passages lead to a dominant pedal of the tonic key from 139–47 which runs into the recapitulation at 148.

So the so-called development section consists entirely of new material except for the first five bars. This is not so uncommon with Mozart; and 'free fantasia' might be a better description of this section.

The first and second section of the first subject in the recapitulation are the same as in the exposition, but the equivalent of bars 22–35 is omitted.

The second subject starts at 170 in G minor and reaches a cadence in F major at 178–9. Bars 180–4 have the same bass as 46–9 but the semiquaver decorations over the top are different.

The second section of the second subject starts at 185 in F minor, and is repeated an octave higher at 193, changing at 197, but ending with a perfect cadence in the tonic key at 199–200.

The codetta, 200–26, is very similar to the codetta in the exposition apart from now being in the tonic key, though 202 jumps an octave higher.

A coda starts at 226, in which bars 232–45 correspond to 22–35, now in the tonic key. This means that the third section of the first subject, which had been omitted at its expected place in the recapitulation, ends the movement.

25 Mozart

Piano Sonata in B flat, K 333

First Movement

The first movement is in the usual sonata form. The first subject has a typical Mozartian flow and ends with a perfect cadence at 9–10.

The transition starts at 10^4 with the same figure as bar 1, but reaches the dominant key at 13–14 and continues in the same style until it ends with an arpeggio on the dominant chord of the dominant key at 22.

The second subject begins in the dominant key at 23. Its first section has syncopation in the third bar, and begins a decorated repetition at 31, though it is modified at 35. The second section starts at 39 with a vigorous tune in quavers; and the third section starts at 50 with a semiquaver figure over simple cadential harmonies. There is a short codetta starting at 59.

The development section begins with the first subject in the dominant key; but at 65 it introduces a new dotted figure, which appears again at 67 and then is repeated three times at 68–9.

Bar 71 is the beginning of an episode which starts in F minor and reaches G minor at 80, continuing in that key up to 86. Bars 88–93 are based on a decorative dominant pedal, leading to the recapitulation.

The first subject of the recapitulation glides in at 93,⁴ and is the same as in the exposition.

The transition, starting at 103,⁴ changes almost immediately and takes seven instead of four bars to reach to the repetition of 15 at 110.⁴ From there it is the same as in the exposition up to 118, except that it is in the tonic key.

The first section of the second subject starts in the tonic key at 119, and is the same as in the exposition, except that it jumps an octave higher at 127. The second section also jumps an octave higher at 137, and the figure from 43 is considerably extended, modulating through C minor, 143; B flat major, 144; F major, 145; and G major, 146, and continuing for another six bars until it reaches its cadence in the tonic key at 151–2. The third section, starting at 153, is almost identical with its appearance in the exposition, apart from the key; and the codetta, starting at 161, is exactly the same. There is no coda.

Second Movement

The *andante cantabile* is in a very regular sonata form, and is in the subdominant key. The first subject ends with a perfect cadence at 7–8, and is followed by a transition which leads to the dominant chord of the dominant key at 13. The second subject follows in the dominant key, and consists of two sections, the second one starting with the last three quavers of bar 21. A short codetta, 29–31, rounds off the exposition.

The development section begins with a chromatic inversion of the first subject; and bars 32–43 are very expressive. They start in F minor and reach a perfect cadence in A flat major at 42–3. The transition figure is then developed, passing through F minor at 44–5 and D flat minor at 46–7. It reaches the dominant chord of the tonic key at 48, thus leading into the recapitulation at 51.

In the recapitulation the first subject is decorated, as compared with the exposition; the transition starts the same in the middle of 58 but is again decorated at 61, and reaches the dominant chord of the tonic key at 63. The first section of the second subject begins at 64 and is the same as in the exposition at first, but again starts decoration at 68. The second section and the codetta are exactly as before, except for the change of key.

Third Movement

The finale is in sonata-rondo form. The first subject, 1–16, is a graceful theme, ending with a perfect cadence in the tonic key.

A transition, 16^3–24^2 leads to the dominant key, in which key the second subject appears, ending with another perfect cadence at 35–6. A short link over a dominant pedal of the tonic key leads to the return of the first subject in the tonic key, 41–56.

A link to the episode starts like the transition at 16, but changes at 61 and modulates to G minor.

The episode begins in G minor at 64^3 but modulates to E flat major at 75–6 where a new dotted theme appears. This leads into a development of the first subject in C minor at 91. It returns to the tonic key at 95 but moves immediately to the tonic minor. A dominant pedal, similar to the link at 36–40, starts at 103 and leads to the recapitulation at 112.

The first subject is exactly as it first appeared in the exposition; and the transition begins the same at 127^3 but soon changes and is longer than before, passing through C minor at 133–4 and E flat major at 139–40. It reaches a dominant pedal of the tonic key at 144, which leads to the second subject in the tonic key at 148^2.

This is modified at 154, though 156–7 is the same as 32–3. But then a cadenza-like treatment over the dominant leads to the link passage first heard at 36–40, but this time it is longer, lasting from 164 to 171. It ends on a cadential 6/4, almost as if it were part of a concerto.

A long cadenza then follows which begins with the first two bars of the first subject in the tonic major, followed by two bars in the minor. Bars 179–82 correspond to 36–40. The music gradually works up to a climax on a diminished seventh arpeggio at 198; and a series of cadenza-like scales leads to the return of the first subject at 200.

This ends with a cadential extension at 207–14. A hint of the first subject is then heard over a tonic pedal; and two short cadential repetitions, *p* and *pp*, lead to three *forte* chords which end the movement.

26 Beethoven

Symphony No 4 in B flat

This is a relatively slight symphony, full of humour and gaiety, sandwiched in between the very long 'Eroica' and the highly dramatic C minor. It was written in 1806 and dedicated to Count Oppersdorf, who had commissioned a symphony for 350 florins, after hearing a performance of the Second. It was first performed at the house of Prince Lobkowitz in March, 1807. Tovey says it is the first symphony in which Beethoven fully revealed his mastery of the sense of movement; and Grove speaks of its extraordinary finish and workmanship. Yet it is almost slight enough to have been written by Haydn or Mozart; and, like many of their works, it only uses one flute. Teachers may be interested to read Weber's sarcastic comments on the symphony, given on pp. 101–2 of Grove's book on the symphonies. Other contemporaries, too, thought the work eccentric, though it certainly does not seem so to us today.

First Movement

The first movement starts with a mysterious, dark introduction. A long, *pp*, unison tonic pedal throughout the orchestra leads to a hesitant figure starting in the violins at bar 6, on which the first subject at 43 is later to be based. The symphony is in B flat major but this introduction starts in B flat minor; and, after a repetition of the B flat pedal at 13, the hesitant figure returns in B minor at 18, by means of an enharmonic change. The long mysterious octaves return at 25, this time starting on B natural and then rising upwards in semitones, while the hesitant figure continues against them. Notice the frequent changes of dynamics in the next few bars, until a sudden crescendo leads to a *ff* dominant chord at 36, which runs into the *allegro vivace* at 39. Bars 36–42 also contain a semiquaver run leading up to the dominant chord, at first of five notes, then four, then two, thus creating a *stringendo* effect. Eventually a triplet leads into the first subject at 43.

The first subject contains two contrasting figures: the *staccato* arpeggios played by the strings that grew from bar 6, and the *legato* crotchet phrase played by the wind, starting at 47. The whole of this is then repeated *ff* tutti at 53–9, and the first subject ends with a perfect cadence in the tonic key at 64–5.

The transition, 65–107, starts with the bassoon playing a *pp* version of the first phrase of the first subject, with little comments in the violins. It makes a *crescendo* up to a *ff* tutti repetition at 81 with the figure in the lower strings, repeated by the violins at 85, and modulating to D minor at 90–1 and F minor at 93–4.

In this latter key a second section of the transition starts at 95. It consists of syncopated wind chords within a dominant pedal, repeated tutti at 98. Bars 103–7 descend gradually over a dominant pedal into the second subject at 107 in F major, the usual dominant major. It is a little strange that it should have been led into by a theme in F minor.

The second subject contains several sections. The first one starts with a gay little figure in the bassoon which is imitated by the oboe at 109 and then by the flute at 111 in D minor. The flute continues into a second, rather more sedate phrase at 113, which is carried on by the violins at 117.

The second section starts with an extraordinary three-minim, cross-rhythm, *staccato* sequence in *pp* unison at 121. It creates a feeling of excitement, working up to a climax and ending at 135–41 with a figure similar to the ending of the first section but more vigorous.

The third section starts at 141 with an ingenuous little duet in canon between clarinet and bassoon, which is taken up tutti at 149. It dies down with imitations at 155–9, and bars 159–77 form an extended cadence whose chief feature is one of continuous changes in dynamics through *pp* to *ff*.

A very definite perfect cadence having been reached in the dominant key at 176–7, the rest of the exposition consists of a codetta, which is based on the syncopation first heard at 95 in the transition. Bars 187a–207a prepare for the repeat of the exposition by using the same introductory figure as at 39–43, now extended; while 207a–8a start the repeat of the first subject. At the second repetition bars 185–7 continue the codetta figure and lead into the development section at 187.

This is a most interesting development section. It starts with imitative entries based on the first two bars of the first subject. The figure passes from first to second violins, four bars over I in F major (187–90), then four bars on ^{7}V (191–4), two bars on I (195–6), two bars on IIb (197–8), two bars on Ic (199–200), and two bars on V (201–2).

At 203 the theme slips down to the 'cellos on a dominant chord of key D. For the next twelve bars there is a *pp* duet between this theme in the 'cellos and hints of the lead-in to the first subject in the violins, first heard at 39–43. The volume increases as the other strings join in at 215, until the dominant chord is resolved on I in D major at 217, and four bars of the first subject are heard in the violins.

As this theme is transferred to the bassoon at 221 a new counter-theme appears. It is played five times, first by violins and 'cellos (221–5), then by wood-wind in G minor (225–9), then by violins in E flat major (229–33), then by clarinet and finally by violins, *crescendo*, still in E flat

This leads to a *ff* tutti in E flat at 241 in which the lower strings have the first subject while the violins again hint at the lead-in to it. But at 245 there is a sudden *piano* and the violins have antiphonal hints of the main subject. Another tutti interrupts at 249 on a chord of G major; but at 253 the violins continue their dialogue, accepting the new chord. Yet another tutti interrupts at 257–61, this time on a diminished seventh; and yet again this is followed by the violin dialogue on the new chord. This time they continue up to 281, dropping down to *pp* at 269 and making an enharmonic change at 277.

So the *ppp* chord of F sharp major comes as no surprise at 281 — until we realise how remote we are from the tonic key, B flat! The *pp* drum roll on B flat at 283 is treated as being A sharp, and occurs again at 287.

Then the second phrase of the first subject, first heard at 47–9, is heard several times in the strings in the key of B major, still *pp*. It ends on another diminished seventh with another enharmonic change at 302–4 and the bass quietly slips down from F sharp (now G flat) to F at 305. Hints of the lead-in to the first subject begin to appear in imitation in the strings, and the B flat drum roll reappears, now really as B flat, first for two bars at 307–9 and then continuously from 311 up to the recapitulation, the whole making a continual *crescendo* of 26 bars. A dominant pedal lead-in to a recapitulation is much more usual than is a tonic pedal, as found here. But this one creates a wonderful feeling of excitement.

In the recapitulation the tutti first phrase is repeated by the oboe as a means of decreasing the dynamics, 341–5; the second phrase, starting at 345 is now played by wood-wind and strings; and a short development of the latter leads to a perfect cadence in the tonic key at 350–1, which marks the end of the first subject.

The transition starts *ff* tutti with the first subject in the bass, and passes through C minor at 357 to E flat major at 361 and G minor at 363 before returning to B flat at 365. This, though using the same material, is treated differently from the first section of the transition in the exposition. But the second section, 369–81, is much more like 95–107, except that it now leads to the tonic key. (It could be argued that 65–95 and 351–69 are both parts of the first subject and that the transitions start at 95 and 369. But the two passages are different: both contain modulation but 95 does not end in the tonic key whereas bars 64–5 and 350–1 do make a definite ending in the tonic key.)

The second subject starts at 381 in the tonic. There are frequent slight differences in the scoring: for example, the imitative figure of the first section is played by bassoon, clarinet and oboe instead of bassoon, oboe and flute; the flute doubles the violins from 391–405; and the canon at 415 is accompanied by horns and drum instead of strings, while the oboe joins the clarinet at 419. Otherwise there are no changes until the coda is reached at 461.

The coda starts with the lead-in figure from 39, goes on to develop the first three notes of the first subject at 467–75 and then the second phrase of the first subject from 475–91, interrupted by two tutti cadences at 477–9 and 481–3. At 483 the theme is transferred to the bass while the violins revert to the lead-in figure. Bars 491–8 consist simply of a *ff* tutti tonic chord.

Second Movement

The second movement is in sonata form with lovely *cantabile* first and second subjects and the frequent use of a throbbing accompaniment, first heard in the second violins in bar 1, which is later transferred to different instruments, and can almost be thought of as a motto figure.

The first subject descends and then ascends by step in the first violins with a counter-theme in the violas. It is repeated tutti at 10 with the melody transferred to flute and clarinets and the motto figure in the strings, the brass and the drums.

The transition, starting at 18, consists of a flowing figure in the violins which is repeated in sequence in C minor at 20 and then appears in a shortened form at 22 over a dominant pedal of the dominant key.

This leads to the second subject in the dominant key at 26. The clarinet now has the theme, accompanied first by a rising arpeggio across the strings and then by a charming light figure in the violins. The first phrase has a tutti extension of two bars at 33. The second phrase starts at 35 in the bassoons and is repeated by full wind. It is accompanied by the motto figure in the basses at first, but this soon spreads over the rest of the orchestra in a *crescendo* leading to the development section at 41.

This rather surprisingly starts in the tonic key, and its first eight bars are a decorated repetition of 1–8. Then, at 50, its first three notes start a series of descending first inversions in E flat minor, every beat being *sf*. At 54 first and second violins have an expressive little cadenza, which leads to the motto figure in the bassoon in G flat at 60. Then, at 61, the first bar of the first subject reappears in E flat minor in the clarinet while the motto figure is transferred first to the 'cello and basses and then to the drum.

This leads to the recapitulation at 65. The first subject is now heard only once, 65–72 corresponding to 9–17, though with the flute playing a decorated version of the theme, and the accompaniment in the strings also being a rhythmic variant.

The transition starts at 73 as at 18, but the sequential repetition at 75 is a fourth higher instead of a third lower as at 20, reaching F minor at 76 and leading to a dominant pedal of the tonic key at 77, instead of the dominant key as at 22.

The second subject starts as in the recapitulation except that it is now in the tonic key. The second phrase starts at 90 in the horns instead of the bassoons, and dies away over the tonic chord at 93–5.

A short coda starts at 96 with the first subject in flute and clarinet. Gentle arpeggios and scales lead to a final repetition of the motto figure in the drum, a most unusual ending. This was the period in Beethoven's life when he was becoming very conscious of the possibilities in the imaginative use of the drums.

Third Movement

The scherzo contains a double repeat: scherzo, trio, scherzo, trio, scherzo. Beethoven did this also in his Seventh Symphony and in several chamber works—perhaps he thought the movement was not long enough to balance the other movements without doing so. In most editions the second scherzo and trio are written out; but as they are exactly the same, some editions may save space by not doing so, in which case the bar numbers will not tally with those given here.

The scherzo opens with a delicious cross-rhythm: 2|1, 2|1, 2|1, 2| 123|1, which is much used elsewhere. It is answered by diminished sevenths in triple time, alternating in wind and strings, which lead to the cross-rhythm again and a cadence in the dominant key.

B repeats the cross-rhythm figure on I (21–2) and V (23–6) in D flat major, followed by I (27–30) and V (31–4) in E flat minor. After these four-bar changes there follows a series of two-bar chord changes (thus tightening up the rhythm) starting with I in E flat minor and continuing sequentially with V I in the minor keys of B flat, F, C, G and D, with the cross-rhythm figure over the top. Three bars of V in the tonic key lead to the repetition of **A** at 53.

This time the violins play the melody an octave higher than before and the wood-wind play it, too. The diminished seventh changes at 61 so that the scherzo shall end in the tonic key. But the ending is extended: four bars of V interrupted by a *sf* discord at 70; the same repeated; and then an interrupted cadence at 75–6, followed by V I. But even this cadence is repeated, with the cross-rhythm figure alternately in the bass and the violins.

The trio, which is slower, maintains a steady, flowing triple time. The wind has a chordal phrase with a dainty comment in the violins at the cadence. This device is repeated and then followed by an eight-bar wind phrase ending with a chromatic comment in the strings. A repetition of all this starts at 107 but with variants in the string comments.

D is built over a dominant pedal and starts at 122 with a reiterated note on the horn below a continuation of the **C** theme in the bassoons and the upper wind, treated antiphonally. By 130 the bassoon anacrusis has become three quavers and it is heard without the rest of the phrase and taken over by the strings at 134. V resolves on I at 139, and a string *tremolo* starts, over which C is repeated in the wind (141–55) an octave higher than before.

Bars 149–55 are repeated at 156–63. The extended cadence which follows returns to hints of the two-beat cross-rhythm, heard antiphonally in violin and wind. A four-beat chromatic link, 175–8, leads to the exact return of the scherzo, followed by the trio.

The chromatic passage linking trio and scherzo is again heard at 353–6, though it jumps an octave higher; and the final scherzo repetition is shortened, consisting only of the second **A**, as at 53–90.

There is a tiny, charming coda for the last three bars, consisting of a horn call followed by a *ff* tonic chord. Tovey says 'the two horns blow the whole movement away'.

Fourth Movement

The finale is a gay, playful movement in sonata form. The first subject starts with a busy semiquaver figure in the strings which is interrupted in bars 3 and 4 by *f* tutti chords. However the semiquavers continue, *pp*, though at 12 the violins start a melodic figure over the top. Notice the repeated Fs at 14–15, which become quite a memorable feature. The theme is transferred to the wind at 15, complete with the repeated Fs; and a repetition of the Fs leads to a *f* semiquaver tutti at 21, which starts the transition.

This reaches the dominant chord of the dominant key at 33 and quietens down into the second subject in the dominant at 37. The theme starts in the oboe and is answered by the flute at 41. It is then transferred to the 'cellos at 45 and answered by the violins at 49. The second stanza of the theme starts in the oboe again at 52; and wind and strings answer each other antiphonally until they join together at 59 and lead to a *ff* at 64.

This starts the second section of the second subject. But at 70 it quietens down to allow a perky, disjointed figure to enter in the violins. These two figures continue alternately until a tonic pedal of the dominant key is reached at 88. This is the beginning of the codetta, which leads back to the repeat of the exposition or on to the development section at 100.

The busy semiquaver codetta figure continues in the strings until a *ff* tutti B interrupts it at 118. But the 'cellos continue unconcernedly with the theme from bar 12, which is taken over in stretto by the violins two bars later and by the wind two bars later again. The repeated-note ending of this is heard in different parts of the orchestra until 131.

At this point the semiquaver figure returns in the strings, as accompaniment to a new figure which starts in the bassoons at 133 and is treated imitatively by each wind instrument in turn. Wind and strings continue in this way, with the strings gradually gaining ascendency until a tutti *ff* climax is reached at 161 over a dominant pedal which continues to 181.

There is a kind of a false start to the recapitulation: the bassoon comes in with the first subject, *p, dolce*, as a preliminary to the real start of the recapitulation at 189.

This begins with fuller orchestration than in the exposition, and there is a cut at 193, bar 194 corresponding to the transition at 25. But, though the first subject is so short, the transition is much longer. It changes at 199 so as to stay in the tonic key and is then extended to 215, when the second subject enters in the tonic key.

The theme now starts in the clarinet, answered by the oboe, instead of oboe and flute; but then it is taken over by the strings as before. The second section starts at 242 and leads into the codetta at 266.

A coda starts at 278 and consists largely of the semiquaver first-subject figure, played by the strings alone at first but soon building up to a tutti. This comes to a pause at 318, but then the semiquavers start again, *pp*, in the 'cellos, while the lilting figure from bar 12 is heard over the top. At 345, after a one-bar rest, there is a delightful Haydnesque augmentation of the first subject ending with a pause. The bassoon takes up the last four notes ending with another pause; then the violins and violas do the same. But, at 350, the violas and 'cellos say 'enough of this' and return to speed with a brisk *ff* ending.

27 Beethoven

Symphony No 6 in F (The 'Pastoral')

This symphony, Op 68, was composed in 1808 and dedicated to two of Beethoven's aristocratic friends, Prince Lobkowitz and Count Rassumovsky. It was first performed at an all-Beethoven concert in Vienna, on 22 December of the same year: the concert included the first performances of the Fifth and Sixth Symphonies and also the G major Piano Concerto, with Beethoven at the piano. What an occasion!

On the whole the scoring of the symphony is light, relying mainly on double wood-wind, two horns and strings. Beethoven uses trumpets in the last three movements, trombones in the last two, and a piccolo for the storm scene.

Parts of the symphony are undeniably programmatic and have occasioned much discussion. Beethoven wrote in his sketch book, with the intention of printing in the preface to the symphony: 'The composer leaves it to the audience to imagine the situations. Recollections of country life. All representation loses when it is pushed too far in music. One can tell what the composer means without resorting to titles.' But all that was finally published was 'Pastoral symphony, or a recollection of country life. More an expression of feeling than a painting'—though there are also titles for each movement.

But there are certainly moods, transformed at times into pictures. Beethoven always loved nature, and did most of his composing in the summer in the country. Once, when discussing this symphony with a pupil, he asked if he had not seen tousled musicians in the villages, behaving just as in the fourth movement. And, sixteen years after composing it, he showed a friend just where he had been in the Vienna Woods, near Heiligenstadt, saying the birds had helped him with its composition, and asking him if a yellow hammer was singing in a certain tree, as it had been at the time. By then he was completely deaf.

But the 'Pastoral' Symphony is a classical symphony, of musical value in its own right, quite apart from the programme. Tovey says it 'has the enormous strength of someone who knows how to relax'. It is spacious, with the use of many little figures, in the style of the older classical composers, and these are repeated frequently as in bird song, and give a delicious feeling of pastoral bliss.

I Awakening of happy feelings on getting out into the country

The first movement is in sonata form and the first subject is built up of five tiny figures, all of which are used later. They are: (a) bar 1; (b) 2; (c) 3 and 4; (d) 6; and (e) 9–11, all heard in the first violin. The second violin starts the second phrase at 5 with (a); and a modification of (d) is heard ten times in the violin starting at 16.

Then the wood-wind decide to join in, the oboe having (a) (b) and (c) at 29–32, the clarinet and bassoon imitating it at 33–6. At 37 a tutti development of (a)–(c) starts over a tonic pedal, followed by a dominant and then another tonic pedal.

The transition begins at 53 with repetitions of (a) in the violin interrupted by triplet chords in the wind; and this leads to the second subject in the dominant key at 67. Its first section contains three figures which are freely interchanged, almost producing a round: (1) bars 67–70 in first violin; (2) 67–70 in the 'cello; (3) 71–4 in the 'cello. The reader can label them himself in all the parts from 67–93.

Then, at 93, the second section of the second subject starts. It contains two contrasted figures: at 93–6 in the strings and at 97–100 in the wind. They are repeated at 100–7; then the second one is repeated at 107–11, followed by a decoration of it at 111–15.

The third section of the second subject, forming a codetta, is heard over a tonic pedal of the dominant key. It begins at 115 and the two-bar figure starting in the violin at this point is heard for the next twenty bars, with a swinging tonic-dominant above it in the wind until 127, when the music quietens down and the tonic-dominant figure is transferred to the violins.

A link, based on (a), at 135–8 leads back to the beginning or on to the development, which is based almost entirely on the working out of figures from the first subject. Figures (a) and (b) are first heard in the violin in the tonic key, followed by a development of (c) at 143 which leads to more repetitions of (a) and (b), now in the wind, over a dominant seventh of key B flat at 147.

Bars 151–86 consist entirely of repetitions of (b): over a tonic pedal in B flat at 151–62, then similarly in key D from 163–86. The figure is tossed about from one instrument to another and gradually builds up to a ff tutti at 175 before sinking into imitations in strings alone, which, in turn, lead to humorous imitations between bassoon and violin of the last two notes from 187–90.

Then the process starts all over again, with (a) (b) and (c) in G major at 191, followed by (b) in G major from 197–208 and then in E major from 209–32, again ending with the bassoon and violin imitations at 233–6. This means that nearly every bar from 139 to 236 has been based on the tiny figures (a) (b) and (c), frequently repeated in exactly the same way for bars on end. But it is a kind of pastoral monotony that is very pleasant and relaxing.

And it looks as if the process is going to happen yet again at 237, when (a) (b) and (c) appear in A major. But at 243 (e) appears in the wind, followed by (d) at 246. Figures (d) and (e) are also part of the first subject but they provide a change from (b). They are used up to 275: in the wind at 241–7, then in the strings up to 263 (passing through D major at 254, G minor at 258), then tutti from 263 to 275 (passing through C major at 263 on the way to the tonic key at 267). Four bars of subdominant harmony provide a rather unusual lead-in to the recapitulation at 279.

The first subject starts in second violins and violas instead of first violins, while the first violins have long notes forming a counter-theme which ends in a charming little cadenza. The subject continues in the second violins at 289 and transfers to wind at 291 and back to second violins at 297, the first violins having decorative triplets throughout. Figure (d), which was heard ten times starting at bar 16, is now heard nine times from 300 to 309 before rising rapidly to the tutti at 312. Bars 312–28 are the same as 37–53; and the transition starts the same at 328 but changes at 340, staying in the tonic key and being slightly longer.

The first and second sections of the second subject are more fully scored than in the exposition and are, of course, in the tonic key. The codetta, starting at 394, is more slightly scored at first; and it is followed by the link at 414–17, but this time leading to the coda.

The coda starts with (a) and (b) of the first subject in the clarinet over the dominant seventh of key B flat and is followed by a *forte* statement of (a) (b) and (c) in the strings in B flat, (c) being imitated by the wind at 426. Then the codetta theme from 115 is transformed into triplets and played by clarinets and bassoons over a tonic pedal in B flat. After two bars of imitation in flute and bassoon at 438–9 it is transferred to the strings in the tonic key with a *forte* accompaniment.

It reaches a *ff* climax at 458 and then descends by step in a *diminuendo* until it is interrupted by (b) in the violins at 470. This is treated imitatively in the strings up to 476, which could be the end of the movement. But Beethoven seems loth to end, and gives the clarinet a charming cadenza based on (c), accompanied first by a bassoon and later by the whole orchestra.

Then, at 492, the violin has (a) (b) and (c) *piano* over a tonic pedal, imitated by the flute at 498, by clarinet and bassoon at 503 and finally by a *forte* tutti at 505, though the movement ends with two *piano* chords.

II By the Brook

This is a spacious and very leisurely movement in sonata form, in which the brook murmurs in quavers or semiquavers almost throughout. The first subject begins with a tentative figure in the violins, but it broadens out into a more spacious melody in bars 5–7. Then, against a monotonous syncopated pedal in the horns and bird-like trills in the violin, the melody is repeated in clarinet and bassoon at 7–13. There is a charming pendant to the theme: a three-bar phrase in the violin repeated by the clarinet, followed by a gently reiterated cadence.

The transition starts at 19 with murmuring figures in the strings and the syncopated pedal in the horns, over which the first subject reappears in the violins at 22. But it moves towards the dominant key at 26, thus leading to the second subject in the dominant at 27.

This contains two sections, the first starting in the violins at 27 and transferred to the flute at 30 and then to the bassoon at 32; and the second, and more memorable, starting in the bassoon at 33, with its first bar leisurely repeated three times before proceeding to the cadence. This second theme is then repeated in flute and violins at 41.

In the codetta, starting at 47, the 'cellos repeat the pendant figure of the first subject, imitated by the violins a bar later and the wind a bar later again. A very leisurely cadence ends the exposition at 54.

Four bars of link follow, in which yet another leisurely little theme is heard, first in the tonic key in the violins and then in the flute modulating to G minor

The development starts at 58 in G major, with the first subject in the oboe and a new little arpeggio figure in the strings which is used considerably as time goes on. The murmuring of the brook and the syncopated horns continue as before. But the oboe theme wanders off into a new continuation at 63, imitated by the flute, and both end with trills, reaching the cadence at 69. The haunting pendant theme from the first subject follows in the violin and then in the flute.

Bars 69–79 are a repetition of 58–69, starting in E flat and with different scoring. The first subject theme is now in the clarinet but has yet another different continuation at 73; and the pendant figure is heard in violas and 'cellos at 77 and imitated by violins at 78.

The music has now reached G flat major and it sounds as if the 58–69 passage is to be repeated yet again, with the first subject theme in the violin. But an enharmonic change reaches B major at 83 and the violin continuation is more like the original for a bar before it fades away, leaving only the murmuring of the brook and the trills of the birds. A dominant pedal starting at 86 leads to the recapitulation at 91.

Bars 91–7 correspond to 1–7 but with quite different scoring: a *piano* tutti with the murmuring brook in the strings and ascending semiquaver arpeggios moving about the orchestra, combined with the slow descending arpeggio figure which was first heard at 58. This is all soft enough for the first subject to be heard in the flute, though the violin joins in at 95. But 96–7 produce an interrupted cadence; and a two-bar transition based on the first subject leads straight into the second subject at 99.

The first section of the second subject (99), the second section (105) and the codetta (120) contain so little change, apart from the obvious one of key, that they require no comment.

But 126 begins to merge into the coda, as the music modulates to E flat; and then follow the famous bird imitations. Beethoven said the passage was intended as a joke; and certainly, here, he has produced deliberate imitations of sound rather than merely evoking a mood. The flute imitates the nightingale, the oboe the quail and the clarinet the cuckoo, and the four-bar phrase is completed by the pendant theme in the violins. The bird themes appear again at 133; and the pendant theme ends the movement with charming imitations in the violins, the bassoon, the clarinet and the flute.

III Peasants' Merry-making

The third movement is a rustic kind of scherzo, full of boisterous merry-making. **A** consists of two sentences, the first in F major and the second, unexpectedly, in D major. The repeat of the whole of this is written out at 17–32 instead of using repeat marks; perhaps Beethoven wanted to be sure the repeat was really played.

B, 32–52, starts with a repetition of 1–4 in D major and then slips down a tone and is repeated in C major. Its second sentence, 41–52, corresponds to 9–16 but is now in C major and is extended to make twelve bars.

Notice that this scherzo has started *pp* in the strings and that instruments are gradually being added all the time. Bars 49–52 make a *crescendo* and lead to the return of **A** at 53, *ff*, tutti (though there are still no trumpets—they are being reserved for later). Its second sentence (59–75), instead of being a repetition of its first in D major, as before, brings in a new tune, even more peasant-like, and stays in the tonic to 86.

The bassoon and horn thirds which have been so much in evidence from 75–86 are now taken over by the violins, *diminuendo*, forming a short link to the trio which starts at 91. The violins continue, as if representing simple rustic fiddlers, and form an accompaniment to the theme **C** in the oboe, a hesitant, syncopated theme which may be meant to represent a village rustic not quite able to play in time. The third instrument in this thinly orchestrated theme, which is true to its name of trio, is the second bassoon which plays *doh soh doh* or *doh soh soh doh*, providing the simplest possible bass. Perhaps this represents a sleepy or drunken player, putting in his two notes at irregular intervals. Certainly we are told that Beethoven was humorously imitating a village band he often heard at Mödling.

At the repetition of **C**, 107–22, the clarinet chirps in twice with three notes; and the clarinet takes over theme **D** at 123, accompanied by two bassoons now taking the place of the fiddles, while the violas and cellos take over the *doh soh doh* bass.

When **C** returns at 133 the theme is played by a horn and the accompaniment by both violins and violas, but the droning *doh soh doh* bass reverts to the bassoons as before. However the theme moves back to the oboe at 141, with the clarinet added at 143, while the horn holds on its last C which grows into an extension of the theme at 145, in which the oboe and clarinet join in at 149.

A codetta, 153–61, rounds off the trio with imitations between the lower strings and the wind.

At 161 we expect a return of **D C**, 123–61, followed by a return to the scherzo. But instead of this the bassoons and basses continue by themselves with the theme in unison, *sempre più stretto*, and lead into a completely new and unexpected section in 2/4 time starting at 165. This is a rough folk dance, *allegro* tutti, with a stamping bass.

After four repetitions of the same four bars the theme moves down to bassoons and violas, while the trumpet appears for the first time, thus crowning the festivities. By 189 everyone is playing *ff* and they continue thus to 203, when they cease abruptly, leaving a trumpet and the violins to drop a third from *ff* to *p*, as if exhausted. (Notice that the whole of this extended trio section, 91–204, is in the tonic key, as befits peasant-like music.)

And now, surprisingly, we have a repetition of the whole of the movement heard so far, from bars 1 to 204. Certainly Beethoven does not intend to cut short the merry-making of the peasants! But he naturally wishes to end with the scherzo, so he starts it once again at 205. However, the second sentence of **A**, starting in key D as before at 213, ends now at 219 in the tonic key; and the whole sentence is repeated in the tonic, starting at 223.

Instead of going on to **B**, another repetition of **A** starts *crescendo* at 231, becoming a *ff* tutti *presto* at 235. Bars 241–64 correspond to the end of the scherzo, 59–82. But instead of a final tonic chord, as at 83, we hear the first rumblings of thunder which introduce the storm and lead into an extra, fourth, movement.

IV Thunderstorm

The fourth movement is pure programme music, with much interesting orchestral colour. The piccolo enters for the first time, at 82 in the middle of the storm, when its shrill notes add to the terror; two (not the usual three) trombones enter for the first time, at 106, when the storm reaches its climax; the drums enter for the first time, at 21, representing the first big roll of thunder, combined with low quintuplets in 'cellos and quadruplets in basses, all helping to give a rumbling effect; the *pp staccato* quavers in 3 in the violins give the effect of the first raindrops; the *ff tremolo* arpeggios in the upper strings in 78–89 produce a feeling of intense excitement; and so on.

Structurally the movement is based on a number of figures which produce various permutations and combinations. The 'cellos and basses start with a *pp tremolo* D flat, figure (*a*), at bar 1, forming an interrupted cadence which joins the third and fourth movements, and giving the effect of the first low rumbles of thunder. Figure (*b*) is the *staccato* 'raindrop' quavers in bar 3 in the second violin, while the first violins enter with the crotchet figure (*c*) at 5. These three figures continue in the strings, making a gradual *crescendo* to 21, when the *ff* drum roll and the excited strings mark the real beginning of the storm. As the effect is primarily that of *tremolo* rolls this can still be considered to be figure (*a*). But a new figure, (*d*), enters in the first violins at 23^4; and (*a*) and (*d*) alternate up to 33.

At 33 another figure, (*e*), consisting of quick rising arpeggios in the violins, is probably intended to give the effect of lightning. And the unison string passage, (*f*), starting at 35^3 may represent the scattering of the peasants for shelter. Figure (*a*) returns *pp* at 41 and continues to 55, with the darting 'lightning' arpeggios, (*e*), appearing at 43, 47 and 51–5 above it. Then the 'raindrop' quavers (*b*) return at 56; and (*a*) and (*b*) continue until they reach a climax at 78.

Here a new, slow-moving theme, (*g*), appears in the 'cellos and basses. At 82 the piccolo enters, and by then everyone is playing except the trombones. Figure (*f*) reappears at 89³; and at 95 a sudden *fp* with chromatic scales, (*h*), in the violins provides a temporary lull, until a rapid *crescendo* leads to the entry of the trombones at 106, (*i*) and the storm reaches its tutti climax, with *tremolos* and drum rolls, (*a*), combining up to 119.

Figure (*g*) returns at 119, combined with *tremolo* arpeggios in upper strings as before, but now in a *diminuendo* as the storm moves away. Figure (*a*) returns *piano* at 130; the last flicker of lightning, (*e*), appears at 140; and gradually the music quietens down to 146, when the quavers of bar 3 reappear as *dolce* minims in the oboe over a dominant pedal of the tonic key—this has been likened to the effect of a rainbow after the storm. And Grove calls the *dolce* violin quavers which lead into the next movement 'a strip of blue sky'.

V Shepherds' Song: Happy and thankful feelings after the storm

The fifth movement is a leisurely sonata rondo. It starts with a jodel 'Ranz des Vaches' introduction in the clarinet, imitated by the horn at 5, with dominant and tonic harmonies played softly together in the strings.

The first subject is played three times: in the first violins, *p*, at 9; then an octave lower in the second violins, *crescendo*, at 17; and finally an octave lower again, *ff*, in the violas and 'cellos at 25, with the theme also played by clarinets and horns and supported by trumpets and trombones.

The transition starts at 32 with a syncopated figure in the lower strings which passes to the violins two bars later and is then used imitatively until it reaches the dominant key and the rather insignificant second subject at 42, which grows out of the transition. A short second section starts at 50 and leads to the codetta at 54, which starts *ff* with a return of the Ranz des Vaches, and then *diminuendos* into the return of the first subject at 64.

This starts in the first violins and is transferred to the second violins an octave lower at 72, as before; but then it begins to modulate to B flat major and reaches the episode which starts the middle section at 80.

This theme is played in sixths and thirds by clarinets and bassoons, with a quiet semiquaver accompaniment. It is followed at 95 by a short modulatory development of the first subject, starting in D flat major and slipping down to C major, the dominant key, at 99. Bars 99–117 consist of a new semiquaver figure imitated between first and second violins over a dominant pedal, and lead to the recapitulation at 117.

The first subject appears three times, as in the exposition, at 117, 125 and 133, getting louder and more fully orchestrated each time. But the semiquavers, first heard at 99, continue throughout, so that it becomes a variation of the original theme.

The transition starts at 140, but changes at 145 so that the second subject is reached in the tonic key at 150. Its short second section starts at 158, and the codetta begins at 162. But it is extended before it reaches the return of the first subject at 177.

However this almost immediately merges into the coda. Imitative entries in the strings lead to a *ff* tutti development of the first subject at 190. At 206 the semiquaver figure takes over, with imitative entries in the strings, combined with imitative entries of the original theme in the wind, and this reaches a *ff* tutti climax at 219.

Then the violins gradually descend by step, getting softer all the while, until they reach a *sotto voce* version of the first subject at 237 in strings alone. This is repeated tutti at 246, and strings and wind imitate each other for a few bars. At 260 a muted horn (a rarity with Beethoven) has the theme, while the strings rumble away *pp* with their semiquavers, until two *ff* chords bring the movement to an end.

28 Beethoven

String Quartet in G, Op 18, No 2

Beethoven's first published string quartets, Op 18, were produced
as a set of six, as was common at that time. They were written
between 1798 and 1800 and published in 1801; they were dedicated
to Prince Lobkowitz. This means that Beethoven was nearly thirty
before he felt competent to deal with such a difficult type of music
as the string quartet. The second quartet in G—which may have
been the first to be composed—is charming and feminine.

First Movement, *Allegro*

This movement is in sonata form and is in G major. The first
subject contains three short two-bar motifs which occur separately
elsewhere, so had better be labelled: (*a*) bars 1–2; (*b*), 3–4; and (*c*)
5–6, repeated on a different part of the scale at 7–8. The rhythm of
(*a*) is repeated at 9–10; then (*b*) is heard in harmony—it was in
unison at 3–4; then (*a*) recurs at 13–14, followed by (*b*), which is
used almost continuously up to the end of the first subject at 20.

The transition starts at 21 with unison crotchets followed by a
semiquaver figure. Then the three lowest instruments repeat the
crotchets in E minor at 25–6, followed by the semiquaver figure in
the violins, which is repeated in D major at 29–30 and in D minor
at 31. It is transferred to second violin and viola at 32–3, while an
upper dominant pedal in the first violin prepares the way for the
second subject in the dominant major key at 36.

The first section of the second subject starts with a chromatic
harmonic passage of the kind often found in Beethoven. It is
repeated at 44 with the second violin having the melody while the
first violin has a counter-theme in semiquavers above it.

This reaches B minor at 51 when the second section of the second
subject starts. At first the violins are in thirds and use syncopation,
while the viola has an inner dominant pedal. This is again repeated at

137

56, with the second violin having the melody and the first violin a counter figure above it.

The codetta starts at 61 and is in D major once more. This time the theme starts in the second violin and is transferred to the first violin in a decorated form two bars later. It reverts to the second violin in this decorated form at 66 and is answered by a triplet figure in the first violin, which changes to octave duplets at 71 and begins to rise to a climax. Two statements of (c) of the first subject, at 78–9 and 80–1 bring the exposition to an end.

The development section starts with the same figure, (c), but now in D minor. Then the transition theme is heard in D minor at 86 and is repeated by the three lower strings in B flat major at 90. The second, semiquaver, part of the figure is then played by the violins at 94, followed by viola and 'cello at 96. The three lower strings play its last three notes four times at 97–9, while an upper dominant pedal in the first violin prepares the way for the introduction of the first subject in E flat major at 101.

Figures (a) and (b) of the first subject are heard at 101–4; and then (b) is transferred to the 'cello in an inverted form and continues for some time. It reaches A flat major at 110 and B flat major at 112, when it is transferred back to the first violin. It reaches B flat minor at 115 and F minor at 117 when it moves to the second violin. At 122 it reaches G minor and is transferred to the viola. It reaches a climax on a diminished seventh at 129, resolving on to ^7Vb in G at 135. It gradually fades away in imitations between upper and lower strings until a *forte* D is heard, played by the 'cello in the treble clef six times in 141–4. This leads to (a) and (b) of the first subject in the tonic key in the 'cello at 145–8, thus anticipating the recapitulation which really starts at 149.

The recapitulation starts like the exposition; but the first subject is cut short, the equivalent of bars 13–20 being omitted.

The transition, starting at 161, is quite different from the transition in the exposition and starts with a development of bar 1, passing through D minor at 162 and E minor at 164, with imitations between the two violins. Then the first subject is heard in E major at 170, figures (*a*), (*b*) and (*c*) being heard in turn. Figure (*c*) is then developed, passing through E minor at 176 and G major at 178. The music reaches a dominant pedal of the tonic key at 179; and this eventually leads to the second subject on the tonic key at 187.

The theme of its first section is played first by the second violin from 187–94, and it is then repeated by the first violin at 195–202. The second section starts at 202 and is almost identical with its appearance in the exposition except that it starts in E minor and ends in G major.

The codetta starts at 212 in the tonic key and is again similar to its treatment in the exposition except that the first and second violins change round in the first eight bars. It ends with two repetitions of (*c*) of the first subject at 229–32, as in the exposition.

A coda starts at 233. Bars 233–40 are based on imitations of (*c*); then (*a*), (*b*) and (*c*) are heard from 241 to the end, as in bars 1–8 except that (*c*) is first heard an octave higher in the violin and is repeated by the viola at the end.

Second Movement, *Adagio cantabile*

The second movement is in C major, and is in ternary form. It opens with a *cantabile* melody in the first violin with unusual phrasing: 3+3+2+2 bars long. The short second stanza starts at 11 in G major and ends at 14 in the same key. Four link-bars return to the key of C and to a return of the idea of the opening bar, though now it is repeated twice and produces a four-bar phrase. A codetta, 23–6, consists of cadence repetitions; and the semiquaver figure used at 23–4 forms the bassis of the *allegro* which follows.

The middle section is a scherzo-like *allegro* in F major. Two preliminary bars lead to **A**, 28–36, continuous semiquavers which modulate to the dominant, C major. This is repeated.

B, 36–44, continues with the same idea, but now starting with imitations, and modulates to G minor at 38 before returning to key F and the return of **A** at 44.

This now starts in the second violin and 'cello, with a pedal C in first violin and viola. But the first violin joins the second with the figure at 46, while the 'cello imitates it a beat later. The music changes at 48 so that the section ends in F major. Then **B** and **A** are repeated.

Bars 52–8 continue the semiquaver figure and return to the key of C, thus acting as a link to the return of the first section at *tempo I*.

But now the melody is given to the 'cello, with arpeggios above it, for the first six bars. Then it is returned to the first violin in an even more decorative form. The second stanza starts at 69, in G major, as before; and it and the third stanza are both more highly decorated than before. The codetta, 81–6, is now five bars long instead of three.

Third Movement, *Allegro*

This is a scherzo and trio. **A**, 1–8, begins and ends in G major; and its chief feature is a little figure treated imitatively between the two violins.

B, 9–16, starts with a scale over a tonic pedal in B major. The figure is repeated at 13–16 over [7] V I, key C, followed by Ic V, key G.

A, 17–30, returns an octave higher, with the lower strings now imitating the upper strings in the first phrase and the other way round in the second phrase. This second phrase changes at 22 and an extension modulates to E minor. This leads to the original figure in C major at 27, with the lower strings imitating the upper, and ending in G major at 30.

A codetta starts at 30 with a new figure, treated imitatively. It continues, at 38–42, with imitations of bar 1 in the three upper strings, and added syncopation over the bar line. It ends with a tempestuous descent, using the figure over the tonic chord.

The trio is in C major. **C** is very short, 44–51, and consists of a rising figure using trills and ending in G major.

D starts with an octave leap, and at 54–5 uses triplets before leaping nearly two octaves at 56–7. The triplets then continue in the first violin, transferring to the second at 63 and to the 'cello at 64.

This overlaps with the return of **C** at 63, an octave higher than before and with the triplets continuing beneath it. It is much longer than the first **C** and changes at 67, staying in the key of C and reaching a cadence in that key at 69–70. Bars 67–70 are then repeated at 71–4 with the melody in the 'cello and the triplets above it. Cadence repetitions, in keys G and C alternately, end at 78–9 with a rising arpeggio in key C.

After **D** and **C** have been repeated there are eight link-bars based on the opening figure of **A** over a descending bass in dotted minims, which end on a dominant seventh of key G and lead to the return to the scherzo.

Fourth Movement, *Allegro molto, quasi presto*

This movement is again in sonata form. Its first subject is based on the first four bars, which are heard alone in the 'cello. After that, the figure not only changes from instrument to instrument, in various forms, but does an unusual amount of modulation for a first subject. By 8 it is in D major, by 16 in E minor, and by 18 in C major. Then, at 21, it returns in its original form in G major, though the violin now has the tune. This time it stays in G and reaches a perfect cadence at 27–8. This can therefore be thought of as the end of the first subject.

A new figure starts at 28 which can be thought of as the start of the transition or as a second section of the first subject. In support of the first proposition is the fact that it moves away from the tonic key, and its next important cadence is at 37–8 in D major. In support of the second proposition is the fact that 28–38 has an exact equivalent in the recapitulation at 274–84.

However, it is quite an important and contrasted theme, so it can be considered to be the beginning of the transition. After its cadence in key D at 37–8 it is followed by a development of the first subject in the 'cello in D minor. (Such a development frequently takes place in a transition.) It continues in D minor up to 45, then the last two bars are repeated in B flat major; and then another repetition leads to the dominant pedal of the dominant key at 50–4, which prepares the way for the second subject at 56.

Its first section starts with the two violins alone, the viola being added at 60. The second phrase starts at 64 in viola and 'cello, with the violins taking over at 66. The two sets of instruments alternate once more at 68–70 and 70–2, and are followed by a *sf* pedal on A which leads to the second section of the second subject at 76.

This bears a distinct resemblance to the first bar of the first subject, inverted. It is frequently repeated and reaches a dominant pedal of key F at 96 which resolves on F at 103 but then moves on to a perfect cadence in the dominant key at 111–12.

The codetta, 112–39, which follows, starts with the first two bars of the first subject in imitation between the second violin and viola and the first violin, over a tonic pedal. By 122 the first bar is heard alone, inverted, and is therefore similar to the second section of the second subject. From 122–8 it is heard in imitation; and then, from 128–39 it is in diminution as well as in imitation; and all this is over the tonic chord of the dominant key. The exposition ends at 139 with a pause on the seventh which is added to the chord, thus implying a return to the key of G.

But the development section does not start with a resolution on the chord of G. Instead, it starts abruptly in E flat major with the first subject in that key. It moves to the transition figure in the same key at 147. Later, this figure passes rapidly through C major (155); C minor (156); F major (157); B flat major (159); C minor (160) and F major (162) on its way to a dominant pedal of key C which lasts from 163–78, with continuous semiquavers above.

This leads to a development of the first subject in C major, starting at 179. It appears in canon at one beat's distance between 'cello and second violin from 187–202, with the first violin joining in with the quavers as well at 190 and 194 onwards, all three being at one beat's distance away from each other between 194 and 202. The viola joins in also with the quavers, but by inversion. From

202–12 the viola and 'cello continue with the quaver figure in imitation, while the violins refer to bar 1 at 206–7, 210–11, and 214.

The first violin continues with an inversion of bar 1 at 215; and gradually the two middle instruments join in with this figure in its descending form, so that it is very much like the second section of the second subject. They are over a dominant pedal of the tonic key in the 'cello from 215–27 and are followed by a hesitant eight bars ending on a chord of E flat.

Then, unexpectedly, the first subject returns in A flat major at 235. The rising quaver part of it is heard three times, and then it appears in augmentation at 243, ending with a pause on a dominant seventh of key G at 245–6. This finishes the development section.

The recapitulation starts like the exposition except that a quaver counter-theme appears in the first violin, while the theme itself is kept to the lower instruments. However the theme returns to the first violin at 267; and 267–74 is the same as 21–8 except for a sudden scuttle of semiquavers in viola and 'cello at 270.

The transition starts in the same way, too, 274–84 being exactly the same as 28–38. But at 284 the development of the first subject in the 'cello appears in G minor instead of D minor: a fourth lower; and it continues in the same way, thus leading to a dominant pedal of the tonic key at 296–301.

The second subject starts in the tonic key at 302. There are only slight differences in the first section, apart from key; and the second section, 322–58 is exactly the same.

The codetta starts at 358. It contains an extension of two bars at 368–9, but otherwise is similar to its appearance in the exposition; and it ends with a pause on the dominant seventh of the sub-dominant key, C, at 387.

The coda starts at 388 with the first four bars of the first subject in C major. But the music returns to G at 394 and the first four bars of the first subject are heard in that key at 396–9. Bars 400 to the end continue with the theme, using first crotchets, then quavers (402–5), then semiquavers (406–9), and ending with three statements of the tonic chord and a bar's pause to complete the last phrase.

29 Beethoven

Piano Sonata in C, Op 2, No 3

There are two main sources of analyses of Beethoven sonatas available in print. One is the Macpherson analyses supplied in the Joseph Williams edition of each separate sonata. The other is Tovey's book of analyses of all the piano sonatas published by the Associated Board. Macpherson's analyses are given in outline only, which means, for example, that the three lines of description of the development section of the first movement of Op 2, No 3 would be insufficient for a Board which asked for an analysis of the development section. Tovey goes to the other extreme, as he gives what he calls a 'bar-to-bar analysis', accounting for the length of every phrase and sub-phrase. This is useful reading for the teacher but would be hard going for the O Level candidate, apart from being unnecessarily detailed.

There are also other differences between the analyses of these two authorities. For example, in Op 2, No 3, Macpherson says the second movement is in modified sonata form while Tovey calls it 'special rondo form'; Macpherson says the last movement is in sonata-rondo form while Tovey calls it rondo, though he really means the same thing. And frequently Macpherson will state that a minuet or scherzo or trio is in ternary form while Tovey will call it binary.

The object here is to give the amount of information that an O Level candidate can reasonably be expected to assimilate; and also to comment on any differences in terminology, realising that where differences do occur, an examiner is sure to accept either interpretation.

First Movement

The first movement is in the usual sonata form. The first subject begins rather squarely—two bars and a pause answered by another two bars and a pause—but then continues in a more flowing style, with a syncopated ending leading to a perfect cadence in the tonic key at 11–12. Notice that the theme from bar 1 reappears in the bass at 9.

The ending at 11–12 is so definite that it appears reasonable to consider that it marks the end of the first subject, particularly as 1–12 is repeated almost exactly in the recapitulation. But the passage which follows, 13–26, does not really modulate; and its second half, 21–6, is the same in exposition and recapitulation. So it is debatable whether to consider it to be part of the first subject, as does Tovey, or to call it a transition, as does Macpherson. It feels like a transitional passage in spite of its lack of modulation; and its scale of G at the end (25–6 and 159–60) can lead equally well to either dominant or tonic key.

It is a showy bravura passage, with its arpeggios and broken octaves, which Beethoven as a young pianist must have enjoyed playing; and its second half, 21–6, is nothing more than a cadential extension, repeating V and I in the tonic key.

The second subject starts at 23 in the dominant *minor*—the listener of Beethoven's day would have expected the dominant major. The six-bar phrase is repeated, starting in D minor at 33 and ending in A minor at 40.

A transition passage, 39–47, using modulatory sequences, leads to the second section of the second subject in the more usual dominant major at 47. This contains an imitative figure between the two upper parts, which is repeated in invertible counterpoint at 55.

A dominant seventh of C major at 60 leads to a reference to the theme in that key starting at 13 (which I propose now to call the transition). The figure from bars 13–14 is used three times, over I in key C, ^{7}V in key G and I in key G. Then the figure from 15–16 is used for two bars at 67–8, followed by a descending, syncopated bass ending on G at 73, and then by four bravura cadence bars.

A codetta starts at 77^3 in which a two-bar figure is used twice, and then the first bar of it is used four times, ascending to a climax and a perfect cadence in the dominant key. The exposition ends with bravura broken chords reminiscent of 15–16.

The development section begins with the codetta figure modulating to C minor (92) and F minor (94). Its first bar is then used four times more and leads to a *ff* bravura passage in broken chords, starting with a chord of B flat at 97 and sliding up by semitones in the bass, no key being established until it dies down into a *pp* statement of the first subject in D major at 109. This key feels very remote (Tovey considers it is really E double flat). After four bars corresponding to 1–4, bar 1 is developed for some time, interspersed with the syncopated figure from 11–12.

This eventually leads to a dominant pedal of the tonic key from 129–38, over which bar 1 is developed in imitation and sequence, thus effectively leading to the recapitulation.

In the recapitulation the first subject is nearly the same as 1–8, and 9–12 is omitted. The transition starts at 147 with a syncopated figure in which the bass grows out of the previous two bars of melody, passing over to the treble at 151. This takes the place of the bravura broken chords heard at 13; but 155–61 are the same as 21–6.

The second subject starts at 161 in the tonic minor but otherwise is exactly as before. So are the link (173–81), the second subject (181–95), the reference to the transition (195–211) and the codetta (211–218).

The coda starts with the interrupted cadence (217–8). A chord of A flat lasts for six bars and is followed by a series of rising diminished sevenths which lead to a pause on Ic of the tonic key at 232. This chord is the typical indication of the start of a cadenza in a concerto; and a concerto-like cadenza does, in fact, follow. After surging upwards to a high E the figure from bar 1 is developed, gradually descending into the usual trill on ^{7}V. (The whole of this cadenza is unbarred.)

After the cadenza there is a return to the first subject starting in its original form but changing at 237 into a series of syncopations that are originally derived from 11–12 but were used more fully at 115–29. They lead to a quiet interrupted cadence and a pause at 248. Three dramatically unexpected *ff* bars are followed by a repetition of the last six bars of the exposition but now in the tonic key, thus bringing the two sections of the movement to an end in the same way.

Second Movement

Macpherson considers that this movement is in modified sonata form. This seems right to me, so I shall proceed to analyse it in this way, and then consider Tovey's alternative afterwards.

Notice first the unexpected key of the movement: E major, quite unrelated to C major, but having a lovely calming effect after the tempestuous first movement.

The first subject is short and consists mostly of one-bar phrases. Bar 5 starts like bar 1 but in F sharp minor; and after some hesitancy the music leads towards a perfect cadence in the tonic key at 10–11.

But the chord at 11 is E minor instead of the expected E major and this starts the second subject in the tonic minor key—an unexpected key for a second subject, though perhaps it has its historical basis in the *minore* sections beloved of Haydn.

This second subject has two sections which are rather alike because both contain a continuous semiquaver accompaniment. The first section contains two three-bar phrases, the first in E minor (11–13), the second in G major (14–16), followed by a two-bar extension. The second starts in G major at 19 with a new syncopated figure in the left hand, and again contains three-bar phrases.

A one-bar link, 25, makes a return to E minor when there is a return to the idea of the first section, *ff*, modulating to A minor at 29 and B minor at 32. The second section theme then returns at 37 over a dominant pedal of the tonic key. This leads quietly into the recapitulation at 43.

The first subject is exactly the same as in the exposition until it reaches the cadence, when it abruptly changes to C major and has two *ff* bars in that key before reaching the first section of the second subject in the unexpected key of C major at 55. But the second section, starting at 59, is in the usual tonic key and is a transposition of 19–24 with two extra bars added at the end.

This leads to the coda, which starts with a decorative version of the first subject, an octave higher, at 67, has a different bar at 72 and an interrupted cadence at 74, followed by a two-bar extension. The melody moves to the bass at 77 with a dominant pedal above it, and abrupt changes of pitch and dynamics lead to the final cadence.

Tovey says the movement is in special rondo form, labelling it: main theme, 1–10; episode, 11–42; main theme, 43–52; repetition of episode, 53–66; main theme, 67–76; coda, 77–82. This, in effect means: **A B A B A** coda. Most people would expect at least two contrasted episodes in a rondo. And it is more usual to call a theme that occurs twice a 'subject', reserving the word 'episode' for a theme which occurs only once. But apart from different labels, the only real difference between this analysis and the one given above is that he calls 67 a recurrence of the main theme and considers that the coda starts at 77.

Third Movement

This movement is quite definitely a scherzo and not a minuet, and is nearly as humorous in effect as the scherzo in the previous sonata, Op 2, No 2. The third movements of all the the Op 2 sonatas should be compared, as an illustration of Beethoven's change from minuet to scherzo.

Macpherson states that this scherzo is in ternary form. Tovey avoids the use of any term to describe its form, which seems much the best way, in view of conflicting opinions about the use of the words binary and ternary. But elsewhere Tovey does state very definitely that when the first **A** in **A|BA‖** form does not end with a perfect cadence in the tonic key and the first section therefore sounds incomplete, the form should be called binary. In this scherzo bar 16 ends in the dominant key; and many analysts would therefore say the form was binary.

A, 1–16, starts with imitative entries in three voices, in the tonic key, C major. Bars 7–8 form an imperfect cadence, and the figure then continues for another eight bars in rising sequences, ending in the dominant key at 16.

B, 17–28, continues to develop the same figure, still using imitation and sequence, and passing through C minor at 18, B flat minor at 20 and A flat major at 24.

A link over a dominant pedal, 28–40, continues to use the figure with sudden changes of dynamics and effectively leads into the return of **A**, 40–55, which is the same as 1–8 except that it now ends with a perfect cadence.

A codetta, 55–64, still using the same figure, brings the scherzo to an end. (Macpherson calls it a coda, but it seems better to reserve this term for the end of the whole movement, where Beethoven has used it himself.)

The trio is in exactly the same form as the scherzo, so again it seems wiser to avoid the use of either binary or ternary as terms of description. Notice that Macpherson begins to number the bars afresh for the trio, while Tovey continues the numbering from the scherzo. The latter method is more generally used today, and will be followed in this analysis.

C, 65–72, which starts in A minor and ends in E minor, consists entirely of simple broken chords.

D, 73–81, continues in the same style, but starts in C major and modulates through D minor at 75 on its way to the return of **C** in A minor at 81.

C, 81–8, starts an octave higher than at 65 and changes at 86 so as to end in the tonic key.

Beethoven writes out the repeat of **D C** at 89–105 because he changes **C** at 100 so as to avoid the perfect cadence in A minor and leads instead, by means of a descending dominant seventh at 102–4, to a return to the key of the scherzo, C major.

F

After the scherzo is repeated the coda, 106–27, starts with the last two notes of the scherzo, repeated *ff* on A and then on F sharp. This leads to a dominant pedal in the bass, built from the opening figure with chords over the top, changing to a tonic pedal at 118 and gradually dying down into a *pp* unison C.

Fourth Movement

This movement is in sonata-rondo form. The first subject, 1–18, contains two ideas, an ascending series of quaver first inversions at 1–8 and a semiquaver passage built over a dominant pedal at 9–16. A two-bar link, 17–18, leads to a return of the first idea at 19, but it changes at 22 and passes through E minor at 23 on its way to G major at 26, reaching the dominant chord at 29, ready to lead into the second subject. Bars 19–29 fulfil the function of a transition, though they are based on the first subject.

The second subject, 30–55, is again based on two ideas, heard at 31–2 and 35–8. The first idea begins to repeat itself an octave higher at 40 but changes to G minor at 43; and the second idea begins to repeat an octave higher in G minor at 45 and is extended by descending sequences until it reaches the dominant of the tonic key at 55.

A link follows, at 55–69. It is based on a dominant pedal until 63, when scale passages lead into the return of the first subject at 69.

This time the first subject, 69–76, is shortened, only its first idea being used. A transition, 76–103, starts with the first subject theme in the bass, reaching D minor at 80, E minor at 84 and A minor at 95. From here it descends in a *diminuendo* into the episode at 103.

This starts in F major and is yet again based on two ideas. The first one has a dotted crotchet theme in the treble, transferred to the bass at 111. The second one, starting at 119, is based on a dominant pedal. The first one is then repeated at 127 in a decorated form, and the second one reappears at 135. The first one returns yet again at 143, changing to the minor mode at 147 and modulating to A flat major at 151 and C minor at 155. Extensions lead into a dominant pedal of the tonic key at 164–7.

A transition, 167–81, based on the second idea of the second episode and then, at 177, on scale passages, leads into the recapitulation.

The first subject begins in the same way as 1–8 but is then repeated with the figure in the bass. Bars 197–206 are exactly the same as 9–18.

The transition, 207–17, begins as in the exposition but changes at 210 so as to lead to the tonic key.

The second subject, 218–45, starts in the tonic key but otherwise is the same as in the exposition up to 231. At 232 the theme is extended for three bars before going on to its second theme, but it reaches a dominant pedal of the tonic key at 245, as at 55.

The link, 245–58, is the same as that starting at 55, up to 253; and the next six bars are similar to 63–9.

A coda starts at 259 with a reference to the first subject in the left hand and a prolonged tonic trill in the right. The hands change over at 265. Bar 269 continues with the triplets, used chromatically at first, and leads to Ic at 281. A rising scale of triplets in the right hand leads to V at 285 with a trill over the top. At 289 a double trill starts, followed by a triple trill at 291. Two bars later the single trill is left to itself for four bars, followed by a pause. Eight bars of a *diminuendo* reference to the first subject, 298–305 lead to a final *ff* reference, which brings the movement to an end.

30 Beethoven

Piano Sonata in D, Op 28 (The 'Pastoral')

The first of Beethoven's piano sonatas to have a title was the 'Pathetic', Op 13, though this title was given to it by its publisher and not by Beethoven. Op 27, No 2 was similarly christened 'The Moonlight'; and Op 28 was given the name the 'Pastoral' by Cranz,

Beethoven's publisher in Hamburg. But many parts of this poetic sonata are not pastoral at all, in the way that Beethoven understood the word. The last movement most nearly approximates to the title, with its peasant-like humour. There is no doubt, however, that to give a sonata a title helps to get it better known, though Beethoven himself was very sparing with his titles. 'Les Adieux' is the only title for a piano sonata that can definitely be attributed to him.

The 'Pastoral' sonata was written in 1801, just at the time when Beethoven was getting alarmed at his increasing deafness. But, on the whole, this is a peaceful and happy sonata. It is in the usual four movements, and is quite regular if one compares it with the two Op 27 sonatas which preceded it.

First Movement, *Allegro*

The first subject of the first movement starts over a tonic pedal with the first two chords, surprisingly, in the key of G, though the first cadence, at bars 9–10, is the usual tonic key. The style is flowing, really more like 6/8 than 3/4, so the phrase norm tends to be eight bars, rather than four, though the first three phrases are irregular (10 + 10 + 9), while the last phrase (29–39) overlaps with the last bar of the previous phrase and is eleven bars long. The tonic pedal is present almost continuously throughout this first subject, and gives a feeling of placidity to it.

The transition starts at 40 and modulates to the dominant major, with an answering sequence (44–48) a fifth higher in E major. These eight bars are then repeated with decorations; and the last two bars of quavers (54–5) are repeated twice more before running down on to a long note on E.

Both Tovey and Macpherson consider that the second subject starts in the mediant minor at 63; and it is quite common with Beethoven for a second subject to start in a key such as the mediant minor. But it is also possible to argue that bars 63–90 are a continuation of the transition, because (i) they feel so similar in style—the bass of 40–55 falls by step while the treble of 63–77 rises by step;

(ii) the repeated note in the bass in these bars has a similarity to the repeated note in the bass of the first subject; (iii) when this section returns in the recapitulation at 337 it is in B minor and not in the tonic key; and (iv) the bars 77–91 have a preparatory feeling, leading towards the second subject in the dominant key at 91.

So it is possible to argue that either 63 or 91 starts the second subject, and that examiners should accept either. The very fact that the entry of the second movement is not so obvious is an indication of how effectively Beethoven welds his movement together.

So bar 91 can be called either the second section of the second subject in the dominant major, or the beginning of the second subject, according to one's feeling about the significance of 63–90. It is a swinging melody, with the second stanza starting at 111. Each stanza ends in an improvisatory style (104–10 and 126–35).

A codetta starts at 136, in which syncopation is a feature. The eight-bar phrase (136–43) is repeated in full at 144–51, more heavily harmonised; then the second half is repeated at 152–5; then the last quarter is played twice at 156–7 and 158–9, the last time continuing the scale downwards, as a link to the return to the repeat of the exposition or on to the development section. Beethoven frequently repeats ever-smaller sections of an original phrase in this way, thus providing greater rhythmic intensity.

The development section starts with four bars modulating to G major. Then the first ten-bar phrase of the first subject is heard in G major, followed by a varied repetition of it in G minor. Notice the new quaver accompaniment in the last four bars in the bass (183–6), because much use is made of it later.

Now Beethoven develops this theme by rhythmic condensation, as he did in the codetta. First, the last *four* bars of the ten-bar phrase (183–6) are repeated in D minor; then they are repeated in G minor again, but with the parts inverted, thus forming double counterpoint (compare 183–6 with 191–4); then the D minor sequence is repeated by inversion (compare 187–90 with 195–8).

Further condensation then takes place by using the last *two* bars,

153

197–8, and repeating them by inversion at 199–200. They are repeated three times more. reaching the key of A minor, and inverting the parts at each repetition.

Then Beethoven compresses the figure into *one* bar, each bar overlapping with the next, and repeats it twelve times, until he reaches a dominant pedal of B minor at 219.

At this point the figure is compressed into *two beats* in the alto part, imitating the one-bar figure in the tenor part. The figure disappears altogether at 240, but syncopated chords continue over the pedal, which continues in a *diminuendo* up to 256.

It is interesting to note how Beethoven has compressed this ten-bar theme; and how, as he shortens it, he repeats it more frequently. Starting at 167 the plan is as follows: ten bars, twice; four bars, three times; two bars, four times; one bar, twelve times; one bar, combined with its two-beat imitation, twenty-one times. This takes one to 240, where the figure disappears, and the music slowly dies down over the dominant pedal. One has only to play this is to realise the mounting intensity caused by this device.

It is also interesting to note that this prolonged dominant pedal belongs to the key of B minor and not to the tonic key, as one would expect towards the end of the development section. Beethoven gets back to the tonic by alluding to the codetta in B major at 257–60, repeating the figure in B minor at 261–5, and then repeating the last half of it over the dominant seventh of the tonic chord at 266–8.

In the recapitulation, starting at 269, the first subject is the same as in the exposition, except for the extra decoration in bars 279–80 and an extended phrase at 304–11.

The transition starts the same, but 316–19 are a note lower than 44–7, thus returning to the tonic key; and bars 324–7 change similarly. This results in bar 328 starting a fourth higher than in the exposition, thus reaching B minor at 337 instead of E minor as at 63, for the passage which has already been discussed as being either the start of the second subject or the continuation of the transition.

From here to the coda, which starts at 438, the only change, apart from key, is an extra bar at 403.

The coda is based on the first subject and is built over a tonic pedal. Again the last two bars are developed, with the first note rising higher each time, until it reaches the top tonic.

Second Movement, *Andante*

Beethoven was said to have been particularly fond of this movement. It starts with an attractive *cantabile* melody, accompanied by a pizzicato effect in the bass.

Macpherson says the movement is in episodical form, Tovey says '*da capo*' form, while other people would describe it as ternary, or minuet and trio form. However, this is just a difference of terminology: they all mean the same thing.

The movement is in the tonic minor key which is unusual for, by this time, it was rare for all the movements of a sonata to have the same tonic.

The first section is in the hybrid form which is called binary by Tovey and ternary by Macpherson. Tovey calls it binary because the first part is incomplete, ending in the dominant key at bar 8. Macpherson calls it ternary because the first part returns at 17, even though it is considerably modified. Perhaps the best method is to avoid either term and to describe the plan thus: **A**. 1–8, tonic, through F major to dominant minor: ‖: **B**. 9–15; link 15–16; **A**. 17–22, beginning and ending in the tonic: ‖. Notice that **B** is over a dominant pedal of D minor, and that bars 10–11 are repeated twice at 12 and 13, and then again in diminution at 14 and 15— rhythmic condensation once more. When **A** returns, bar 18 is treated sequentially, passing through C major (18–19), D minor (19–20) and G minor (20–1) before reaching the cadence in the tonic key at 22, thus extending a four-bar phrase into six bars.

The episode (or middle section, or trio section, according to varied terminologies) is in D major, and is in binary form, whatever terminology is adopted. Its basis is a three-times repeated chord followed by an arpeggio. **C** (23–30) begins and ends in D major, though with a modulation to the dominant in the middle. **D** (31–38) starts in G major and returns to the tonic.

When the first section returns at 39 each half is first heard as at the beginning of the movement, but the repeats are written out because considerable decoration is added in each case.

The coda starts at 83 and refers to the first section at 83–8 and the second section at 89–93, before a few cadential bars bring the movement to an end.

Third Movement, *Allegro vivace*

This is a scherzo and trio, in minuet and trio form, with a whimsical rhythm. Like the first section of the second movement the scherzo can again be called hybrid, binary or ternary, as you wish. The repeat of **A**, 16–32, is written out because the harmonies are fuller than the first time; but each time it modulates to the dominant. **B**, 33–48, starts in G major and rises in sequence through A major (37–40) and B minor (41–4) before pausing on a dominant seventh of the tonic key. The first part of A^2 (49–56) corresponds to the second **A** at 16–24, but then it changes so as to end in the tonic key at 64. There is no repetition of **A**, but a cadence extension then continues to 70. Notice the silent bar at the end, which is essential to complete the rhythmic phrase.

The trio is in the relative major and is more flowing in style. **C** modulates to D major, and **D** (which is very like **C**) returns to B minor, with the repeat written out because the harmonies are different. There is no return to **C**, so the trio is certainly binary.

Notice that when the scherzo returns it must be played in full, as Beethoven does not say 'ma senza repetizione'. This is because the repeat of the first section, **A**, is written out, so the second section must be repeated also, for the sake of balance.

Fourth Movement, *Allegro ma non troppo*

This rondo is in sonata-rondo form. The decorative pedal of D which starts the movement in the bass is the basis of the first subject and is used elsewhere at times too. A short figure is heard over it at 3–4, which is repeated at 7–8. The answering phrase, starting at 9, is repeated decoratively at 13, and the first subject ends at 16.

The transition, 17–28, is a series of broken chords which leads to the second subject in the dominant key at 29. This starts with imitative entries and is again repeated with decorations at 32. The cadence chords are then repeated four times (37–40) before the final slower-moving cadence at 41–3. A broken octave link then leads to a return of the first subject at 52, which is identical with its first appearance except for an additional treble part at 56–7.

Bars 68–79 form a link to the episode and they are based on the bass figure of the first subject, but now in the treble part and played by inversion.

The episode, 79–101, starts in G major in three part counterpoint. If one calls the top part (*a*), the middle part (*b*) and the lowest part (*c*), then they reappear at 83 in the key of D in the form (*b*) (*a*) (*c*), from the highest to the lowest. Then, at 87, (*a*) appears in the bass with two new parts above it, starting in G and modulating sequentially through A minor (88), B minor (89) and C major (90), reaching G minor at 91.

The next phase (91–5) is rather like 79–83, except that it is in the minor, the harmonies are thicker and it is built over a tonic pedal. It modulates to D minor and the last phrase of the theme (95–101) is extended to six bars.

Another link (101–13), over a dominant pedal with broken octaves above it, which is very similar to the link at 43–50, leads to the recapitulation.

The first subject is the same as at the beginning except that the treble interjection at 118–19 is even more elaborate than it was at 56–7. The transition starts the same as at 17, but it changes at 134, is longer than the first time, and ends at 144 on the dominant chord of the tonic key.

The second subject starts at 145 in the tonic key, but its cadence repetitions at the end are more frequent. The link passage is the same as 43–50 except that it is in the tonic key.

A coda starts at 168, instead of the final repetition of the first subject. It has the same relationship to the previous link passage that 43–50 had to the return of the first subject at 52, so this means that it starts in G major. It is based on the first subject; but now we see how much more important the bass was than the treble, because the treble part has vanished completely. At first the bass has syncopated chords above it; then, at 177, it reaches a dominant pedal, with chromatic harmonies above it. It returns again *più allegro* at 193, now with semiquaver decorations above it, and the decorative tonic pedal continues from 193 to the end.

31 Beethoven
Piano Sonata in E minor, Op 90

This sonata was dedicated to Beethoven's friend and patron Count Lichnowsky on the occasion of his engagement. It contains only two movements, the first full of passionate energy that Beethoven called a contest between head and heart, while he called the second 'happy conversation with the beloved'. It is one of the earliest of his sonatas to use German, rather than Italian expression marks.

First Movement

This movement is in E minor but although the first subject, 1–24, begins and ends in E minor, it modulates considerably during its course. It contains two main themes, starting at 1 and 9, and the first one is developed at 17, leaping two octaves in its course. Notice the dynamic contrasts—perhaps showing the contest between head and heart.

The transition, 25–55, starts *pp* in E minor, but a dominant seventh followed by a scale passage lead to C major at 32, and similarly to A minor at 34. A new theme in B minor is reached at 45, and this leads to the second subject in the dominant minor at 55.

This consists of a flowing theme in octaves with a semiquaver broken-chord accompaniment, ending with a perfect cadence in B minor at 66–7. A short codetta, 68–81, making a continuous *diminuendo*, brings the exposition to an end.

The development section starts with a *pp* development of the first subject, over internal quaver pedals, in rising sequences. At 92 a sudden *f* on E flat starts to develop the rhythm of bar 1 over a wide range and unexpected chords. It dies down over a dominant pedal of C, starting at 100, and this is followed by a few mysterious bars in which the two hands cautiously approach each other in unison contrary motion, 104–7. Bars 110–14 restate 9–12 in C major and this theme is then developed in the left hand in a gradual *crescendo*, reaching Ic in the tonic key at 130.

Imitative *ff* semiquavers at 132 are repeated in *p* quavers at 133, then by crotchets at 134, and finally spread out over minims at 136. Then the figure gradually speeds up again until quavers lead into the recapitulation at 144. This extraordinary augmentation and diminution of a simple figure turns out to be an ingenious use of the first bar of the first subject.

Very little needs to be said about the recapitulation. There is no change in the first subject, 144–67; the transition starts in C major at 168 instead of the tonic key, but bars 172–9 are identical with 29–36, while 180–88 modulate so as to end up a fourth higher than 37–55, in the tonic key; and the second subject, 198–210, and the codetta, 211–22, are almost identical with 55–67 and 68–79, apart from change of key.

A coda which starts at 223 begins by repeating the previous six bars an octave higher and sounds as if it is going to repeat them an octave higher again but changes its mind at 232 and has six bars of the first subject before repeating 17–24 as an end to the movement.

Second Movement

This movement is in sonata-rondo form and is in E major, which means that the two movements share the same tonic but not the same mode.

The first subject is on the plan: (a) 1–8; (b) 9–16; (b) an octave higher 17–24; (a) with the second half ornamented 25–32.

A transition, 33–40, starts in C sharp minor, with ps and fs alternating, and leads to the second subject at 41 in B major.

This contains two themes: (c) 41–8, which has a varied repeat starting a third higher at 49–56; and (d) 60–8, the two being joined by a link.

An exact repetition of the first subject follows at 70–101.

A repetition of the previous two bars at 102–3 starts the beginning of the middle section, which is largely development. The same phrase is repeated twice more in the minor mode at 104–7 and then the hands move outwards in a *crescendo*, landing in C major at 114.

The second theme of the first subject, (d), first heard at 60–4, is next played four times: in C major, 114–7; C minor, 118–21; C sharp minor, 122–5; and C sharp major, 126–9. Ten bars of dominant harmony of the tonic key then lead to the recapitulation at 140.

The first subject, 140–71, is exactly as before. The transition, 172–80, is modified at 174 so as to lead to the second subject at 181 in the tonic key. This is almost identical with its first appearance until 208, apart from the change of key.

Then three bars of a diminished seventh lead to a modulatory digression, starting in C major, based on bar 3. This eventually reaches dominant harmony of the tonic key at 222, which quietly leads back to the first subject at 230.

Bars 230–52 correspond to 1–22 except that the tune alternates between left and right hands.

The coda starts at 252 as the music starts to develop the cadence bar over a dominant pedal. This continues to 262 when three bars refer to (d) of the second subject. But after a short pause the music returns to the previous cadence bar which is used up to 276, when 1–4 returns in its original form. At 280–4 the previous two bars are repeated twice. The figure then appears briefly with imitative entries in four voices, followed by *accelerando* semiquavers, slowing down in the last two bars, and ending *pp*.

32 Schubert

Piano trio in B flat, Opus 99

Schubert wrote some of the most loved chamber music of all time. One has only to mention the 'Trout' quintet, the octet, the 'Death and the Maiden' quartet, to realise this. But, to pianists at any rate, the two trios for violin, 'cello and piano have a particularly warm place in their affections. And these two were written in 1827, the year before Schubert died. What other fine works would he have written, one wonders, if only he had lived a little longer. The B flat trio is a gay Viennese-like work, full of Schubertian melodies and delightfully unexpected modulations. Like the E flat trio it was written for three fine performers who had become closely associated with Schubert: the pianist Bocklet, the violinist Schuppanzich and the 'cellist Linke.

First Movement, *Allegro moderato*

The opening of this movement is particularly gay, with its swinging triplets in octaves in the strings, heard against repeated quaver chords in the piano and a dotted figure, often leaping an octave, in the left hand. The first phrase is five bars long; and the answering phrase, starting in C minor and ending in B flat major, is seven bars long.

Then follows a passage, starting at 12, which makes much more use of triplets and the dotted figure, heard earlier. It therefore grows out of the first subject but without its actual melody. It feels transitional; and when it begins to modulate, as it does, to C minor at 16 and D major at 18, one feels in no doubt that the transition did start at 12, after the perfect cadence in the tonic key.

But, unexpectedly, bars 24–5 modulate back to the tonic key; and 26–33 are very similar to 1–8, except that they are *pp* instead of *f* and that the parts are now changed round, the piano having the tune and the strings the accompaniment. This sounds very natural, but it creates difficulties over formal nomenclature. However, this passage does not end with a perfect cadence in the tonic as did 1–12: instead it makes frequent changes of key but never returns to B flat. So this fact, combined with the transitional feeling produced at 12, inclines one to say that the transition does start at 12, though it contains a restatement of the first subject in the tonic key.

This restatement changes at 34 and reaches the expected dominant key of F major at 37, but it does not stay there. It changes its mode to F minor at 42, then modulates every bar: to C major at 43, C minor at 44, G major at 45, G minor at 46, D major at 47 and D minor at 48, reaching A major at 49. This time it stays in one key for nine bars, ending with a high tonic in the solo 'cello at 57. This note is played five times, poised alone, high in the air, with a *crescendo* and a *diminuendo*. Then the fifth time: lo and behold, it becomes the mediant of F major, the dominant major key, and settles down to a lovely *cantabile* second subject. Its *tessitura* is so high for the 'cello that it is not very easy to play; but it is a magical moment which any player must enjoy.

The violin joins in with the melody an octave higher at 63, accompanied by happily flowing triplets in the piano. The tune is repeated in the piano at 68 and continues to 79, with little interjections in the strings.

The second section of the second subject starts at 79. Violin and 'cello imitate each other, starting with an upward leaping octave or seventh which bears a resemblance to the upward leaping sixths and sevenths at the beginning of the second subject, while the piano accompanies with dancing triplets as before. The piano takes over the imitations at 81 while the triplet accompaniment is played by the strings; and they reach A flat major at 85.

Then piano and strings change round again, and change back yet once more at 91, by which time they are returning to the key of F. The leaping melody returns yet again to the strings at 93, and all three instruments work up to a climax which ends with a *diminuendo* and a sudden bar's silence at 99.

The codetta starts at 100, with the same leaping figure in the 'cello but now *pp*, and with a syncopated accompaniment in the violin. It is answered *pp* by a new phrase in the piano at 102. Then the parts change round at 104, the octave leaps being in the bass of the piano while the answering phrase appears in the strings at 106.

Bar 108 really marks the end of the exposition; but four link-bars, based on the first subject, lead back to the beginning or on to the development section.

This section starts with the first subject in B flat minor in the strings, reaching D flat major at 120, when the theme is transferred to the bass of the piano. It returns to the strings at 123 and reaches E flat major, a tone higher than at 120, when the theme is once more transferred to the bass of the piano. Yet again it moves to the strings at 129, a tone higher than at 123, and resolves on to F major at 132.

The next six bars are based on the triplets and the dotted figure of the transition, and end on the dominant of F in the bass, which slides down to B flat and then to A flat at 139, when the first section of the second subject appears in the 'cello in A flat.

This is combined with the triplets from 12, as a counter-theme in the violin. Then the two string parts change over at 143, and modulate to the remote key of E major, in which key the two themes appear at 147 in the same form in which they occurred at 139.

Once more they change round at 151, and reach C major at 155;

and the violin continues the main second-subject theme through D minor at 157 until it reaches F major at 161.

At this moment a pedal starts on F in the piano, which gradually assumes the position of the dominant pedal of B flat minor. Over it the second-subject theme continues in the violin, becoming twice as fast (diminution) at 167. The pedal ceases at 172 but the violin continues similarly, passing through B flat major until F major is reached at 175.

Now the main second-subject theme appears *ff* in 'cello and piano leaping an octave rather than a sixth or seventh; and it has an answering figure in the upper reaches of the 'cello at 177. This is repeated at 179–82, but with the answering theme now in the violin.

At 183 we reach a dominant pedal of B flat minor, over which the rhythm of bar 1 of the first subject is heard in imitation between the strings. It reaches G flat major at 187, and the whole first-subject theme appears in the violin, passing to the 'cello in A flat minor at 192, and on to D flat major at 196. It moves to the violin again, still in D flat major at 198, and is transferred to the 'cello in E flat minor at 203, passing through B flat minor at 206, D flat major at 207, B flat minor at 208, and B flat major at 209 before finally reaching the recapitulation at 211.

What a development section this has been, passing so freely through so great a number of keys! The description has inevitably been long, but it could have been even longer, if every little development or counter-theme had been mentioned. Schubert's invention seems inexhaustible.

However there is comparatively little to say about the recapitulation which, like many of Schubert's recapitulations, follows similar lines to the exposition. The first subject is differently scored, with the theme in the piano and the accompaniment in the strings. The transition, starting at 222, changes at 226, there being a considerable curtailment, with the repetition of the first subject, which occurred at 26, being omitted.

But 228–35 are similar to 41–7. Then 235–43 stay in D major

instead of moving to A, as in the exposition, so that the repeated tonic of D at 241–3 becomes the mediant of the tonic key when the second subject starts at 244, in the same way that tonic changed to mediant at 57–9.

The second subject starts in the violin instead of the 'cello, but both strings join together at 248, as they did at 63. The second section follows at 262, and the codetta at 285; and there is little change until the coda is reached at 293.

This consists of loud chords and the triplet figuration played alternately in piano and strings until they reach a *fff* in A flat at 305, followed by a pause.

The piano then continues *pp* with syncopated chords in the strings; and the transition figures return at 311, to end the movement.

Second Movement

This movement is an *andante* in the subdominant key, E flat major. It is in a loosely-knit ternary form, in which the first subject returns at 82 in A flat instead of E flat and modulates to several remote keys before it returns to the tonic. The whole movement is full of lovely chromaticisms and unexpected modulations.

The piano starts with a gently swaying accompaniment above a tonic pedal, over which a haunting *cantabile* long-phrased melody is played by the 'cello. It is high for a 'cello and is written in the treble clef but, of course, it sounds an octave lower than it is written. Notice the bass part of the piano moving downwards in semitones at 10–12.

At 13 the violin repeats the 'cello melody an octave higher, while the 'cello has a counter-melody against it and the piano continues the swaying accompaniment. It changes in the last bar (22) so as to end in the dominant key. All this is then repeated.

The piano then takes up the melody at 23, beginning in the dominant key, modulating to B flat minor at 27 and ending at 32 with an imperfect cadence in that key. The semitonal movement is again heard in the bass at 29–32, and the string instruments have little swaying counter-themes.

The melody returns to the strings at 33, in imitation and in an ornamented form, while the swaying accompaniment returns to the piano. This part starts in E flat major again and changes to E flat minor at 35 and to G flat major at 37; and the bass then again moves down in semitones at 38–41 before returning to E flat major at 42. Bars 42–6 form a short codetta over a tonic pedal; and bars 46a and 47a are a link leading to a repetition of 23–46. Bars 46b and 47b then form another link leading to the middle section starting in C minor.

This middle section begins with two bars of syncopated accompaniment before the melody enters in the right hand of the piano part, while the syncopated accompaniment continues in the strings. By 52 the melody is played in octaves. At 55 it changes to thirds and is answered by runs in the violin, over a dominant pedal in C minor. By 57 the piano is moving in octaves again and the music has reached A flat major, passing on to G flat major at 61 before it reaches a cadence in E flat major at 63–4. Now the melody is played alternately by violin and 'cello and reaches C major at 66 before returning to the piano at 67, in which key it reaches a perfect cadence at 68–9.

Bars 69–79 are very similar to 48–56. They start with the syncopated accompaniment figure in the piano, and the melody appears in imitation between the string instruments, now in C *major*. The parts change over at 76 but are still in C major and end with a cadence in that key at 79.

Two link bars at 80–1 lead to a simple but lovely change of key to A flat major (Schubert loves to drop thus to a key a major third lower), in which unexpected key the first theme returns at 82. Now the melody starts in the violin, with a broken-chord accompaniment in the piano. It reaches the even-more unexpected key of E major at 88; and it moves to the 'cello in that key at 92, with a counter-theme in the violin, reaching C major at 98.

At 102 the melody is transferred to the piano, still in C major, with little counter-themes in the strings as at 23, but returns to the tonic key at last at 104; and 104–23 are very similar to 23–42 except that they begin in the tonic key and therefore modulate to E flat minor at 108. The music reaches E flat major again at 114, as at 33, but moves through E flat minor at 118 instead of G flat major as at 37, before reaching a perfect cadence in the tonic key at 122–3.

Bar 123 starts a codetta similar to that at 42, but it is extended at 127 until it reaches its final cadence at 132.

There are few more satisfying movements than this one, either to listen to or to play.

Third Movement, *Scherzo* and *trio*

This movement returns to the tonic key. The piano starts **A**, with bars 3 and 4 imitated by the violin at 5 and 6 and by the 'cello at 7 and 8. Bars 9–14 have the strings and piano moving mostly in opposite directions by step. The cadence occurs at 15–16 in the dominant key, but is extended by imitation and repetition up to 20. Violin and 'cello then continue in unison for four beats, ceasing abruptly and acting as a link to the repetition of **A**.

After the repetition of 1–20 the imitative link continues from the second quaver of 20 up to the third quaver of 25 and is followed by **B**, which starts on the fourth quaver of 25.

It begins very like **A** but is now in the key of A flat major, with the figure in the strings, and the piano providing the accompaniment. Bar 29 falls instead of rising, as at 6; and after the cadence at 30–1 the phrase starts again in the violin an octave higher than at 25–6. But this time it falls in thirds twice sequentially, though it is still in A flat major when it reaches the next cadence at 34–5. The falling sequential figure is then repeated in the 'cello and the bass part of the piano and reaches D flat major at 38–9. Rising quavers in the violin, falling quavers in the 'cello and falling chords in the piano, ending with syncopation in the violin, lead to a dominant chord of the tonic key at 41.

Bars 41–53 form a link passage back to **A**, starting with imitations in the strings, followed by the strings mostly in unison from 45–50, and ending abruptly on the second quaver of 53, as did the short link at 20–1.

When **A** returns it starts with the strings in unison, accompanied by the piano. Bars 62–71 are the same as 9–18 except that they now lead to a cadence in the tonic key at 68–9 instead of to the dominant. The cadence is repeated twice as before; but the second time, at 72–3, it modulates to G minor, thus starting a long modulatory sequential extension, passing through E flat major at 74–5 and G minor again at 77–8 before reaching a cadence in the tonic key at 82–3.

A codetta starts at 83 and consists of imitations between strings and piano, with all coming together for the final cadence at 94–5.

Bars 95a–100a form a similar link to that starting at 22 and lead to a repetition of **B**, starting with the last three quavers of bar 100. After **B** and **A** have been repeated they end at 95b.

The trio is in E flat major and the melody is played by the strings with accompanying chords in the piano throughout. **C**, which bears a slight resemblance to the main theme of the slow movement, starts in the violin and is repeated in the 'cello at 104 with the violin joining in two bars later and modulating to G minor.

D again starts in the violin at 112, but the 'cello joins in after two bars this time, and the two move forward together, reaching a cadence in B flat major at 126–7.

C returns at 128, again in the violin, with the 'cello joining in two bars later; but now it modulates freely, passing through B flat major at 130–1, A flat major at 132–3, B flat major again at 134–5, C minor at 136–7, A flat major again at 138–9 and F minor at 140–1 before returning to the tonic key at 142–3.

Bars 144–51 form a short link in the same style, moving round the dominant chord preparatory to the return of the scherzo.

Fourth Movement, *Rondo*

This, like many finales written at this period, is called a rondo, but it is not in rondo form: it can perhaps be said to be in a very free sonata form.

The first subject starts gaily in the violin with a piano accompaniment of broken chords. The drooping figure at 15–16 is imitated by the 'cello at 17–18; and likewise the violin figure at 19–20 is imitated by the 'cello at 20–1. Then both string instruments combine to finish the first stanza in unison at 23–6.

The second stanza starts in the piano in octaves at 27, with the broken chord accompaniment now in the violin. It begins in the dominant key but vacillates between dominant and tonic keys. Bars 41–52 correspond to 15–26, though differently scored.

The second subject starts at 52 in G minor instead of the more usual dominant major, and consists of two contrasting ideas: (*a*), which is first heard in a *f* unison at 52; and (*b*), a gay dotted figure which is first heard in the violin at 56. Here the latter is combined with (*a*) in the bass part of the piano; and thereafter the two are combined for a long time in all kinds of ways.

Figure (*a*) is heard in unison again in all the instruments at 64; then, at 68 it is heard in the 'cello while the piano plays a triplet variant of (*b*), ending in F major at 75. Then, at 76, (*a*) is heard in imitation in violin and 'cello against *tremolos* in the piano. At first the imitations are at two bars' distance but, at 86, they are only one bar away from each other.

They lead to a new, more flowing theme in A flat major in the violin at 88 which is a variant of (*a*) and is heard against continuing *tremolos* on the piano. This ends in F major at 116, and is followed by (*a*) played *pizzicato* in the 'cello combined with (*b*) in octaves in the piano. After a cadence in E flat major at 122–3 (*b*) is transferred to the violin while a variant of (*a*) is heard in the piano. They lead to a cadence in B flat major at 130–1.

Bars 132–50 are the same as 68–86; and 152–75 are the same as

169

88–111 except that they are in F major instead of A flat major and are differently scored.

At 176 (*a*) appears in unison in the strings again, passing through D minor at 176, G minor at 180, C major at 184 and B flat major at 186.

Then (*a*) is transferred to the piano at 188, passing through E flat major at 192 and reaching D flat major at 196, when all three instruments play (*a*) in unison, reaching a cadence in B flat major at 205–6. Bars 208–13 then repeat 202–7.

A codetta starts at 214; and 214–30 consist of repetitions of V and I in F major. A repeated tonic for four bars then leads to (*a*) in unison once more. Bars 238–45 repeat 230–7; but 245–6 make an interrupted cadence, and four *decrescendo* bars of the repeated tonic lead into the development section at 250.

This starts with a variant of (*a*) in the 'cello in D flat major in 3/2 time, over a tonic pedal, with a gay counter-theme in the violin. Bars 252–3 repeat 250–1, and 256–7 repeat 254–5. Then, at 258, (*a*) moves to the violin while counter-themes are heard in 'cello and piano. The violin part at 266 is similar to that at 251; then the figure is transferred to the bass of the piano at 267 and to the treble of the piano at 268.

At 269 all three instruments play (*a*) in unison again, now in C minor; but the figure from 251 reappears in imitation at 272 between 'cello and violin, while the piano continues with (*a*), in G major. A repeated tonic in the violin at 277–8 moves upwards to a repeated dominant of E flat major in 279–80, and this leads into the recapitulation at 281. The development section has consisted entirely of the second subject and variants of it, in 3/2 instead of 2/4 time.

But in the recapitulation the first subject starts in E flat major, the subdominant key, instead of the tonic key, not a very uncommon device in this period, though Schubert does not make use of it to repeat the exposition in its entirety a fifth lower as sometimes he does elsewhere. However bars 281–318 are the same as 1–38 except for this change of key.

But at 319 the music changes and the first subject is considerably extended. The theme is transferred to the violin at 319 and to the piano again at 321; then, from 322–6 the two hands of the piano part imitate each other. And so it continues, the theme continually changing from one part to another and modulating freely until, at last, at 342, the music returns to the tonic key.

And at 345 the first subject is at last heard in the tonic key. Bars 345–70 correspond to 1–26, though the theme changes to the 'cello at 353, and violin and 'cello change round freely thereafter.

At 370 this leads straight into the second subject as it did at 52. The theme is in the tonic major key, as expected; but what is not expected is that it appears in 3/2 time, as in the development section at 250. Figure (a) is in the violin and figure (b) in the cello, and the one-bar figure falls a third for five successive bars until the two parts change round for three successive bars at 375–7.

Bar 378 starts six bars of close imitations at one beat's distance between violin, 'cello and piano, until all play together at 384.

At 388 the second subject returns in its original form in 2/4 time; and 385–92 are the same as 52–9. But, although the change to the original time signature has the effect of making one feel one is reverting to normality in the recapitulation, the key is still G minor, which is far from normal. Thereafter it modulates to E flat major at 396 and to C minor at 400. Bars 397–547 correspond note-for-note with 64–214 except that they are a fourth lower, which means that the theme which was in A flat at 88 is in D flat at 421, and that the music does reach the tonic key, at last, at 485.

Bars 547–82 form the codetta, which is the same as 214–49 except that it is now in the tonic instead of the dominant key.

The coda starts at 583; and bars 583–94 are the same as the development section at 250–61 except that they start in G flat instead of D flat major. Then, at 595, the pedal bass slips down from G flat to F, becoming the dominant pedal of the tonic key, and moving to a tonic pedal at 599–610, with the (a) and (b) figures of the second subject heard above in 3/2 time throughout.

A final presto starts at 611 in 2/4 time. It begins with (a) of the second subject, starting in the tonic key but moving rapidly through G minor at 615 and C minor at 617, then rising by semitones until it reaches E flat at 621-3.

From here to the end consists of a series of the chords V and I in the tonic key, combined with occasional use of the reiterated note which was originally heard in the codetta, starting at 214, and the figure from bar 1, which is used in imitation between the two string instruments. The movement ends with two *ff* chords.

33 Mendelssohn
Five Orchestral Pieces for 'A Midsummer Night's Dream', Op 61

When Mendelssohn was only seventeen he was so inspired by reading a translation of Shakespeare's *A Midsummer Night's Dream* that he wrote a famous overture to it. (An analysis of this will be found in Book 1 of this series.)

Sixteen years later, at the height of his fame, when Mendelssohn was in the service of the King of Prussia, he was commissioned by the King to write incidental music for the whole of the play. He wrote thirteen pieces in all, including six melodramas (background music to words) and the songs 'You spotted snakes' and 'Thro the house give glimmering light', which latter, together with another melodrama, form the finale. Anyone fortunate enough to hear the play with Mendelssohn's music throughout will realise how marvellously it catches the spirit of the words. But the five orchestral pieces analysed below are quite separate pieces, and are often given concert performances in their own right.

This incidental music was finished in 1842 and was first performed with the play in the Potsdam Palace in 1843.

I Scherzo

This occurs after the first act, and sets the scene for the entrance of the fairies in Act II, scene 1. It is one of Mendelssohn's most delightful scherzos, and well depicts the frolics of the fairies.

It is in G minor, in sonata form, and is scored for the standard classical orchestra. But the wind play alone for the first sixteen bars, with a tonic pedal for the first eight bars and a dominant pedal for the next eight, when the horns enter.

The strings enter at 17, repeating the first eight bars, *p*, in full orchestra, except that there are no drums. Then, still using the rhythm of the first subject, the music begins to modulate, reaching C minor at 26 and B flat major at 30, and then passing through a kind of no-man's-land, where key is concerned, until it reaches a perfect cadence in B flat at 47–8.

Bars 25–48 might be considered to be a transition, as they modulate, and end in the relative major key. But, on the other hand, they continue with the opening figure throughout, and the theme is so persistent that it seems advisable to consider that the first subject lasts to 48, in spite of ending in the relative major key.

The second subject could have started at 48; but 48–70 feel more like a transition. The semiquavers continue to run round as before, but a new figure appears at 54: C F sharp G in the violins with the dotted crotchet F sharp marked *sf*; and this continues in varied form and in different parts of the orchestra up to 70.

The second subject starts at 70, *pp*, in unison strings. It is very similar in style to the first subject, with bustling semiquavers running round in circles; yet it is a distinct theme in its own right; and it ends with the first violins alone running from 93 to where the development section starts at 99.

This begins very like the first subject, and is again scored for wind alone in the tonic key. But at 115, when the strings enter, the theme appears in the violas and 'cellos, with long notes in the wind, and works up to a *ff* climax in D major at 129. Then it subsides, with the semiquaver figure moving from flute to clarinet, to viola and to 'cello against *pizzicato* violins and violas.

Bar 137 starts like 115 a fourth higher and more fully orchestrated, with a soft timpano roll now added to the score; and it builds up to another climax at 151.

Yet again the semiquaver figure, starting quietly, is transferred from one instrument to another, against *pizzicato* strings. Bar 159 starts like 33, but now ascending in semitones instead of descending, with *sf*s at the beginning of most bars building up to another climax at 177.

Gradually the music subsides until a *pp* entrance of the second subject at 188, starting in E flat major. The first half of this is developed at 202, and finally only the first bar of it is left at 214, treated imitatively.

At 220 the timpano enters with a *pp* dominant pedal of the tonic key. The first subject is developed over it, and then the *sf* figure first heard at 54–6. Yet in spite of the occasional *sf*s, the music remains *sotto voce*. Finally, at 250, the semiquaver figure runs up through all the strings in turn until it reaches the recapitulation at 258.

This time it is varied and shortened. It changes at 266, when an upper tonic pedal appears high in the violins. The *sf* figure from the transition reappears at 274; and it leads into the second subject in the tonic major at 297.

This merges into a coda at 323, in which a figure in the oboe, which has appeared before in the middle of the texture is now clearly heard. It is answered by flute and clarinet with a figure like the cadence figure of the transition. The two figures are repeated, and they lead to a long and very difficult continuous semiquaver passage in the flute. Tovey says: 'Listeners who wish to appreciate what this involves may be recommended to pronounce 240 intelligible syllables at the uniform rate of nine to a second without taking breath.'

At 377 the second flute joins in with the first subject, answered by the two clarinets; finally the whole orchestra ends in a breathless *pp*.

But this is not really the end of this delightful scherzo. As the curtain goes up snatches of it appear between the speeches of the fairies in the melodrama which follows. They are not, however, played in the concert version.

II Intermezzo

This is really No 5 of the complete incidental music. It comes after the end of Act II, when Hermia wakes from a horrible dream and finds herself deserted by Lysander. She cries: 'Either death or you I'll find immediately', and runs off through the eerie darkness of the wood, which is full of strange echoes and midsummer madness.

The music is marked *allegro appassionato* and is in A minor. Over *tremolos* in violin II, viola and 'cello and occasional *pizzicato* notes in the double basses there is a pathetic, meandering figure of five quavers in violins and oboes imitated by three quavers in flutes and clarinets. At bar 7 the same instruments use an imitative crotchet-quaver figure; but the original two figures return at 9 and continue up to 23, when a *sf* climax is reached once more; and this section comes to an end in E minor, the dominant minor, at 35.

The middle section starts at 35 with agitated *tremolo* strings over which a new figure is heard, first in violins and oboes, then in flutes and clarinets. The instruments alternate in this way, starting in A minor and passing through C major at 41 and B flat major at 48, and returning to A minor at 52.

A dominant pedal of the tonic key is reached at 56 and continues with the agitated figures above it, up to the return of the first section at 73.

This has an additional *cantabile* theme in the 'cellos and basses and bassoon; and twice it has a C sharp instead of a C natural in the flute. Otherwise it is the same up to 85, when it rises to a climax and the oboe joins the 'cellos and bassoon with the *cantabile* theme, which now descends in semitones until 90. Bar 91 is a Neapolitan sixth which leads to Ic V I in A minor. The semitonal descent from 85–90 is then repeated. An extension follows in which the quaver figures

175

are tossed from one instrument to another, in growing agitation, up to 111.

A coda starts at 111 with the tune in the bass, first heard at 74, alternated twice with the quaver figure. But at 125 the quaver figure takes over completely, being played imitatively in strings and wind up to 135, when the violins and clarinet ascend in quavers for two bars, *pp*, followed by the two flutes ascending even higher, and then by clarinet and violin descending again. Finally, at 142, the 'cellos have a slow phrase to themselves, ending with a pause at 147.

After the pause the music changes to *allegro molto commodo*, as the Athenian workmen enter, in order to rehearse their play. The theme is very peasant-like and is played by two bassoons, with two clarinets joining in at 165, two horns at 172, and two oboes at 176. Until 180 the strings have played a quiet accompanying role; but, at 180, they all join in with the *ff* semiquavers, and then take over the tune. Three quiet chords in the woodwind bring the movement to an end.

III Notturno

This is No 7 in the complete score and comes at the end of Act III, after the four lovers have been chasing each other in the darkness and finally lie down exhausted, unaware that they are so near each other. This nocturne expresses the comfort of sleep to tired mortals.

It is in episodical form in E major. But the episode is a development of the main theme, though with different orchestration, and it begins in the same key, so that it might almost be said to be in 'unary' form.

The opening theme is played by two horns and two bassoons, and is a famous example of horn playing. A modern composer, with four horns at his disposal, would probably have written it for four horns, and not used the bassoons. This first theme is on the plan **A A B A**, with **B** built over a dominant pedal except for the cadence and its extension at 23–6.

The episode starts with an impassioned reply to the horns in the strings, *crescendo ed agitato*, with the second phrase, starting at 38, giving a soft answer in the clarinets. *Forte* strings and *pp* clarinets continue to alternate; and at last the music begins to modulate: to C sharp minor at 47 and to F sharp minor at 54. The flutes answer the violins instead of the clarinets at 59, and gradually they lead to the return of the first section at 73.

But, though the music is still soft and soothing, and the horns and bassoons still have the theme as before, they are now accompanied by slurred quavers in the woodwind and slurred triplets in the strings. An oboe starts to double the horn tune an octave higher at 84; and an extension to the theme starts at 87, in which the violins join at the climax, 103, and then fall to the cadence at 109.

A coda starts at 109, in which the horns and bassoons play the first phrase, which is based on the opening theme. The next phrase, starting at 112,[3] heralds the return of the fairies, with two flutes playing *pp*, joined by the violins, and mostly built over a tonic pedal. The last bars fade away to nothing, as the first violins play a high tonic pedal with *pp pizzicato* notes in the lower strings. Daybreak dawns, to show Titania and her fairies with the four lovers still lying asleep.

IV Wedding March

This is No 9 in the complete score, and is an introduction to the fifth act, which takes place in the palace of Theseus, and celebrates the wedding of Theseus and Hippolyta. The Wedding March is known to everyone, but very few know of its association with this play.

It consists of a triumphal march with two trios; and starts with a fanfare of *three* trumpets (an unusual number in Mendelssohn's music.

The main theme is a tutti in C major on the plan **A**:‖:**B A**:‖, using three trombones and the now obsolete ophicleide; and, in addition to timpani, cymbals are used when **A** returns at 22.

Trio I starts at 30, with **C** in G major and **D** in B major. The percussion is silent, except for one drum stroke when **C** returns at 40.

The main march then returns at 44, but now consists of **A** only.

Trio II modulates from C to F major and starts at 52. It is a quieter theme, in which trombones are silent; and it is in binary form, with **F** starting at 59.

Bars 68–84 form a link which builds up a *crescendo* and leads to a triumphant return of **A** at 84, as the curtain rises and the wedding procession enters. Brass and percussion are used continuously now throughout **A A B A**.

The coda starts at 108 with another fanfare and is followed by imitation between trombones and strings from 112–19. A final grand cadence lasts from 120–9.

V Dance of the Clowns

Theseus chooses Bottom and his players to entertain them; and No 10 in the complete score is a melodrama which introduces the prologue, and includes a short funeral march which comes after the death of Pyramus and Thisbe.

This is followed by No 11 'A Dance of Clowns', the last item in the five orchestral pieces, which Theseus chooses in preference to the epilogue. It is based on bars 194–222 of the overture, in which the donkey's bray is heard. Horns, ophicleide, drums, 'cellos and basses start with heavily accented Bs, over which the first phrase of the melody is played by upper strings and woodwind, including the leaping ninth at 7–8. The second phrase starts at 9; and these two phrases alternate right through the piece, with many repetitions.

There is a quieter section starting at 21, when violas and clarinets play the first phrase; but 29 returns to the noisy *ff* of the beginning. At 45 clarinets and violins play the second phrase more quietly, dying down to 52. But the first phrase returns *ff* at 53, and is played brusquely three times to finish the movement.

34 Schumann

Piano Quintet in E flat, Op 44

Schumann and his wife were both pianists. This work is therefore written more from a pianistic point of view than from that of the strings. Clara Schumann popularised the work by public performances, and it is dedicated to her.

Its first public performance took place in January 1843 in the Gewandhaus, Leipzig. It was written soon after his three string quartets (in which he was learning to write for strings), the First Symphony, and the first movement of the piano concerto. He wrote the piano quartet and the piano trio later in the same year. This was the first piano quintet ever to be written, though Mozart had written two piano quartets; and all Schumann's later chamber works included his beloved piano.

Grove says this work will always keep its place in the rank of musical masterpieces. It has brilliant originality and innate power, which grows throughout the work. The work made a great impression on contemporary musicians. Berlioz heard it performed in Leipzig and carried its fame to Paris.

As so many of the themes start anacrusically, particularly in the later movements, it may be as well to remind the reader that the bar number given is always that of the first complete bar.

First Movement

The first movement is an *allegro brillante* in sonata form. Its forceful chordal opening with its striding intervals is orchestral in conception: the string writing is often very simple and doubles the piano part in this way. In other words, the parts are less contrapuntal than they would be in an earlier classical work, and the whole conception is simpler and more full of colour.

After the initial opening, with its tutti effect, the opening bars are developed in imitation, starting with the piano at 9 and moving through the string parts in turn. All the parts come together again at 17, now over a dominant pedal instead of over a tonic pedal, as at the beginning.

The dominant note strides up four octaves in 25–6 and leads to the transition, which grows out of the octave leaps but makes an unexpected modulation to G flat major and is more lyrical—unusually so for a transition. It is repeated sequentially in the piano in E flat minor at 31; and then the violin takes it over at 35, with the keys changed round, E flat minor and then G flat major. Further development, starting at 43, works up to a climax, leading up to a perfect cadence in F major at 49–50.

A short link, 51–6 (it may be thought of as a continuation of the transition, if wished), in which the octave leap is still present in the 'cello in a subdued form, combined with a hint of the first subject, leads to the second subject in the dominant key at 57.

Now the 'cello starts the theme, with the piano having a syncopated chordal accompaniment. The viola imitates the 'cello by inversion, and the two instruments appear again in the same way, leading to a climax in the 'cello at 69. It drops down to a cadence at 73, and 50–73 is then repeated but with the violins now adding little interjections, and all instruments join in the climax, as compared with the first time.

Bar 95 looks as though it is going to start yet another repetition, but it breaks off after four bars and the codetta starts. It begins with a syncopated, augmented version of the first two bars of the first subject; then the third and fourth bars of the first subject at 106–7 lead to the first subject in the dominant with quavers added. The end of the exposition sounds quite like an orchestral tutti.

The development section is almost entirely based on the first subject: the transition and the second subject are not used at all. It starts with a quiet, syncopated form of the first bars of the first subject, with the rising seventh between the first two notes changed to a falling second. It appears in imitation in every instrument except the first violin, but is interrupted at 128 with a tutti statement of the first subject in A flat major. Bars 132–3 form another variant of 3–4.

This leads to a long passage in which the piano has bars 3–4 in diminution, producing continuous quavers, while the strings have imitations of the first two notes of the first subject. It is built over a series of tonic and dominant chords, starting in A flat minor at 134 and passing through E flat minor at 138, B flat minor at 142, F minor at 146, C minor at 154 and F minor at 158. Strings and piano then imitate each other at 162–6.

The whole of 128–61 is then repeated in a different key, with minor modifications. It starts in F minor instead of A flat major, and 132–3 is extended to four bars at 171–4, leading to the equivalent of 134 a tone lower than before. But now the strings no longer refer to the first subject: they just have accompanying chords. In fact, the piano steals the limelight throughout the development section.

The music changes at 203 as compared with 162, the piano continuing its quavers in a *crescendo* until it reaches the recapitulation at 207. There are slight changes in the first subject, and the transition changes at 236, becoming a sixth higher than before at 237 and a fourth higher at 241, thus leading to E flat instead of B flat for the second subject, which starts at 263.

The second subject is the same as in the exposition, except for key, until it reaches 321, when it merges into a coda. This continues with the same figure, and is over a tonic pedal from 332 to the end.

Second Movement

The second movement is a funeral march in the relative minor. It is in sonata-rondo form, but very much broken up into sections, and therefore easy to follow.

After two bars of piano introduction the first subject starts with its sad theme in the first violin. It is on the plan **A**:‖:**B A**:‖. The repeat of the first **A** is written out because the harmonies are varied, and it ends in the tonic key. The tune of **B** starts at 11 in the second violin, but is soon transferred to the first violin; and **A** returns in the viola (thus sounding even more mournful) in the tonic key at 18, and is again played twice. Notice that the end of **B** and the beginning of **A** overlap. A short codetta, 25–9, rounds off the first subject.

The first subject is one of those sections where opinions differ as to whether to call it binary or ternary; and the same situation occurs with all three themes in this movement. All three end their first sections in their own tonic key, though the episode does not end it with a perfect cadence. Tovey would therefore call the first and second subjects 'ternary' and the episode 'binary', because the ending of its first section was unfinished. Others would call all three 'binary' because of the division into two repeated sections, while others would call all three 'ternary' because in each case the first theme returns at the end of the second section. Perhaps it is best to avoid the use of either term, and to say they are in a hybrid form.

The second subject, 30–61, offers solace by being in C major. The *cantabile* melody is in the first violin throughout, while the piano has an accompaniment in triplets against a cross-rhythm of four quavers in second violin and viola. The plan is **C**:‖:**D C**:‖, with the repeat of the first **C** written out because the first time it ends with an imperfect cadence while the second time it ends with a perfect. **D** moves into E minor, and when **C** returns the harmonies are changed.

There is then an exact repetition of the first subject, thus bringing the exposition to an end.

Bars 85–92 form a link to the episode, and are based on 116–27, the beginning of the development section of the first movement.

The episode, 92–109, is in F minor and is *agitato*. The strings accompany the piano, which has triplets based on a decorated form of the first two bars of the first subject. The plan is **E**:‖:**F E**:‖, with the second **E** written out because the piano is an octave higher than the first time and is differently accompanied. Both run on without a finished cadence: in fact, the piano triplets are kept up throughout the episode.

When the recapitulation starts at 110 the piano triplets continue, though they are less agitated. This time the viola starts the first subject, so it is even more mournful than at its first appearance. There is also a short figure, periodically appearing in various instruments, which is based on the theme of the episode. When **A** returns after **B**, at 126, the theme is transferred to the piano; and the end of **B** and the return to **A** overlap, as before.

The second subject returns at 133 in F major, not in the tonic key. The strings are as at the first appearance of the second subject, but the piano continues the quaver triplets, instead of having crotchet triplets, as before.

The first subject returns at 165 in F minor instead of C minor, and the triplets stop at last. But 170–1 change, so as to get back to the tonic key, and the ensuing **B** and **A** are as before.

Bars 186–93 form a coda. They are really a cadential augmentation in the strings, under which the piano has the beginning of the first subject for the last time. A tierce de Picardie brings a ray of light at the end.

Third Movement

The third movement consists of a scherzo with two trios, a device which Schumann also uses in his First Symphony. And in the Fourth Symphony he repeats the trio as well as the scherzo, as does Beethoven in his Fourth Symphony. Both devices have the effect of providing a better balance in length between the third movement and the other movements.

As with the third movements of his predecessors, Schumann returns to the tonic key, but there is great freedom of key within the movement, which is typical of his work.

The scherzo consists entirely of rapid scale passages, ascending and descending in turn. It is again a hybrid mixture of binary and ternary form.

A ends in the dominant key; and **B** introduces a new crotchet-quaver rhythm, which it combines with the triplet scales. It modulates through a number of keys before returning to **A** at 33, which is fuller than before. It is also shorter, and it changes at 39 so as to end in the tonic.

Trio I is in C flat minor, a major third below the tonic key, i.e. *doh* becomes *me*. This is a change of key much favoured by Schubert. But Schumann does not change the key-signature—and, in any case, B major would be easier to read than C flat major. The theme, **C**, has a resemblance to the first subject of the first movement, in an inverted form, and the viola plays it in canon with the first violin. **D** slips down a semitone to B flat minor, and the canon continues. But this time the second violin provides a third imitation, though it is hardly long enough to be called a canon; and even the 'cello has two bars of it. **C** returns at 69. Then a two-bar link, 77–9, leads to an exact repetition of the scherzo.

Trio II is in A flat minor, but with a signature of A flat major. It increases the tension by using four notes to the beat instead of three, and is a very 'busy' section. It is much longer than the scherzo and trio I. In **E** the first violin and the 'cello play the semiquavers in octaves while the piano plays a chordal accompaniment. **F**, 131, makes an enharmonic change into E major, and the second violin and the viola have the semiquavers. It ends in C sharp minor, and **E** returns at 139, with the theme an octave higher than before and played now by the first violin, the viola and the piano.

Just when we are expecting the end of trio II a long development occurs, starting at 147. The semiquaver figure now becomes the accompaniment to a new quaver *pizzicato* figure starting in the second violin and viola, and a new crotchet figure starting in first violin and 'cello, the crotchet figure becoming more important as the movement proceeds. There are a series of sequences—the whole movement is full of sequences and the keys change so rapidly that it might have been better to have had no key-signature at all. Certainly a sharp signature would have been preferable to a flat one.

E starts again in F sharp minor at 163, now busier than ever, and combined with the two new figures. At 178 the first violin part is written in G sharp minor while the piano and 'cello are in A flat minor. After further sequential development **E** returns yet again at 183, in the tonic key, A flat minor, but an octave higher and fuller than ever, as everyone but the 'cellist is now playing the semi-quavers; and at 190 even he joins in.

The scherzo is then repeated again, exactly as before; and a coda starts at 241, based on the scherzo and built over a tonic pedal.

Fourth Movement

The finale is in sonata form, but it is very free, particularly with regard to keys. The first phrase begins in C minor and ends in G minor, and the music does not settle into the tonic key until 22. There are two distinct themes to the first subject, the second starting at 22, where the tonic key is first established, and this is built over a tonic pedal. Then the first theme returns at 30, now starting in G minor and modulating to D minor. The second theme returns again at 38, now in B flat major.

This leads straight into the second subject, starting in the unrelated key of G major. It begins with a diminution of 22 in the piano, followed by a new quaver figure accompanied by *pizzicato* chords. These two figures alternate for some time, combined with a new crotchet figure in the viola at 52, which is imitated by the second violin in 54 and the first violin a bar later, and which has a resemblance to the crotchet figure at 22. The music rushes on inexorably, passing through A minor at 57, C major at 58, A minor at 64, G major at 66 and the unexpected key of E flat major at 68, but returning to G at the double bar line at 77.

Bars 78–93 may at first give the impression that the movement is going to be in sonata-rondo form, because they start with a return to the first subject. But they begin in the remote key of E minor, modulating to B minor, and by 85 the music is running down and we realise that this is the codetta. An extended cadence ends in B major at 93, and in spite of the remote key, this appears to mark the end of the exposition.

The development section starts at 94 with a short figure in the strings which is heard twice more, at 101–3 and 105–7. In between its repetitions there is a low quaver rumble in the piano, the first time lasting for four bars, the second time for two, and the third and fourth times for one bar only. This grows out of the second subject at 46–7. Over the first rumble the viola plays the figure from the second subject which started at 52.

At 115 the viola begins to play it again, but two bars later it is playing the second theme from the first subject, first heard at 22. Notice how effectively the two themes merge into one. This combined theme is transferred to the 'cello at 123 and to the first violin at 127; and by 131 it is played by everyone, and continues up to the recapitulation.

But at the same time a completely new theme has appeared, starting in the first violin at 115 in E major. It is transferred to the second violin and viola at 123; and the two themes run together from 115–30.

The recapitulation starts at 137, but in C sharp minor, a semitone higher than in the exposition! And it modulates to many unexpected keys before it finally settles down in the tonic for the second subject at 179.

The first phrase of the first subject ends in the dominant, as it did in the exposition, but now it is G sharp minor. It continues as in the exposition but a semitone higher until it reaches 149, when it appears in G sharp minor, modulating to D sharp minor.

The second first-subject theme appears at 157 in B major, an augmented fifth higher than at 22, when it was in E flat.

Then the first of the first-subject themes reappears at 165 in E flat minor, modulating to B flat minor, while the second first-subject theme reappears at 173 in G flat major. This is still very remote from the tonic key, so it comes as a surprise to find the second subject appearing in the tonic at 179. Altogether a very unexpected start for a recapitulation, and yet it all sounds quite natural.

The second subject is a sixth higher, as compared with the exposition. Otherwise the only change is that the theme which appeared in the viola at 52 now appears in the 'cello at 187. The codetta, 213–20, is also the same as at 78–85, except for key.

However the equivalent of 86–93 is omitted, and in its place there is a very long coda, 221–427, which is almost as long as the whole of the rest of the movement.

It starts with a variant of the previous bars, leading to E flat major. Then, at 225, a syncopated theme appears in the piano, which bears a resemblance to 52, while the strings play a syncopated chordal accompaniment.

At 249 the first section of the first subject reappears in C minor in the piano against a counter theme in quavers which first appears in the second violin. This is the beginning of a contrapuntal section in which these two themes are passed from one instrument to another, in the style of a fugato.

Then, at 275, the combination of themes heard in the development at 115 occurs in E flat major, instead of E major as before. It reaches A flat major at 285. By 287 the first section of the subject appears in the piano, followed by the second section two bars later.

This latter figure appears in rising sequences, reaching a climax at 300, when the first violin begins to hint at the leaping figure of the first subject of the first movement, against reiterated chords in the rest of the strings, giving a tutti effect. The resemblance continues to grow up to the pause in 318.

Then the first movement theme appears in full, in augmentation in the right hand part of the piano against a variant of the first subject of the last movement in the left hand and the second violin. The two themes continue to combine in different instruments in turn. A dominant pedal is added at 355, and a climax is reached on a diminished seventh at 375–8.

Then the material from 225 reappears, and this leads to a tonic pedal at 402, over which the first subject of the finale appears. At 410 the pedal stops, and everyone plays in unison up to the last few cadence bars.

Schumann never reached greater heights of formal construction than in this last movement.

35 Schumann

Kinderscenen, Op 15

Everyone knows of Schumann's courtship and marriage to the pianist, Clara Wieck. They had eight children, but *Kinderscenen* were written by Schumann two years before his marriage. They were intended for A. W. F. von Zuccalmaglio, but the dedication was not printed. They may well have been an expression of a young lover's longing for a home and family of his own; but they are probably intended to be played *to* children, rather than *by* children, as they are quite difficult.

Ten years later, when Schumann had been happily married for eight years, he wrote his famous *Album for the Young*, containing forty-three pieces, many of which are playable by children.

Schumann is therefore one of the earliest composers to provide attractive music for the young. It should be pointed out, however, that he always wrote the piece first and added the title afterwards, so there seems little point in trying to relate the title too closely to the piece. There is a simple, child-like quality about the compositions as a whole, and the titles certainly suit the pieces.

1 'Von fremden Ländern und Menschen'

This is a simple little piece in ternary form. **A** grows out of the first two bars, in which the chromatic second chord is a feature, and it ends in the tonic key. The melody of **B** is entirely in crotchets, and consists of a four-bar phrase which sounds as if it is about to modulate to the relative minor, but is then extended to six bars and ends in the tonic key after all. The second **A** is an exact repetition of the first.

2 'Curiose Geschichte'

The plan of this little piece is also **A** :‖ : **B A** :‖, but in this case the first **A** modulates to the dominant key, while the second **A** stays in the tonic. This is therefore a form which is called binary by some analysts, such as Tovey, because the first **A** is incomplete, and ternary by others, such as Macpherson, because the **A** returns. Perhaps it is wise to avoid the use of either term. **B** is only four bars long, and is in the subdominant major.

3 'Hasche-Mann'

Again the plan is **A** :‖ : **B A** :‖, but this time **A** is four bars long and ends in the tonic key, B minor, while **B** is eight bars long and modulates to G major, E minor and C major before ending on a dominant chord of B minor, preparatory to the return of **A**. It can safely be said to be in ternary form.

4 'Bittendes Kind'

Although this piece is very short it has a little more variety. Every phrase is two bars long and the plan is **A** :‖ : **B** :‖ : **C** :‖ : **A** :‖. **A** ends on the dominant chord of the tonic key, D major. **B** is built on a pedal on D and modulates from G major back to D major. **C** is in A minor. The final **A** repeats the dominant chord at the end to make an extra bar, and adds a seventh above it, thus ending on a discord.

5 'Glückes genug'

This piece grows entirely out of the seven quavers which start the melody. They are imitated a bar later in the left hand and are used in the left hand again in bar 5, being imitated a bar later in the right hand this time. The melody is then continued in sequence. A repetition of 1–8 occurs at 9–16. Then the seven quavers are used in F major, again with an imitation in the left hand. Bar 21 starts a repetition of 17, but this time the music returns to the tonic key, to end the piece at 24.

6 'Wichtige Begenbenheit'

This is a vigorous, chordal piece, the octaves in the left hand fitting the title 'Important Happening'. It is in ternary form, with bars 5–8 repeating 1–4 an octave lower. **B** is in the subdominant key, D major, though it modulates to G major in the middle.

7 'Träumerei'

This little gem is one of Schumann's best known and most loved pieces; and it certainly fits its title of 'Dreaming', though it is surely the dreaming of an adult, rather than a child. The piece grows out of the first phrase; and **A** consists of two four-bar phrases, the first one in F major, the second modulating to D minor on the way to the dominant, C major. **B** continues with the idea of **A** but modulates to G minor (11), B flat major (13) and D minor (15) before returning to **A** at 17. The second **A** is eight bars, as was the first, but this time it stays in the tonic key.

8 'Am Kamin'

A consists of a four-bar phrase repeated, and ends in the tonic key. **B** is built over a dominant pedal of the tonic key, but modulates to G minor over it and then, sequentially, to A minor. The music returns to F major at 17, when **A** returns an octave lower, though the melody jumps back to the original octave in the second bar, and its ending rises to a climax. After the repetition of **B A** there is a short coda, consisting of a four-bar phrase which is repeated an octave lower.

9 'Ritter vom Steckenpferd'

Syncopation and pedals are features of this piece. **A**, in C major, has a dominant pedal in the bass and a tonic pedal in the right hand. **B** modulates to F major and D minor before leading back to C major for the second **A**. This repeats bars 5–8 twice, instead of 1–4. The syncopation suggests movement, yet the pedals keep the music on the same spot, which fits the rocking horse in the title.

10 'Fast zu ernst'

Syncopation again, yet this time giving the impression of being 'almost in earnest'! The syncopated figure continues throughout the piece, which is in G sharp minor. The first stanza (1–8) modulates to B major and is repeated a third higher at 9–16, thus modulating from B major to D sharp minor.

A four-bar link on the dominant pedal of the tonic key leads to the second stanza, which is similar to the first. But it lasts from 22–34 and modulates from G sharp minor to B major, then back to G sharp minor, followed by B major again.

The first stanza then reappears at 35–42 but in B major, as at 9–16. It is followed by the same link as before (17–21).

The second stanza follows on at 48–57 but it is shorter than at 22–34, and changes at 53 so as to end in the tonic key.

Every section of this piece ends with a pause, and then starts again with the same idea. Perhaps Schumann thought this gave the impression of 'try, try, try again'!

11 'Fürchtenmachen'

This piece is full of chromaticisms, which are perhaps intended to give the impression of fear.

A, 1–8, is in G major and ends with an imperfect cadence. **B**, 9–12, starts in E minor and ends in C major. It has the melody in the bass. **A**, 13–20, is an exact repetition of the first **A**. **C**, 21–4, starts in A minor and ends in F sharp minor. It consists of a semiquaver figure followed by *sf* chords. This is followed, not by **A**, as might have been expected in a suspected rondo form, but by another new phrase, **D**, with a crotchet *legato* melody, which starts in E minor and ends in B major.

A now returns exactly as before, and is followed by **B**, also exactly as before, and by a final **A**, which is the same as the three previous **A**s, except that it now ends with a perfect cadence.

This produces an irregular kind of rondo form in which **B**, as well as **A** recurs. Alternatively it could be regarded as a miniature minuet and trio form in which the trio, **C D**, consists of eight bars between the two minuet sections. But the form is clear enough, and it is really quite unnecessary to give it a name.

12 'Kind im Einschlummern'

This piece has a rhythmic ostinato in the bass, presumably meant to give the impression of the slumbering child.

A, 1–8, has an imitation of the ostinato figure a beat later in the right hand. It is in E minor and dies down at the end to a dominant chord.

B, 9–16, is in E major and consists of three repetitions of tonic and dominant chords, an octave lower each time, followed at 12, by a perfect cadence in the dominant key. The whole of this is then repeated.

C, 17–24, starts in B minor but moves to B major at 20 and to G major at 22. It then dies down and leads to a modified repetition of **A**. This reaches its climax at 27 and then falls, in a *diminuendo*, to end with a plagal cadence.

13 'Der Dichter spricht'

'The Poet Speaks' is a coda to the whole work, in the key in which it began, G major. There are three solemn phrases, the first ending in the tonic key, the second in A minor and the third pausing on a diminished seventh in E minor. This is followed by a *pp* cadence. The first two phrases of the piece are then repeated, and the final phrase returns to the tonic key, ending with a slow IV V I.

36 Borodin

Overture to 'Prince Igor'

Borodin was the illegitimate son of wealthy parents, who gave him a good education and many opportunities of travel. He was trained as a chemist and this became his profession, in which he held various high offices.

But he had always been interested in music as an amateur, and gradually he became friendly with other musicians and devoted his spare time to composition.

In 1869 he became interested in the story of *Prince Igor*. He wrote some words and music for it but then lost interest and transferred some of the music to the B minor symphony. In 1874 his interest in the story revived and he wrote the Polovstian March and the popular, colourful Polovstian Dances the following summer. In the next few years he wrote an occasional number for the projected opera but then lost interest again. However in 1887 his interest revived once more, and he wrote a few more numbers for the opera and composed the overture; but he died suddenly in February of that year.

Prince Igor was completed and orchestrated by his friends Glazounoff and Rimsky-Korsakov who had frequently helped with advice or completion of his works in the past. So it is hard to tell how much of the work is really Borodin's. But it is generally agreed that he had great musical and lyrical gifts; and it seems tragic that so little of his life was really devoted to music.

The completed opera was produced in St Petersburg (Leningrad) in 1890. Borodin never wrote down the overture but he had frequently played it to his friends on the piano, so Glazounoff felt he could orchestrate it from what he had heard and what he found among the composer's papers. The overture is in sonata form and uses several themes from the opera.

It starts with an *andante* introduction in D minor. The 'cellos fall by step while the violins rise by step, and they are soon joined by the wood-wind. A new cross-rhythm theme appears in the wood-wind at 22, but at 31 the lower strings resume their stepwise downward movement.

The *allegro* starts at 40 in D major with a fanfare taken from Act III in the opera, heralding the Polovetz. It is heard imitatively in the brass over a dominant pedal and drum roll, at first at one-bar intervals, then with imitations at a crotchet's distance, over a rising *crescendo* which finally leads to the first subject at 68.

This is an exhilarating scalic figure which comes from the duet between Prince Igor and his wife, Yaroslavna, in their reunion in Act IV. By 76 the pulsating vigour is reminiscent of accompaniment figures heard in the Polovtsian Dances. The first subject dies down into a perfect cadence in the tonic key, D major, at 82–6.

The transition starts at 86 with a *dolce* clarinet melody drawn from the trio in Act III. It is still in D major at first, but changes to A major at 103 when the flutes join in with the melody. It is transferred to the strings at 110, with a *diminuendo* and then a *crescendo* which leads to a climax at 122 and ends with a cadence in the tonic key at 131–2. A passage for horns leads to a *ff* tutti at 142 in B flat, which gradually dies down to the second subject at 166 in the unexpected key of B flat major.

This is taken from Igor's aria in Act II and is a long haunting melody played by the horn. A flute joins in at 190, and the tune is taken over by the wind at 194 and then by the violins, *con anima*, in octaves at 214.

A codetta starts at 242 which is based on the second-subject theme but is now heard in canon in clarinet, oboe, bassoon and horn over a tonic pedal of B flat. This canon was discovered among the composer's sketches after his death. Another nineteen bars (261–79), mainly in the strings and still over a tonic pedal, lead to the development section at 280.

This starts with the transition theme in the bass in G flat major and continues for some time, modulating freely and combined with hints of the opening fanfare. It reaches B flat major at 296 and G minor at 301 and then begins to work up in rising sequences, with the fanfare coming more and more to the fore until it reaches a tutti climax at 430 and the fanfare is heard *ff* in the brass, leading to the first subject in G major at 339. This, too, is treated in rising sequences, starting on G at 339, on A flat at 347 and on A natural at 351.

Bar 355 introduces the accompaniment figure from Konchak, the conqueror's, aria in Act II, heard over a most peculiar bass progression found on a scrap of paper after Borodin's death. It consists of a descending diminished fifth followed by another one a semitone lower and so on; and it is combined with scraps of the first-subject figure, heard in the violins at 359, 363 and 367. Gradually the reiterated accompanying figure and the peculiar bass gain the ascendancy until they reach the recapitulation at 399.

This starts with the fanfare as before; and the first subject, starting at 426, is also unchanged. But the transition, starting 455, has the melody in the violin instead of the clarinet. Then, at 459, where the melody is transferred to the violin in the exposition, it is heard in the clarinet. At 461 it is played by flutes, clarinets and violins but is now a third lower than in the exposition, so that it is in F sharp major. It changes at 468 and is shortened, so that 473 corresponds to 122. The equivalent of 132–41 is omitted. Bars 485–92 correspond to 142–9, but then the music moves straight into the second subject, the equivalent of 150–65 being omitted.

The second subject, starting at 493, is in A major (the dominant, not the expected tonic key) and the tune now starts in the 'cello instead of the horn. At 521 it transfers to the violins (it was in the wood-wind in the exposition) with a fuller accompaniment than before. The repetition of the melody (starting at 242 in the exposition) and the canon (starting at 242) are omitted in the recapitulation.

Instead a coda starts at 541, in which the second-subject theme is heard in the 'cellos against the transition theme in the clarinet; this combination also was found among the composer's papers after his death. At 549 the parts change round, the transition theme being played by violas, 'cellos and bassoon and the second subject by the upper wood-wind. At 557 the violins join in with the latter.

An interrupted cadence is reached at 569—it could be considered an alternative position for the beginning of the coda. A development of the transition theme is now heard in the bass while the fanfare figure is heard above it, and both grow in intensity. The transition figure is transferred to the violins at 589 and a great tutti climax is built up until a perfect cadence in D major is reached at 605.

From 605 to the end at 628 has been supplied by Glazounoff and is a grandiloquent cadence with *tremolo* descending scales combined with the fanfare figure.

37 Brahms

A German Requiem

This *Requiem* is not the usual type, based on the Roman Catholic mass for the dead. Brahms was a philosopher rather than a theologian, though he was a great reader of the Bible. And he compiled the text for his *Requiem* from a number of quotations in the Old and New Testaments and the Apocrypha, based on Luther's translations. But there is no reference to Christ and no prayers for the dead, which are usually the essence of a requiem mass. The words plumb the depths, but also offer consolation. No. 6 ends with a quotation from Revelation which forms a musical climax full of praise and glory; and it has been suggested that No 7 was added only because it was impossible to end a requiem in a mood of jubilation.

It is thought that Brahms compiled the words in 1865–6 at

Winterthur, with the help of Frau Rieter and her daughter, and possibly also the pastor, Dr Löwe, of Zurich. But some, at least of the music was written earlier. The second movement, the funeral march, was originally the tragic scherzo of a symphony in D minor, written in 1854, but never published—two of its other movements were later transferred to the piano concerto in D minor. And he may have composed the first movement of the *Requiem* at the same time as his serenade, Op 16, in 1859: in both the violas are the highest string instruments used. Most of the work was completed by 1866 but No 5, containing the soprano solo, was not composed till 1868. The first complete performance was given in the Gewandhaus, Leipzig in 1869, and did much to establish his fame.

It has been said that the work was first inspired by the death of Schumann in 1856 and that it received a further impetus by the death of Brahms's mother in 1865.

The translation of the German referred to here is that of Ivor Atkins, in the vocal edition published by Novello. But the teacher or student may also care to refer to the Eulenberg full score, in which the English translation is different. There are occasional references to the orchestral scoring in this article, when it is of interest, though many students may study it in the vocal score.

No 1 'Selig sind, die da Leid tragen' (Blessed are they that mourn)

Perhaps the most remarkable thing about this number is that no violins are used at all. Violas are the highest string instruments and this produces a heavy, most poignant sense of tragedy.

It starts with a tonic pedal of repeated crotchets. The 'cellos are divided into three parts, the third 'cellos playing the pedal with the basses, the second 'cellos playing mournful semibreves in descending semitones and the first 'cellos playing theme (*a*) which starts in bar 3, imitated two bars later by the second violas and two bars later again by the first violas. This means that the lower strings are divided into six parts.

The voices enter at 15 with theme (b) which starts in semibreves but, after an interruption of two further bars of (a) in the strings, develops into a longer theme. The altos become prominent at the end of the sentence 25–7, the last six crotchets of which can be labelled (c). This figure is then repeated in the orchestra.

The second sentence starts at 29 with a falling sixth, an inversion of the rising third at the beginning of (b); and when it ends at 37 the oboe takes up a plaintive theme rising by step, (d), which is taken up by the sopranos at 39. Theme (c) brings this sentence to an end in the tonic key in the sopranos at 43–5, repeated by the wind at 45–7.

But 46–7 make an interrupted cadence, and 47 begins the second section of the number in D flat major. It starts quietly with a crotchet figure but works up to a *forte* at 'shall reap in joy'. Bars 51 onwards in the soprano can be called theme (f). The section ends quietly in D flat at 63 in the voices, and the orchestra drops down, using the same figure to 65 when the tonic pedal of F, with which the number opened, returns. Then follows a short return to the first section, using figure (a), now in the voices but to the words 'Who goeth forth and weepeth'.

But at 80 the music returns again to the key of D flat, and at 84 theme (f) returns to the words 'and beareth forth precious seed shall come again rejoicing and bring his sheaves with him'.

Five link bars over a tonic pedal of D flat with theme (a) above them, 96–100, lead to theme (b) on 'blessed' and to the return of the first section yet again, in key F. Theme (b) is heard in its entirety in the orchestra at 106–11 (it is noteworthy that this theme also re-appears in the final number of the *Requiem*). The voices take it over at 111. Theme (d) reappears at 127 in the orchestra followed by the voices as before, and theme (c) reappears at 133–5.

A coda starts at 145 and this is also used to end the whole work. It is based on theme (c) in the voices and theme (b) in the orchestra.

No 2 'Denn alles Fleisch es ist wie Gras' (Behold all flesh is as the grass')

The key of this movement is B flat minor, a fourth higher than No 1. Each movement is in a higher key than the previous one, until the original key of F is reached for the final number. So, from the sombre effect of the first number, the movement is always higher, thus raising the spirits.

As a further lightening of effect the violins are used in No 2 for the first time, though the effect is still solemn. And when the voices enter the sopranos are not used immediately, so the colour is still dark.

The orchestra has a long introduction, which can almost be thought of as a solemn processional march, though in triple time. It is for full orchestra, though everyone is playing softly and the strings are muted. It contains two themes, both played over a solemn bass: (a) at bar 2, and (b) at 13 which is rather more lightly scored, with a rhythm which is almost dance-like, and in the dominant key.

The three lower voice parts enter on the last beat of 22 with a solemn chorale theme in unison against (a) in the orchestra. (Notice the dark effect of the C flat in the altos at 24 and 20.) When (b) returns in the orchestra at 33 the sopranos and altos sing alone in thirds for the first phrase, though all the voices join in, in four-part harmony, at 36, and end at 41 in F minor with a tierce de Picardie.

Then, at 42–54, the orchestra has another passage to itself, based on (a), first in F major, then in F minor, over a tonic pedal, and making a gradual *crescendo*, which returns to the tonic key and a *ff* entry of the whole choir with its first chorale phrase at 54. The second phrase follows at 65, against (b) in the orchestra as before, but this time ending in the tonic key.

The next section of the movement starts in chorus and orchestra on the last beat of 74 in D flat major, *poco più mosso*, to 'and therefore be patient'. Bars 83–6 repeat this new theme in the orchestra alone, but the choir joins in again at 87. The theme continues at 91—notice the touch of D major at 99 and the enharmonic change at 100 leading to B flat major at 102–3. The harp starts a quaver accompaniment at 105. A cadence in G flat major is reached at 118–9. The voices end this section *pp* with the horns softly imitating them.

The first section returns at 126, and 126–97 is an exact repetition of 1–73.

Then follows a short section to the words 'But yet the Lord's word standeth fast for evermore'. It is *un poco sostenuto* and lasts from 198–206. The strings starts in syncopated arpeggios and continue in broken chords, while the trombones play in solemn chords and the trumpets foreshadow the theme (*c*) which is to follow at 206. All this acts as an introduction to another big new section of this gigantic chorus, *allegro non troppo*.

It starts with a fugue-like theme (*c*) in the basses in the tonic, B flat major, to 'And the ransomed of the Lord'. The other three voices enter with a similar version of (*c*) at 212.

A modulatory section, starting on 'gladness' at 219 passes through E flat major (221) and F major (223) and is followed by a Neapolitan sixth at 225–6 which leads to an elongated cadence in F major at 227–31.

Another new theme (*d*), starts at 233, which is sung by the sopranos at one speed simultaneously with the tenors in augmentation of the same theme. It is heard again in the altos at 245, against the basses in augmentation; and the first part of it is treated imitatively by the altos at 249, the tenors at 250 and the sopranos at 251.

Another chromatic modulatory section, this time on 'sorrow and sighing' passes through B major at 257, B flat minor at 261, G flat major at 263 and E flat minor at 265. An unexpected chord of B major then leads to C major at 267–8.

Starting in this key imitative entries of (*c*) are heard in various voices and instruments, passing through F major (270), B flat major (273), E flat major (278), B flat major again (279), C minor (281), A flat major (282), E flat major again (288–9), and ending in the tonic key, B flat major at 290.

A passage similar to 219–31 follows at 291–303 but now ending in the tonic instead of the dominant key.

Then a coda begins, built over a tonic pedal from 303 to the end of the movement at 337. Over it are heard (c) and a modified version of (d) in various voices and instruments, building up to a great climax at 333 and then dying away to the end.

No 3 'Herr, lehre doch mich' (Lord, let me know mine end)

This starts solemnly with a pedal A on the horns and drums. The baritone soloist then enters with the words of Psalm 39. He begins in D minor and reaches a perfect cadence in that key at 16.

The chorus then repeats this, with an augmentation of the final cadence, and ending with VI instead of I. The scoring is fuller, though it is still low and subdued, using only *pp* horns, trumpets, drums and strings.

The baritone soloist continues at 33–48 with a second stanza which, starting with the interrupted cadence in D minor, passes through E flat minor at 35 and unexpectedly reaches B minor at 41 and E minor at 43 before ending with another interrupted cadence in D minor at 48. At first he is accompanied by the wood-wind, but the rhythmic figure he used at 35 is taken up by the strings at 39. Then the section ends with the wood-wind chords with which it began.

The chorus again repeats the soloist's part, 48–66, though this time the music changes at 52 so as to stay in E flat minor. The first part has a triplet accompaniment in the strings, and the string figure from 39 appears in the wind at 54. After several bars in which no key is established the dominant of D minor is reached at 62, and it looks as if the chorus is going to end with a perfect cadence in D. But, instead, it ends over a dominant pedal (a *pp* timpani roll) over which the baritone soloist enters again at 67.

He repeats the first section, 1–16, but now the accompaniment is more urgent, with disjointed string chords, and the drum roll continues throughout.

Instead of finishing, as at 16, the chorus enters at 81 and they continue together, thus providing a codetta for this first section of the movement. When the voices end at 93 the orchestra continues, *ff*, with the figure first heard at 35 repeated three times, an octave lower each time, getting softer over a tonic pedal, and ending with a *pp pizzicato* D.

A new section starts at 105 with the baritone singing 'Verily, every man living is altogether vanity', but now he is accompanied by a lovely counter-theme in the wood-wind. The music starts in D major but moves to D minor at 118.

The chorus again repeats the theme, starting at 129, but this time in F major, with a syncopated quaver accompaniment in the strings which is not shown in the vocal score. Bars 129–38 correspond to 105–14, there being no minor section. The counter-theme in the wood-wind continues from 138–42.

The next section feels recapitulatory, as it returns to the tonic key and uses previous material, though it uses new words 'Now, Lord, what then do I hope for'. The soloist begins with his first theme from 2–4, but the chorus takes over at 144, using the repeated minims of this theme for 'Now, Lord', but also the theme first heard in the wood-wind at 105. Both are used imitatively up to 153, and then 'Now, Lord' is imitated in stretto for two bars.

The orchestration has been getting fuller throughout this section, with continuous accompanying quaver triplets in the strings; and a climax is reached at 156, with a *ff* drum roll and crotchet triplet repeated chords in the wind, against quaver triplet chords in the strings. The voices reach their climax at the same time, and then the music gradually dies down until only the wood-wind chords are left, ending on a *pp* chord with a pause at 163.

Finally this part of the movement ends with a short coda in D major, 164–73, with the consolatory words 'My hope is in Thee'. The word 'hope' is treated with imitative entries of a rising crotchet figure.

The movement ends with a fugue, which starts at 173, and is built over a tonic pedal throughout. Brahms has written some magnificent long pedals—another long pedal is that of the whole of the development section of the sonata in D minor for violin and piano. But the latter is over a dominant pedal, while this fugue is over a tonic. There is an independent, continuous quaver accompaniment almost throughout, though it heightens the tension by changing to triplets towards the end. The quaver figure is frequently based on parts of the fugue subject.

The fugue subject is unusual because it starts in G major, the subdominant key, moves to the tonic key in the second bar, and ends in A minor. The answer, beginning in the alto, at the end of 175, starts in the tonic key, D major, and moves to A major. So it is 'real' up to the fifth crotchet in 177. Then it changes, becoming 'tonal', so as to end in the tonic key. The sopranos enter with the subject again at 178 and the basses with the answer at 180. The exposition of the fugue ends with the last note of the bass entry on the second crotchet of 183.

The middle section starts with an episode in which the sopranos have a variant of the subject which soon merges into coloratura on the word 'torment'. A middle entry appears in C major in the altos in 187, followed by another entry in the tenors in stretto in G major at 188. The second half of the subject is modified in both cases.

Another modified middle entry occurs in the sopranos at 191 in D minor, and this is followed by two more entries in stretto, in G minor in the tenors at 193 and in A major in the sopranos later in the same bar.

The final section starts at 196 in the tonic key. All four voices enter in stretto, starting with the answer in the basses, and followed by the subject in the tenors, the answer in the altos and the subject in the sopranos.

A coda begins at 201. It vacillates between G major and D major, thus giving the effect of a prolonged plagal cadence.

No 4 'Wie lieblich . . .' (How lovely are Thy Dwellings)

The smooth *cantabile* style of this much-loved number reaches the heights of sublimity. It opens with a tranquil melody in flute and clarinet which is an inversion of the melody (*a*) in the soprano part which follows. The style is harmonic at first, but theme (*b*), which starts in the violins at 23 in the dominant key, B flat, consists of canonic imitations. Theme (*c*) starts at 46 and also contains imitative entries. It begins in F minor and ends in D major at 62.

Theme (*d*), starting at 66, reverts to the harmonic style of the opening and modulates freely but ends in the tonic key at 94, when the music returns to the opening with theme (*a*). It changes at 112 so as to end in the tonic key at 118. Theme (*b*) then returns in the tonic key (thus behaving rather like a second subject in sonata form) but changes at 126 and ends with an imperfect cadence at 132–3.

Now follows a double fugue. Assuming that S and A stand for subject and answer the exposition entries are as follow: S^1 in soprano 133; S^2 bass 134; A^1 alto 135^3; A^2 tenor 136; S^1 tenor 141^3; S^2 alto 142; A^1 bass 143^3; A^2 soprano 144. In other words the first subject moves downwards through the four vocal parts at the same time as the second subject moves upwards.

At 146^3 the tenor starts the middle section of the fugue with a modulatory middle entry of the first subject; and from here to 163 a number of partial entries of both subjects are used, ending with the dominant chord of the tonic key.

Then, instead of a final section of the fugue in which the subject returns in the tonic key, there is a lovely coda based on the inversion of (*a*) from the first section, starting with the orchestra as at bar 1 in the tonic key but carried on now by the voices, soprano and tenor in octaves followed by alto and bass in octaves. The music ends with a quiet six bars in orchestra alone.

No 5 'Ihr habt nun Traurigkeit' (Ye now have Sorrow)

Thr *Requiem* was first performed in 1867/68 without No 5, which was written in May 1868 and was inspired by Brahms's memory of his mother, who had died three years earlier. It was first performed with the rest of the work in Leipzig in 1869. It is a soprano solo with a very high tessitura, accompanied by chorus.

The strings begin with theme (a) in quavers, but when the soloist enters at 4 with theme (b) her part is slower-moving. She speaks of sorrow up to 14, and then a two-bar link to the word 'but yet' leads to (a) in her part in the original quavers at 'I will again behold you'. At 18 the chorus sings 'Thee will I comfort' to (a) augmented into crotchets, while the soloist soars above. This part is in the dominant key and is almost like a second subject.

The middle section starts at 27 in B flat major, the soloist singing (c) which reaches a cadence in B major at 34–5. Then the choir again sings 'Thee will I comfort' but to a new theme, (d), sung first by the men, then by the women. The soloist then takes up (d), and is joined by the chorus with the same theme at 44, and the latter sinks down and back to the tonic key.

The first section returns at 49 with (a) in the orchestra in the tonic key, but when the soloist enters with (b) she modulates frequently: to C minor (53); A flat major (54); B flat major (56); E flat minor (56); B flat major (57); and D minor (58). The two-bar link on 'but yet' over the dominant of the tonic key leads to the second subject (a) in the tonic which is now heard in its original form in the solo part combined with its augmented form in the chorus.

A coda starts at 73 in which the chorus sings (d) then (a) in the tonic key while the soloist sings softly above.

No 6 'Denn wir haben hier keine bleibende Stadt' (For here we have no abiding City)

The previous number was written for soprano solo and chorus: it expressed grief and offered consolation. No 6 deals with triumph over death. It is the longest number in the work, and it provides a glorious climax. The final number, 7, 'Blessed are the dead', is expressive of tranquility in death and is, musically, a kind of coda. It contains a reference to the first movement, thus rounding-off the whole work.

The prevailing key of the first section of No 6 is C minor. It begins with the chorus singing in a simple, harmonic style. At bar

18, the opening figure returns, but now it is treated imitatively.

The baritone solo enters at 28 with the words 'Behold, I shew you a mystery'. There is a lovely, mysterious modulation over a *pp* drum roll, which exactly suits the words. He ends in D flat major, which is enharmonically changed to C sharp major, and this leads to the next section in F sharp minor, starting with 'We shall not all sleep'. Notice the diminished third in his voice part at 36–7, which occurs again at 50–1. He is answered by a counter-melody in the wood-wind on each occasion. In between the two entries, the chorus enters at 40, singing *pp* in a *parlando* style, while the baritone's melody in diminution over *tremolos* in the violas, and this works up

When the soloist enters again at 62, the violins have his first melody is transferred to the strings. The same thing happens at 54.

When the soloist enters again at 62, the violins have his first melody in diminution over *tremolos* in the violas, and this works up the trombones: and at 76 the drums enter *ff* and the violins rush up and down the dominant chord of C minor, thus leading to the next section in that key.

This consists of a short, vigorous choral section, 82–104, with the chorus singing in harmonic style against a *ff* tutti accompaniment, including energetic semiquavers in the strings.

A drum roll, starting at 108, brings in the soloist again, but his entry is quite short and leads, at 128, to a repetition of the previous chorus (82–104) to different words: 'Now death is swallowed up in victory'.

At 152 the chorus continues in an even more exultant vein: 'Death where is thy victory' continuing with what Newman calls 'a challenging roar' at the repetitions of 'where' at 192–200, and ending 'where is thy sting?' The harmonic style and tutti accompaniment remain the same, though modulations occur frequently, starting in F sharp minor at 152 and ending in an exultant C major at 207.

The movements ends with a fugue—there has already been a fugue at the end of the consoling 'How lovely are Thy dwellings', but this one, though very expressive, is in a grand, *maestoso* style, starting with the words 'Worthy art Thou, Lord, of praise and glory'.

The subject starts in the alto voice, with the answer in the soprano at 212, another entry of the subject in the bass at 216 and the answer in the tenor at 220. There is a counter-subject in the alto at 213, in the soprano at 217 and in the bass at 221, to the words 'For Thou, Almighty, hast created all'.

The alto starts another entry of the subject at 224, but it changes in the third bar; and it is followed by entries in the soprano at 226, the bass at 228, the tenor at 230, and yet another entry in the soprano at 231. But all these entries are partial and modulatory. So, although 224–34 sounds like a counter-exposition, it is of a rather unusual kind.

But the fugue has an independent orchestral accompaniment. The violins have a continuous crotchet figure against the first entry of the subject at 208, which bears a resemblance to the counter-subject. The crotchets are transferred to the violas at 212 and to the 'cellos and basses at 216. They change to broken-octave triplets at 224, as the organ enters and these continue to 234, the end of the counter-exposition.

An episode starts at 235, to the words 'For by Thee were all things created', while the strings revert to the crotchet accompaniment again. At first the voice parts are in the style of the subject, but at 242 they take on the style of the counter-subject. However, they are not based on actual figures from the subject and counter-subject, as they would probably be if they were episodes in earlier classical fugues.

Another entry of the subject appears in the sopranos at 244. But although this must be classed as a middle entry, it is, surprisingly, in the tonic key, as is also the next partial entry in the bass at 248.

A short episode, based on the second half of the subject, lasts from 251–6. It is interrupted by another entry in the bass at 257, starting in C major and ending in G major. Another episode, based on the second half of the subject, starts at 262. It is harmonic at first, but imitative entries begin at 267.

Four more partial and modulatory entries of the subject now appear in stretto, in the soprano at 271, the alto at 272, the bass at 273, and the tenor at 274.

Then the episodic material based on the second half of the subject returns, but for longer this time. It reaches a climax at 289, by which time the whole orchestra is also playing *fortissimo*.

Another theme appears at 291, sung quietly by the tenors to the words 'By Thee were all things created'. It is answered by the soprano at 294, and the three upper voice parts continue to 304.

Then the bass enters again with the subject, answered by all the other voice parts in turn, in stretto. The second half of the subject is next treated in stretto, starting in the bass on the last beat of 310.

The theme first heard at 291 reappears in the alto at 316, starting in E major, and it is again sung by the three upper parts, though the basses join in with an independent part at 320.

The final section of the fugue starts at 330, with the subject in the bass in C major and repeated in stretto, though, even now, with occasional modulations. It is repeated immediately in an even closer stretto. But it is the second half of the subject that brings the movement to a triumphant close in the elemental key of C major.

No 7 'Selig sind die Toten' (Blessed are the Dead)

The final number returns to the key and to some of the themes of No 1. The strings gradually soar upwards in a gently swaying figure over a tonic pedal, while (*a*), a long, broadly flowing phrase, is heard in the sopranos from bars 2–10. This is not unlike an inversion of (*d*) from No 1 at 37–9, when it was played in the oboes and imitated by the sopranos in 39–42. The string figure continues up to 37.

The soprano phrase is answered by the basses at 10–18, starting on the dominant and passing through C major at 11–13 and G minor at 14–17.

This leads to the entry of the full chorus at 18 with (*b*), which is over a pedal G from 18–22 and refers to (*e*) from bar 47, the beginning of the second section of No 1, at 28–9, before ending with a perfect cadence in C major at 33–4.

The first section ends with (*c*), which is heard in the wood-wind at 34 and is imitated by the first violins at 36. Bars 34–9 are all built over a tonic pedal of C major, and they end with a *pizzicato* unison C.

The middle section contains two contrasting ideas. Figure (*d*) is a recitative-like figure sung by the lower voices and accompanied by horns and trombones. It lasts from 40–7 and modulates to E major.

Figure (*e*) starts at 48 with the change of key signature to A major. A gently swinging figure in the strings accompanies imitative entries of (*e*) in the voices in a smooth vocal style reminiscent of (*a*). In bars 54–7 they are unaccompanied; and then figure (*e*) starts in the oboe and passes to the flute before the voices enter again. They modulate to E major at 58 and F major at 64 before returning again to E at 65.

This part ends with an interrupted cadence at 70, when (*e*) enters in first violins, flute and oboe, hinting at F major again, before the voices return once more at 72 to E major and, this time, end with a perfect cadence in that key at 73–4, repeated in the orchestra at 75–6.

Figure (*d*) then returns with the voices singing softly on low notes against horns and trombones as before. This time it passes through B major at 79 and G sharp major at 83–7.

From this remote key the tenors and basses return to (*e*) in A major at 89. Bars 89–95 are similar to 50–6; but then an extension starts, during which (*e*) is heard high in flute and oboe in 97–9. The voices reach a cadence in A major at 101.

Two modulatory bars lead back to the beginning in key F. Now the tenors start (*a*) instead of the sopranos; and they are followed by the whole choir singing (*b*) at 112, as at 18, but now staying in the tonic key and being built over a dominant pedal up to 116.

Bars 117–20 do not establish any key but lead to another dominant pedal of the tonic key at 120; and this part ends with a perfect cadence in F major at 127–8.

It is followed by (c), as at 34, but now in the tonic key, starting in the orchestra alone but with the voices joining in at 132.

However the music moves abruptly to E flat at 133 and this starts the coda, which is based on (b) and (c) from the first chorus and also on its coda. (All the references to (b) and (c) which follow refer to (b) and (c) of the first movement, not of the last.) The wood-wind and horns have (b), (No 1, bars 15 and 144); and the tenors enter with (c), (No 1, bars 26, 145 and 147), followed at 138 by the sopranos with (b). Bars 133–42 are in E flat major. Then, at 143, (c) enters in the strings in D flat major followed by (b) in the voices at 144, (c) in the flute at 145, (b) in the voices again at 146, and (c) in the oboe at 147.

Bars 147–50 return again to F, with (b) in the wood-wind and horns; and imitative entries of (c) are heard in the voices from 151–6.

Bars 156–67, the end of the movement, are identical with 147 to the end of the first movement, except that the words are different. This brings coherence to the work as a whole, and makes the ending of this wonderful *Requiem* have an even greater impact.

38 Brahms

Op 119; Nos 1 and 4

(Nos 2 and 3 are analysed in Book 2 of this series)

No 1 *Adagio*

This intermezzo consists of *molto legato* arpeggios making figures which mostly rise or fall by step, though sometimes they skip an octave up or down. It is in ternary form.

The first section begins in B minor, modulates to D major at 7, and begins to repeat itself at 9, but changes at 11 so as to reach F sharp minor at 12, in which key it ends at 16, with a tierce de Picardie.

The middle section starts in the brighter key of the relative major and passes through E minor at 22 and F sharp minor at 23 on its way to its climax in D major at 24, after which it falls by step and jumps an octave lower at 29, before starting, like the first section, to repeat itself at 31. The repetition changes at 33 and moves to G major, again rising to a climax at 39, then falls an octave twice at 40 and 41 and rises an octave twice at 44 and 45, thus leading to a repetition of the first section at 47.

This is a variant in which triplets are sometimes used. The repetition of the section, starting at 55, remains in the tonic key though it is very chromatic; and it gradually falls, in stepwise figures to a *pp* cadence.

No 4 *Allegro risoluto*

This rhapsodie is in a free kind of sonata-rondo form. The vigorous first subject in E flat major has a cadence of crotchet chords with repeated notes at the top at 5–7 which comes again in G minor at 9–10, and again in the tonic key at 14–15. The music moves to E flat minor at 17 and the repeated notes occur again in the bass at 19–20, and at the top of the chords at 21–2.

Soon it is realised that the chords at 21–2 form the beginning of the second subject in the dominant major. They are heard again in the bass at 24–5 with semiquaver figures over the top and are transferred to the top at 26–8, leading to C minor. The same figure at 31–3 leads back to B flat major at 34, to C flat major at 49, and to the tonic key at 51, when the first subject returns.

The first subject is the same as at its first appearance until 55, when it moves to C minor. It ends with V VI, an interrupted cadence, at 60–1; and four link bars lead to the episode at 66.

This starts in C minor and is really in 6/8 time up to 84, though it is still written in 2/4. Its theme is repeated an octave higher in C major at 83. It ends at 84; and a similar link to 60–4, but now twice as long, 85–92, leads to the middle section of the episode starting at 93. This is a graceful arpeggiando subject in A flat major; and another eight-bar link, 109–16, leads to a repetition of 93–126, when the music changes and leads back to the first section of the episode at 133–52, in which there are small changes, as compared with 65–84.

The recapitulation starts at 153 with the first subject surprisingly in C major and in a varied form: the first three bars starting with a rest, then *pp*, and lower than before. A dominant pedal in C minor from 168–86, over which the repeated note figure is much in evidence, leads to the second subject at 188.

But this starts in another surprising key: B flat major, the same as in the exposition. However it modulates to C flat major at 195, to D flat major at 209, to E flat minor at 205 and D flat major at 209, modulating freely as one might expect from its title 'rhapsodie', until it finally leads to the return of the first subject in the tonic at 217.

This changes to E flat minor at 232 as before, but leads to a coda at 237. The coda is in E flat minor, the tonic minor, throughout, and contains two new figures, the first at 237 and the second at 248, the latter starting a tonic pedal and working up to a *ff* climax.

39 Dvorak

Sonatina for Violin and Piano

This work was written in 1893, when Dvorak was in New York, at the same time that he wrote the 'New World' symphony and the 'Nigger' quartet. But, although belonging to the period of his maturity, it is not one of his greatest works, though it has the advantage that it is so slight that it can be played by inexperienced chamber-music players. But Dvorak wrote little for two instruments; and some, at least, of his trios, quartets and quintets are very much finer works.

First Movement

The first movement is a simple example of sonata form. The first subject is shared between violin and piano, and its first sentence ends in the tonic key at 8. Then a repetition begins with the parts changed round; but the music changes at 13, so that the second sentence ends in B minor at 16.

A second section of the first subject begins at 17 over a dominant pedal in the tonic key; and again the instruments change round at 21. This section ends on a dominant pedal of E minor, at 32–6.

The movement, so far, has not divided itself into a clear-cut first subject followed by a transition. The first sentence ends with a perfect cadence in the tonic key at 8, but it is followed by a repetition which starts in the tonic key and does not sound like a transition, though it has moved away from the tonic by the end of the sentence. Then 16–31 are still in the tonic, and feel more like a second section of the first subject than a transition. But 32–6 might be thought of as a small transition, if wished.

The second subject starts in the relative minor at 37, with the melody in the piano, imitated by the violin. At 45 the parts again change round, and a climax is reached at 50.

A codetta starts at 52, and the parts again change over at 56: it begins to look as if Dvorak is determined to be scrupulously fair in letting the instruments have equal shares. The exposition ends with a reference to the first subject at 60, still in E minor.

The development section modulates to B flat major, and a reference to the first subject starts at 68 in that key in the left hand of the piano. After using bars 1–2 it skips to 5–6, and then the right hand does the same thing. Bars 5–6 are passed to the violin at 75–6.

H

The violin goes on to 7–8 at 78–9 and this is transferred to the piano at 79 and leads to D flat major.

At 80 the violin has bars 1–2 followed by 5–6 in D flat major. Then the piano imitates 5–6 and goes on to 7–8. This starts a series of imitations of 7–8, in piano and violin alternately, passing through a number of keys until the music reaches a dominant pedal of the tonic key at 108–12, which leads to the recapitulation. The development section has consisted entirely of repetitions of different parts of 1–8 of the first subject, and is rather mechanical.

In the recapitulation the first subject starts as in the exposition, but changes to the tonic minor at 120; and at 124 the violin and piano parts change round, as compared with the exposition, and lead to D minor.

Bars 128–47 correspond to 17–36 except that they start in the unexpected key of B flat major and lead to the tonic key, therefore dropping to the key a minor third lower, as in the exposition.

The second subject starts at 148 and seems, at first, to be unsure whether it is in the major or the minor key, but it soon settles for the major. However, at 152, it decides to refer to 25 from the first subject. But it returns to the fold with the codetta at 159, which contains a reference to the first subject at 167, as in the exposition.

This merges into a coda at 175, which begins by repeating 167–70 but then refers to 5–6 and 7–8. An extended cadence leads to the end of the movement.

Second Movement

The second movement still has G as its key centre, though it is now in the minor mode. It is unusual at this stage in musical history, for a work in several movements, to have the same tonic for all its movements, and it inevitably produces a sense of monotony.

The subtitle of the movement, 'Indian Canzonetta', presumably has a link with the American Red Indians, as had other of Dvorak's works written in America.

The first theme is primitive and plaintive and contains many repeated notes. Bars 1–4 are repeated at 5–8 with a varied ending, and then 1–16 is repeated exactly. So far the violin has had the melody throughout.

The second theme starts at 17 in the relative major. Its first section is given to the piano but its second section, starting at 25, moves back to the violin over a dominant pedal, though the piano repeats it at 29. Then the first section of the theme returns at 33 but now in the piano over a tonic pedal. However it moves at the end to a dominant pedal in the tonic key, 39–43.

This leads to a third theme, 44–70, in the tonic major. It is built over a tonic pedal and is even more primitive. The piano has the theme while the violin has a two-note ostinato. At 56 the instruments change over, and there is an extended cadence at 59–63. The first two notes of the theme are repeated several times, and lead to a repetition of the first theme, differently harmonised, at 72–80.

A coda, 80–7, uses the first bar of the first theme, mainly in the bass.

The plan of the movement as a whole is **A B C A**—a very simple form that has no specific title.

Third Movement

The third movement is a scherzo in minuet and trio form. **A**, 1–16, ends in the tonic key. **B**, 17–32, begins with the figure from bars 1–2, but a new melody grows out of it. It ends in the dominant key; and a link, 32–40, leads to an exact repetition of **A**.

The trio is in C major. **C**, 56–63, ends in C major. **D**, 64–70, changes to the minor; and a link, 70–78, leads to a repetition of **C**.

Then the scherzo is repeated.

Fourth Movement

The finale is in sonata form, with simple, folk-like tunes in which syncopation, produced either by quaver-crotchet or quaver-dotted crotchet rhythms, is a feature.

The first subject contains three figures in its first two bars which are so much used in the development section that it is an advantage to label them: (*a*) bar 1, in the violin; (*b*) bar 1, the quavers in the middle of the piano part; (*c*) bar 2, in the violin. Notice the syncopated figure in bar 3 of the violin part.

The first subject is in ternary form. Its first section, 1–8, is repeated at 9–16 with piano and violin parts changed round. Its middle section, 17–34, grows out of the syncopated rhythm first heard in bar 3. Bars 35–42 are a varied repetition of 1–8.

The transition starts at 43, and is based on the first three notes of the first subject, treated imitatively between right and left hands of the piano and the violin. It leads to an upper dominant pedal of the relative minor at 58 which, in turn, leads to the second subject in that key—the same key relationship as in the first movement.

The second subject, like the first, is in ternary form. This is unusual, but is in keeping with the song-like nature of the movement. The jerky rhythm of its first section is continuous, played first by the violin and then by the piano. Its middle section, starting at 78, uses another rhythmic figure, and is mainly in unison. Then the first section returns at 90, though it is now eight, instead of sixteen, bars long. A cadence extension, 98–105, seems to be codetta-like, and to be leading to the end of the exposition.

But then, surprisingly, another theme appears at 106. It is a song-like theme, very reminiscent of themes in the 'New World' symphony, and is *molto tranquillo* in E major. At first one might think it was an episode, but it reappears in the recapitulation. The most sensible thing seems to be to call it a third subject, because it is so completely contrasted to the second, not appearing to belong to it, and because 98–105 seem to be so cadential. Yet it is undoubtedly part of the exposition. It can, of course, be called a second section of the second subject, but third subject seems more logical, unusual though it may be to have three subjects in sonata form. Its ending, 130–49 is an example of phrase-construction, consisting of 4+4+ 2+2+1+1+1+1 bars.

The development section starts at 150 with a development of the first two bars of the first subject against a bass descending in semi-tones. By 158 the first figure (*a*) is being used alone; then, at 162, (*b*), the middle voice in bar 1, is heard in the violin against (*a*) in the piano. These two figures alternate up to 167 when (*c*), from bar 2, is heard in the violin against (*b*). After eight bars of this the rhythm (*c*) takes over, being heard alternately in piano and violin.

Triplets (new material) appear at 184, but (*c*) reappears in the piano at 188, and then these two figures are heard alternately for a few bars.

At 200 a rhythmic variant of the first subject starts in C sharp minor. It reaches G major at 208, and a dominant pedal continues from here up to the recapitulation at 220.

The first section of the first subject is the same as in the exposition except that it is not repeated; and this applies also to the middle section, 228–35. Bars 236–9 repeat 228–31 in the dominant key, and this leads straight into the transition at 240 without a return to the first section. But at 240 the melody is played softly against triplets, whereas at 43 it was played loudly with imitation. It ends, however, very similarly, and leads to the second subject in the tonic minor at 251.

Both the second subject and the third subject are the same as in the exposition, except for key, the third subject now appearing in the tonic major at 295.

A coda starts at 339. The first four bars are like the beginning of the development section, except that they are in the tonic key. But then the music changes and leads to a repetition of the first two bars of the first subject at 353. An extended cadence brings the movement to an end.

40 Debussy

Piano Suite, 'Children's Corner'

Debussy (1862–1918) married a dressmaker in 1899. But in 1904 he left her for Mme Emma Bardac, 'a woman of superior culture', whom, after a divorce, he married in 1905. Claude Emma Debussy (called by her pet-name 'Chou-Chou' in this suite to whom it is dedicated) was their only child, and she could have been little more than a baby at the time it was written, in 1906–08. But Debussy must have anticipated her being able to play it when she became a little older, as there is not a single octave, struck as a chord, in the whole of the suite.

This is the only piano work completed in 1908, the previous one being *Images*, written in 1905–07.

1 'Dr Gradus ad Parnassum'

This is an opening prelude in C major, rather like a study, which will help the learner to graduate to the heights of Parnassus. It is possible that Debussy had in mind Bach's opening prelude in C major of 'the 48'.

Notice that, as in all Debussy's music, he uses mostly French rather than Italian musical terms, though the commonly used Italian terms, *p*, *pp*, *crescendo*, and *a tempo*, appear also. Anyone who is not sure of a French term should look it up in a dictionary. The only one that may cause a little puzzlement is *en dehors* (found in bar 21 of 'Jimbo's Lullaby') which, in effect, means that the part concerned should stand out from the rest of the texture.

This piece is based entirely on the opening figure, though it changes to half-speed in bars 33–44. It gains its main variety by the use of modulation, moving to A minor at 11–21, returning to the opening bars in C major at 21, then moving to E minor at 24, touching on B flat major at 33, then D flat major at 37 with the opening figure in augmentation, before returning to C major with the opening figure at 45.

Bars 45–54 are the same as 1–9 which thus gives the piece a feeling of being in ternary form. But bars 55–6 are different; and from 57, where it is marked *en animant peu à peu*. the music begins to feel like a coda. It gradually descends to *très animé* at 67, when it begins to rise to its climax at 71. Then it falls to an unusual form of extended plagal cadence, *ff*, at the end.

2 'Jimbo's Lullaby'

This is pictorial music. The piece is mostly pitched very low and moves slowly and clumsily—*un peu gauche*—as befits an elephant. It is based on three figures, **A**, **B**, **C**, and derivatives of them. There are also a number of pedals, and the interval of a harmonic second is a marked feature throughout.

A starts as a unison melody, low in the bass, with the interval of a second making a brief interruption in bars 3 and 4.

B starts at 9 with a pedal G, which lasts for six bars, the interval of a second frequently recurring, and an inner melody making an augmented second in semibreves, which is transferred to the bass at 15.

A two-bar link of seconds, 19–20, leads to a return of the melody of **A**, now two octaves higher, and accompanied by the ever-present seconds. By 24^4 it is three octaves above the original version at $5.^4$

Bars 29–32 form another link based on seconds, and lead to **C** at 33, a series of first inversions over a recurrent decorative pedal on A flat.

Bar 39 reverts to another version of the augmented second theme from **B**, accompanied by a broken octave figure in the bass.

The rhythm and chordal effect of **C** returns at 47, starting with the melody falling in semitones and built over a pedal of D flat. **C** moves to the bass at 54 and then to the melody at 57, though it is still in the bass clef.

This leads to a return of **A** in the tonic key at 63, combined with **C** in the middle voice, over a pedal chord at first and then, at 67 onwards, over the ubiquitous seconds. **C** is transferred to the bass at 70; and gradually the music dies away, the seconds having the last word.

3 'Serenade of the Doll'

This piece imitates the sound of the lute, which is generally used for serenades. But it is a miniature serenade· with the soft pedal used almost throughout. It has two bars of introduction, consisting of a *pp* double tonic and dominant pedal, and then **A** appears in the left hand under the double pedal, which is now syncopated. It is a disjointed tune, with an acciaccatura before every note.

At bar 9 the same tune appears a fifth higher in the right hand, but with the same two notes as a syncopated pedal, now in the left hand.

B starts at 14 with a *pesante* but still disjointed tune, now in the left hand again, while the right hand plays syncopated tonic and dominant pedals of the dominant key, though the dominant pedal is dropped at 19.

A returns at 30 in the tonic key, but the tune is now heavier and has lost its acciaccaturas. Also it is in the right hand and the harmonies are fuller, though the syncopated tonic and dominant pedals are still there. But there is also another counter-theme in the bass.

C starts at 35 and consists of a frequently repeated one-bar figure containing a dotted crotchet. It is an ostinato on C sharp and D sharp in the right hand with varied harmonies below it, the bass slipping down by step and the tonality being vague. The ostinato moves into the middle of the texture at 39 as the bass reaches a dominant pedal of the dominant key which leads to *a tempo* at 43, when the two bars of introduction recur, now in the dominant key.

They lead to yet another figure, **D**, in the left hand with a tonic pedal below it and the usual syncopated repeated tonic pedal above it. At 51–2 the music appears to be leading to key C, but 53 avoids establishing any key. The tune continues in the middle of the texture, with long notes beneath it and the repeated syncopated chords above it, ending with a run of *pp* staccato quavers at 61–2 and *staccato* chords at 63–4.

After a bar's pause at 65 a repeated ostinato harmonic interval of a second appears in the left hand, over which **E** appears at 69, but with still no established key. Bars 69–72 are repeated a tone higher at 73 and lead to *sf* discords at 78, 80, 81 and 82, which prepare the way for the return of **A** in the tonic key at 84.

But it is not the same as the first **A**. The tune is an octave higher and in a different rhythm; and F sharp and A make the pedal for four bars, followed by varied discords which lead to a coda at 94.

This starts with a new figure, **F**, over a tonic pedal. But **A** returns at 107, using the theme as first heard at 9–10 over a broken tonic and dominant pedal. At 115 the chordal accompaniment is left to itself, and the music dies away on a tonic arpeggio, followed by a bar's silence.

4 'The Snow is Dancing'

This piece is in D minor and is very impressionistic in style. The semiquaver movement, representing the snow, never stops dancing. In a sense, there is no harmony in this piece: a slow-moving tune in unison or octaves, with an ostinato figure as an accompaniment. The ostinato starts in bar 1 in quavers, then changes to semiquavers in bar 2, and the tune starts in semibreves in bar 3.

At bar 14 it changes to a series of minim triads; and at 22 the tune is in octaves outside the continuing ostinato. The first section ends with two bars of the ostinato in C minor at 32–3.

The middle section, 34–56, starts with a little counter-theme which is added to the ostinato at 34, while another fragment of tune is added at 40. Then the first counter-theme reappears at 44.

The first section returns at 57, with the ostinato in its original form, and the semibreve theme making a tonic pedal for the first four bars, as at 7–10.

The coda starts with the second fragment of counter-theme, first heard at 40, at 68. But bars 70–4, which are built over a tonic

221

pedal, revert to the quaver figure of bar 1, plus the ever-present semiquavers.

5 'The little Shepherd'

This is very improvisatory in style. It starts with four bars of unaccompanied introduction, like the sound of a primitive shepherd's pipe, without any feeling of tonality.

The main figure of the piece, **A**, starts at 5. It ends with a cadence in A major at 9–11, the first time that one is aware of a clear tonality.

B starts at 12 with a contrasted melody, but still improvisatory in style; and it ends with a cadence in E major at 16–18.

Two link-bars lead to the return of figure **A** at 21, with the tune a third higher than before and with different harmonies. But 27 returns to the figure at the original pitch; and 27–31 are the same as 7–11, thus again ending in A major.

6 'Golliwog's Cake Walk'

This is perhaps the best-known piece of the suite. The 'cake walk' was a popular dance at the time the piece was written, and the golliwog's performance of it is both clumsy and humorous.

It opens with four bars of a very syncopated melody in octaves anticipating **A**. Then, after an unexpected bar's rest, there follow four bars of the chord of E flat with an added second, a common device of Debussy's. They are full of syncopation and unexpected *p*s and *f*s.

A starts at 10 with a syncopated melody, which is still mostly built over a chord of E flat. But it ends at 25 in the dominant key.

B begins at 26 and contains humorous repetitions of a bass figure at 30–33. But, after a *ff* chord at 40 it reverts to the chord of E flat plus the added second for six bars.

C starts at 47 in G flat major. It is entirely *pp* and contains syncopated chords preceded by acciaccaturas.

D begins at 61 with two slow bars of a mock-emotional theme followed by *pp* quaver chords *a tempo*. The two contrasted ideas continue in alternation until the emotional theme takes over at 79. This is followed by hints of the introductory bars which lead to a return of **A** at 90.

B follows at 106, and continues up to 117, with slight changes at 110–13.

Bars 118 to the end of the piece form a coda based on the introduction. And the piece ends with a humorous run down to two *ff* E flats.

41 Ravel

Introduction and Allegro for Flute, Clarinet, Harp and String Quartet

Ravel was a student at the Paris Conservatoire and he early showed his individuality. He won the second Prix de Rome award in 1901; but, in spite of a number of his early works becoming well-known, he was never given the highest honour, the first Prix de Rome, and this resulted in an outcry in 1905, just at the time he was writing his *Introduction and Allegro.*

This is therefore an early work, but one which shows his peculiar blend of atmospheric impressionism with the utmost finish and clarity in the use of classical forms. It is, in one sense, a sextet, in another sense, a miniature concerto for harp, because the harp is the most important instrument in the combination. Yet every instrument is used with a full realisation of its possible colour effects, both by themselves and in combination, so that the result is deliciously satisfying as a work of art and a study in tonal colours.

The analysis which follows refers to the guide numbers which occur every few bars throughout the miniature score, rather than to bar numbers.

The slow introduction contains the germs of themes which are used later in the *Allegro.* It is tonal but the tonality is, at times, most elusive. Is the opening in G flat major or E flat minor? There are chromatic notes in both keys and neither key is firmly established with an old-fashioned tonic-dominant opening. But the prevailing key of most of the introduction is surely E flat minor. Figure (*a*) starts in this key in the first bar in flute and clarinet in thirds, answered by the strings in unison with figure (*b*) in the third bar. And the harp enters a bar later with a cadenza-like passage, to end the first phrase.

The whole of this is then repeated with different instrumentation starting at the seventh bar. 'Cellos and violas have figure (*a*) in thirds in C sharp minor (a tone lower, enharmonically changed), with the 'cellos playing above the violas; and figure (*b*) enters two bars later in flute, clarinet and first violin in unison in the same key, with a harp arpeggio rounding off the phrase, as before.

At 1, marked *moins lent*, figure (*c*) appears in the 'cello, in E flat minor again, with very light arpeggios above in flute, clarinet and violins. Note the *pizzicato* of the second violins, which adds to the ethereal quality, and the *pp* double-tonguing of the wind instruments. The harp joins in with the arpeggios four bars later, as the music speeds up and begins to move towards G flat major.

Figure (*d*) appears in the first violin and viola in octaves two bars later again, at *modérément animé*, while the arpeggios continue, starting with a dominant seventh of G flat major. Gradually the music quietens and slows down; and two bars before 2 figure (*d*) is transferred to the wind, and answered by the violin a bar later, over dominant harmony of G flat major.

The *Allegro*, which is in sonata form, starts at 2 in G flat major. The first subject grows out of figure (*b*) in the Introduction, but is subtly changed in both rhythm and tonality—it now starts on the supertonic whereas it started on the tonic in the Introduction. A new figure, (*e*), appears seven bars after 2. Both (*b*) and (*e*) and the sweeping arpeggios which accompany them are played by the solo harp; and the first sentence ends two bars before 3 in the dominant key, D flat major.

The second, answering sentence, based on the same ideas, starts at 3. It returns to the tonic key, G flat major (though written as F sharp major in the strings), and the tune now starts on the dominant and is played by the flute, accompanied by *tremolos* and *pizzicato* arpeggios. The harp joins the flute four bars later; and, four bars later again, the theme is transferred to the clarinet. It seems loth to end; and, as it dies down, it is taken over by the harp one bar before 4. The first violin has the two-bar phrase twice before it is once more transferred to the harp.

Four bars later, at *a tempo*, the first subject theme appears once more, starting on the supertonic in the tonic key, as at 2. Now it is played by the flute and viola, accompanied by yet another variety of instrumental colour: harp semiquaver arpeggios, using a harmonic on the first note of every beat, *pp* triplets in the violins, and *pp pizzicato* chords in the 'cello. The whole produces a lovely shimmering effect.

At 5 a variant of (*e*) is transferred to the first violin and clarinet in octaves, while the arpeggios continue. Four bars later the tune moves to the flute and both violins, again in octaves, and the phrase ends with a harp arpeggio.

This leads to the second subject, (*f*), at 6 in E flat minor, the relative minor. The theme is a new one (not present in the Introduction) and it starts with flute and clarinet in octaves, accompanied by *pizzicato* chords in the violins. Four bars later the theme is transferred to the violins in octaves, accompanied by *pizzicato* arpeggios in the lower strings and double-tongued arpeggios in the wind. Four bars later again the first bar of the second subject theme is played in inverted form (*g*) by the flute six times, interrupted twice by harp glissandos in chords. Then it is transferred to the clarinet, four bars before 8 and two bars later again to the harp, playing harmonics, now unaccompanied. This marks the end of the exposition, in E flat minor.

The development section starts at 8 and consists of new variants of the previously-heard themes, in new instrumental colours. A variant of figure (a) starts in muted first violin and viola, accompanied by a repeated *pizzicato* figure in second violin and 'cello forming the tonic chord of E flat minor, and this pedal continues up to 10.

Starting at 8, two bars of this repetition of figure (a) is repeated four times, and at its third repetition it is combined with a variant of (b), the first subject theme, played by the harp and starting on the supertonic, with the rhythm changed. It is transferred to the violins five bars before 9, now starting on the dominant, while a variant of (e) is heard in the wind. It moves back to the harp at 9 starting on the tonic, and is repeated two bars later starting on the submediant. Notice that, during these four bars, the violins are playing *pp tremolo sur la touche.*

Four bars after 9 an inversion of figure (g), which grew out of the second subject and was first heard at 7, is heard in the flute, and is then passed to some other instrument every two bars: to the clarinet, the flute again, the viola, the clarinet and second violin accompanied by the harp glissando first heard two bars before 7, the flute and viola plus harp glissando again, flute and viola for a second time, then first violin and viola. During this time the music changes speed, moving slower then faster.

This repetitive figure finally leads to a harp cadenza two bars after 11, which starts with the second subject, (f), in its original form. It is built over a dominant chord of G major, which key is implied but never established.

The (g) variant recurs at 12, played by flute and clarinet, then by harp, then by the violins, then harp again, then violins, then viola and 'cellos at 13, and finally by solo flute, before it leads into the second subject, (f), four bars after 13. During this time it is frequently interrupted by delightful *pp* arpeggios.

The repetition of the second subject, starting four bars after 13, is played over a pedal B flat (or A sharp) until two bars after 15 and gradually builds up a *crescendo*, passing from the clarinet to the first violin, accompanied by an augmentation of (b), the first subject, in the harp, then to flute and clarinet at 14 accompanied by an augmentation of (e) in the first violin and (b) in the viola, in which the harp joins four bars later.

At 15 (f) is played by harp, violin and viola, while (b) is played by flute and clarinet; and this builds up to 16, when (f), the second subject, is played by flute and clarinet while (b), the first subject, is played by the violin.

A *fff* climax is reached at 17, when a variant of (b), the first subject, is played by the violins, *très animé*, against continuous glissandos in the harp.

This leads to a harp cadenza, which starts with a long *ff* arpeggio and then continues with the first subject, (b), in chords, marked *lent*, followed by another arpeggio. At *très lent* figure (a) reappears, followed by another arpeggio; and then (c) is played in harmonics, accompanied by glissandos. The recapitulation begins at 18.

It has been a wonderful development section, with all the figures combined in ever-changing ways and providing the most fascinating variety of tone colours.

The recapitulation, too, uses different tonal combinations from those of the exposition, as well as being considerably altered in proportions. Figures (b) and (e) start in the harp as before, but now with *tremolo* accompaniment in wind and strings. The wind joins the harp with (e) when it arrives, seven bars after 18; and the whole sentence, which again ends in D flat major six bars after 19, is two bars shorter than in the exposition.

The answering sentence, beginning seven bars after 19, starts like 3 but is, at first, played by the harp alone, though the clarinet joins in at 20. The figure is repeated again five bars after 20, starting on the dominant of B minor and played by flute and viola, with the violins taking it over two bars later; and the figure then drops down, in imitations, until it reaches 21, which corresponds to one bar before 4 in the exposition. These modifications result in an extension, there being six bars more than between 3 and 4 in the exposition.

The nine bars after 21 correspond to the eight bars starting one bar before 4, though the harp is silent and the imitations are between wind and strings.

But the repetition of the first subject, starting eight bars after 4 in the exposition is completely omitted in the recapitulation; and the second subject starts ten bars after 21.

The harp, having been silent for the last few bars, starts the second subject on its own. It is in B flat minor, a fourth higher than in the exposition, but this is still not the tonic key. The *Allegro* certainly begins and ends in G flat major, in spite of the vague tonality of the introduction and the shifting tonalities elsewhere. B flat minor is therefore the mediant minor; and the music does not move towards the tonic key until six bars before the coda starts at 24, and even after this it continues to shift until a dominant pedal of the tonic key is reached five bars after 27.

To return, however, to the second subject: after four bars of the harp alone the tune switches to the wind at 22, with dancing figuration in harp and strings.

Five bars later the first bar of the second subject—an inversion of (*g*) as it appeared four bars before 7—continues as before, but with the theme starting in the strings and answered by the wind, instead of the other way round, and the harp glissandos adding colour as before, but now occurring three times instead of twice. This section is longer than in the exposition, six bars before 23 up to 24 being eighteen bars long as compared with fourteen bars. It ends with the solo flute instead of the harp.

The coda starts at 24 with a decorative version of the second subject, (*f*), in the harp accompanied by light *pizzicaro* chords. At 25 the flute joins in with (*g*), rising for five bars and then falling for six bars. The *pizzicato* chords change to *arco* triplet chords five bars after 25 in first violin and viola, and the harp has sweeping arpeggios, thus adding to the excitement.

But 26 returns to the relative quietness of 24, though with the addition of *ppp* trills in the wind. 27 also corresponds to 25, though the music rises higher and reaches a dominant pedal of the tonic key in *forte* arpeggios, five bars after 27. The music accelerates, too, and the theme is in the wind, appearing in quaver diminution two bars before 28, and then in augmentation at 28.

A tonic pedal starts two bars after 28 and continues to the end. The music is based on the first two bars of the first subject, (*b*), with the theme still in the wind, and occurring in diminution seven bars after 28. The last two bars are given glowing colour by a six-note chord glissando in the harp.

42 Strauss

Till Eulenspiegel

This is a programmatic tone poem which was started in 1894 and finished in 1895, when Strauss was thirty. According to one report it was performed in Frankfort in September 1895; according to another its first performance was in Cologne in November 1895. Although he had written several tone poems before, notably *Don Juan* and *Death and the Transfiguration*, this was perhaps the first work to bring him world-wide fame.

'Tyl Owlglass' (the English translation) is based on an old German story of the fourteenth or fifteenth century. Till's native village is Möllen, near Lübeck, and his tombstone, dated 1350, is pointed out to visitors. Till is a popular German figure of the middle ages, just as Robin Hood is for England. But his pranks were purely mischievous, and had no relation to good deeds.

The work is subtitled 'An old Rogue's Tale, set in rondo form for full orchestra'. It begins with a prologue and ends with an epilogue, as befits an old tale; and in between the story is told in a very free rondo form, with Till's two themes appearing in many guises, and contrasted with episodes concerned with other people and the merry pranks he played on them.

The work is scored for a large orchestra. One expects a classical work to be scored for double wood-wind, and a work written at the end of last century to be scored for triple wood-wind. But this one is scored for 3 flutes and piccolo (=4); 3 oboes and cor anglais (=4); 3 clarinets, 2 in B flat 1 in D, and bass clarinet (=4); 3 bassoons and a double bassoon (=4).

As far as the brass is concerned Strauss starts with 4 horns in F, but later two are changed to E; and at the climax he writes for 8 horns. Similarly he starts with 3 trumpets but requires 6 at the climax. And he uses the usual 3 trombones and tuba.

For percussion he uses 5 timpani, requiring two players, a triangle, cymbals, a bass drum, a side drum and a big rattle. And, at the climax, just before Till is brought before the judge, all the instruments are used at once, except the rattle which is reserved for the market scene.

The prologue begins with theme (a), played quietly and leisurely by the violins, and giving little indication of the sprightly humour which it develops later. It ends with arpeggios in the two B flat clarinets.

Till's second theme, (b), starts at bar 6, played by the first horn accompanied by high *tremolo* violins. The theme is droll, even at this preliminary stage, partly because of its syncopation and chromaticisms, and partly because of the way it plunges downwards at the end. It is interrupted by two *staccato* tutti chords and is then repeated more quickly by the first horn, interrupted this time by one tutti chord. It is transferred to the oboes at 21, to the clarinets at 26, to all the bassoons and lower strings at 30, and then it gradually extends to the full orchestra, reaching a climax at 39, which is continued with disjointed short phrases separated by pauses, until the prologue ends on a unison, *ff*, C at 45.

The rondo starts still more quickly with a lusty bar of theme (a) on the little D clarinet, followed by a discord on the oboes, then by a *staccato* downward leap of a diminished seventh in the violins, with *ff* trombones sliding up a semitone.

Then Till sets out on his career of mischief with a *staccato* theme on the strings and trombone, starting at 50. It reaches a climax at 63, but continues gaily on its way, with gradually fuller orchestra, ending with a semiquaver scale rising two octaves and a fifth over 69 and 70.

Theme (*a*) returns at 71 with even greater exuberance, starting high in the woodwind, transferring down to the violins in the next bar and then to the lower strings in the following bar, before rising again in a tutti.

It dies down at 80 and leads to a mockingly polite variation of theme (*a*), which presumably shows him in disguise. It starts with two flutes, with a sedate continuance in the strings, ending with a little trill on the bass clarinet. The flutes and violins appear again in the second phrase, starting at 82, but this time they are interrupted by the D clarinet, then by the B flat clarinet and finally by a *pp* scalic run upwards in the violins. The quieter variation continues in this way until it reaches a slower *espressivo* theme in flutes and violins at 89. The imitative entries continue, in clarinets at 91, first violins at 92, flutes at 93 and second violins also at 93, until they reach a *pizzicato* chord at 96.

Then he appears to take fright and runs away with short variants of (*a*), in the piccolo at 96 and the flute, starting at 97 and continuing in rapidly rising repetitions of the figure, until it is transferred to the clarinet at 102 and the violins at 103.

But off he goes again, *ff* at 105, all the wind playing in unison, and continued by the violins, then by a trill in the oboes at 108 and ending with a descending arpeggio in the clarinet at 110.

We have temporarily reached repose; and under and over a quiet *tremolo* in the violas a two-note semiquaver figure ending with three longer notes appears, first in the lower strings, then in the flute and then in the violins. At 123 the longer notes take over; and after being repeated three times have an *espressivo* longer phrase in contrary motion in the strings.

Bar 129 sounds as if all this is going to be repeated, with the viola

231

tremolos and the hesitant figure in the lower strings; but suddenly Till decides on another prank and, starting with a run up in the bass clarinet, he is depicted in a tutti, riding through the market place and driving the shrieking women away on all sides. The big rattle joins in the *mêlée* at 136; and from 135 to 153 all is noise and confusion, with theme (*a*) appearing *ff* in the strings at 136 and again at 145.

A bar's pause at 154 is the prelude to his running away, with little *pp* semiquaver runs in all the instruments in turn, discordant minor seconds appearing now and again in various wind instruments, and rising quaver runs making a chromatic scale. The music dies down to 179 and ends with four repeated notes on the horns.

In the next episode, starting at 179, he appears dressed up as a priest; and a mock-solemn theme appears in clarinets, bassoons and violas. But his own theme (*a*) breaks through at 189 in the strings—almost as if one can see his own mocking face, half-hidden by the cowl.

However, he has misgivings about this; and a little figure, repeated three times in the violin at 194–5, leads to a repentant triplet figure at 196 in horns, trumpets and violins, which is to appear again later in the story. The music continues with four bars of a drum roll at 199–202, but the repentant figure is repeated again at 202–6, with a solo violin at the top.

But this mood cannot continue for long; and a downward *glissando* in the solo violin at 207 leads to his setting off again, this time to make love to all the pretty girls. Theme (*a*) appears in the clarinet, then twice in the oboe, then in the violins and then the oboe again, as a prelude to a broad, swaggering theme which starts in horns and 'cellos at 222. It grows out of theme (*b*) and is transferred to the violins at 229, continuing up to 255, with little interjections of (*a*) in different instruments at first (223–6) and with the original theme (*b*) in the horn at 244.

The theme works up to a great tutti climax, with semiquaver and quaver interjections in many instruments as the girls make fun of him, so that he bursts out angrily at 263, with trumpets, trombones, 'cellos and basses playing a dotted quaver theme (an augmentation of (*a*)) in unison. This theme is transferred to other parts of the orchestra, and is combined with downward semiquaver scales, presumably mocking shrieks, in the upper wood-wind, until the dotted quaver theme is played tutti, ending at 287.

Now he retires, momentarily, to lick his wounds, with a few notes of theme (*b*) in the horns, followed by a few notes of theme (*a*) in the clarinet, and then a downward chromatic scale in the 'cellos.

Next, starting at 293, he meets some stodgy professors, depicted most aptly in the bass clarinet and the bassoons. He answers them with theme (*b*) in the strings, starting at 299. By 307 the themes are combined, and soon the effect is of them all talking at once. It reaches a climax with the professors' theme *ff* at 344 and Till cocking a snook at them with theme (*a*) in flutes, clarinets, trumpets and violins at 345. This continues until an even greater climax is reached at 366, with Till's theme now triumphantly winning.

But after the pause on the trill at 370 and a moment's hesitancy, Till trips away, whistling a swaggering street-song, starting at 374 in the clarinets and violins. This dies away at 386, however, and there is again a moment's hesitancy, depicted by the fall of the seventh at 387–9, and repeated at 391–3, perhaps expressing a feeling of boredom. This is followed by a quiet augmentation of (*a*) in equal notes (minims).

From now onwards Till continues his antics, which become more and more boisterous until he is finally caught and brought before the judge. But we are not told of any particular stories: instead the themes continue to develop in ever-new guises.

The tempo becomes a little slower, and theme (*a*) is played repeatedly in a different rhythm, *pp*, by cor anglais, horns and trumpets against semiquaver runs in upper wood-wind and strings up to 424. This is followed by two statements of the rising stepwise quaver figure first heard at 82, now played by oboes at 426 and 428.

Then, at 429, theme (b) is played twice in its original form by the horn, with similar *tremolos* in the violins, so that bars 429–42 are very similar to 14–19 played twice, with different harmonies the second time. Theme (b) is then heard in the D clarinet, at 443, followed by the violin and by the basses.

Starting at 449 theme (b) is again played four times by the horns, with semiquaver runs against it as before, gradually working towards a climax.

A series of imitative entries of theme (a) begin at 465 in the horns; and snatches of the first few notes are heard in all parts of the orchestra until a ff climax is reached at 475, when violins and upper wood-wind play the full theme in unison.

A new, slower version of (b) starts at 485 in horns and trombones, combined with snatches of (a), and continues up to 500.

Then themes (a) and (b) are cleverly combined, (a) being in oboes, clarinets and violins at first, while (b) is in horn and violas. The scoring is light; and, at 508, reaches a pp, from which it very gradually builds up, using both themes, until it reaches a ff of (a) at 532.

From now onwards the dynamics ebb and flow, but more and more instruments take part, until the drums start a ff dominant pedal at 544, which leads to a tutti dotted minim climax at 553. From here to 573 the music is in a state of exuberance, with (a) predominating up to 566, and then the theme first heard at 179 being played by all eight horns, six trumpets and three trombones at 567, until there is a crash at 573 and a great bang on the bass drum.

This is followed by a ff menacing side drum roll, over which the judge sternly rebukes Till with five ff dotted minim chords on lower wind, four horns, trombones, tuba and basses, plus intervening ff chords on the other four horns and the rest of the strings. This short passage ends with a timpani roll, and Till answers cheekily with theme (a) on the shrill D clarinet. The judge sternly rebukes him again; and Till again answers in the same way.

But the third time the judge's pronouncement is heard, at 594–7, it is shorter, and Till's reply is now an octave higher, *ff*, and sounds frightened. Also it is cut short; and when the judge speaks again there is no answer from Till. After a short pause the judge speaks yet again (602–4) and this time we hear the sound of frightened repentance from Till, with the figure first heard at 196 when he had misgivings about dressing up as a priest. Now it is played *ff* by oboes, cor anglais, muted horns, trumpets and violins, and then repeated four times, *mf* by muted horns, trumpets and violins, with the oboes and cor anglais joining in the last repetition and rising higher.

But his repentance is of no avail. A *tremolo* chord on the lower strings is interrupted by a *ff* downward leap of a seventh in the brass, which is his sentence of death. Till's (*a*) theme is heard, rising higher on the D clarinet as the hangman's rope quivers convulsively. Then oboes, cor anglais and the D clarinet move slowly down in discords as Till's death rattle is heard in a high *ff* trill on the flute. The discords continue downwards until six soft *pizzicato* string chords, supported by a muted horn chord, end in silence. Till's life has come to an end.

Now we have the epilogue, which comments kindly on poor old Till. It starts like the prologue with theme (*a*) in the violins, but now it continues for longer, in a warm-hearted, romantic style. At 644 clarinets and horns have a delicate variant of (*b*), ending with a pause on a minim chord.

But, after this kindly musing, the tone poem ends with a very quick tutti, in which theme (*a*) is played *ff* by upper wood-wind and violins at 652. And a series of disjointed chords end with a *fff* tutti *staccato* tonic chord.

43 Vaughan Williams

Benedicite

Vaughan Williams wrote every kind of music in the course of his long life. But he has always been particularly associated with music for the church. He was interested in hymn tunes and wrote tunes for *The English Hymnal*, *Songs of Praise*, and the *Oxford Book of Carols*, all of which books he helped to produce. He also wrote larger works such as church services, motets, two 'Te Deums' and a mass; and sacred choral works with orchestra, of which 'Benedicite' is one.

'Benedicite' was composed in 1929 and had its first performance at the Leith Hill Festival in 1930. The words are taken from the Benedicite used for morning service in the *Book of Common Prayer*, combined with a poem by Jane Austin. It is scored for a large orchestra, but the following analysis is based on the vocal score, from which most students will probably study it. The vocal parts are for soprano solo and S A T B chorus; but soprano and alto parts frequently divide, thus making a six-part chorus. There is also an arrangement for female voices only, so it is to be hoped that some schools, at least, will be ambitious enough to get to know the work by performing it.

The work has an affinity with the sacred choral works of the Tudor composers, notably in the very large use of stepwise movement. But fourths are also very prominent, and sometimes they are augmented fourths, which would not have been tolerated in Tudor times. There are also occasional uses of adjacent major and minor thirds in the style of Purcell; and many passages when the parts move so independently of each other that they would only be tolerated in the twentieth century. Yet the whole fuses together in a style that is unmistakably that of Vaughan Williams.

The work is built on a series of figures, often very similar to each other. Frequently a new figure is associated with a new set of words, as in the works of earlier contrapuntal composers; and repetitions of words are associated with the same figure. Figures return, particularly towards the end of the work, when they are fused together. The work is in four sections. The second and third sections introduce the soprano soloist, and the final section is a short return to the ideas of the first section.

The only way this work can be analysed is to label all the figures. The teacher or student is advised to number the bars and follow the course of these figures as they are analysed here, marking them in the copy. In this way he can get to know the work thoroughly and understand its structure. But if a teacher is short of time, or his candidates are not of high calibre, he may decide against going into so much detail with them, merely pointing out how the work is built up on figures, and referring to a few of the more important ones.

Figure (*a*) starts in the orchestral introduction and consists of the first nine crotchets, which are mostly stepwise, though a fourth occurs between the third and fourth notes. Notice that they start on the second crotchet of the bar—in anacrusic rhythm.

After a repetition of this, (*b*) appears over the top of (*a*) in bars 4–6.[1] Notice that it starts with a chord of B major, and that D sharp is followed immediately by D natural twice in bar 5—a Purcellian touch. In fact, the music of bars 1–51 is a mixture of B minor and B major. B minor predominates at first but there are four bars of B major at 28–31. A dominant pedal on F sharp starts at 7,[4] over which figure (*c*) appears. Like (*a*) it consists of nine crotchets starting anacrusically on the second crotchet of the beat, but now it is a series of descending fourths, and it is developed in a series of imitations over the dominant pedal until the singers enter at 13.

The male voices enter in unison with a slightly different version of (*b*). It is now in D major, but the rhythm is the same; and (*c*) continues in the orchestra below the voices. The crotchet figure starting in the voices at 16 is used frequently enough to be given a new label, (*d*). Notice that, unlike (*a*) and (*c*), it starts on the beat.

As they finish at 18 the orchestra enters with a new figure in contrasted rhythm, (e) which makes use of dotted and tied notes and also continuous quavers which are frequently used later. Figure (c) continues underneath.

Bars 21–7 are a repetition of 13–19 but now with female instead of male voices.

At 28 the voices combine in six parts, the men singing (b), now in B major, while the women sing a new figure, (f), with canonic imitations between the two soprano parts. By 32 the quavers from the end of (e) enter in the female voices, in imitation between soprano and alto parts, and then in the orchestra at 34. The voices converge at 34⁴ and by 35⁴ they are singing (d) in unison.

At 38 the voices take up (e) in imitation; and when they finish at 44 the orchestra takes it up, combined with (a) at 44 and with (a) and (b) at 46. Imitative entries of (c) occur again at 48–51, and lead to a section in F sharp minor.

This starts with a variant of (b) in the altos followed by a variant of (a) in the sopranos at 54 and in the tenors at 57. A new figure, (g), starts in the sopranos at 58 with coloratura on 'showers', imitated by the basses at 60 with coloratura on 'winds'. During this a variant of (a) is heard in the orchestra and is also sung by the altos at 59–60 and the sopranos at 62–3. 'Fire and heat' produces a new figure, (h), in imitation between tenors, altos and sopranos, marked *forte*, using fifths and fourths, including an augmented fourth, and aptly fitting the words. It is answered at 64–5 by a repeated note figure, (i), in the men's voice parts to the words 'bless ye the Lord', which also appears frequently later.

The altos start a new figure, (j), at 65, which is taken up by the sopranos at 69. All the voices join in with an augmentation of (i) at 74 against a discordant quaver ostinato in the orchestra combined with dotted semibreve chords which move quite independently. Figure (h) is heard in crotchet diminution by inversion, sung *f*, in close imitation by the voices at 78–9, combined with a quaver diminution of it in the orchestra. This climax is followed by (i) at 'bless ye the Lord'.

Four bars of orchestra alone, combining (e) and (c), lead to a return of (b) in the voices at 84, now in B flat major and minor, combined with a variant of (e) in the orchestra.

A new figure, (k), starts in the altos at 90. It is transferred to the tenor at 95, the alto again at 98 and to the bass at 101, while (e) is heard in the soprano at 93 and again at 96, in the tenor at 98, the alto at 101, the soprano again at 103, the tenor in stretto one beat later, the alto again at 105, the tenor again at 106, and the alto and tenor again at 109 and 111.

In the meantime the second half of (k) is heard in augmentation in the soprano at 105, in the bass at 107 and in further augmentation in the soprano at 109.

This *tour de force* reaches its climax at 114, when a return to earlier figures rounds off the first section of the work. Figures (b) and (c) are heard in the orchestra at 114 and 118 and (a) is heard at 122; while an upper dominant pedal of key D is heard in 126–9 against a slowly descending bass which leads to (d) at 130.

During these bars the voices sing (e) in unison at 116 and again at 120, (d) at 124 and the second half of (f) in stretto, starting at 126. They finish with 'praise him and magnify him for ever' at 131–4.

The second section is *lento* and starts with an oboe solo hinting at figure (l) which is heard in full, sung by the soprano soloist at 139. The second half of her phrase at 142–4 is heard so frequently later that it requires another label, (m).

The female voices of the choir then sing (l) and (m) at 144–50, while the soloist decorates with embellishments. The male voices enter with (l) and (m) at 150–5, while the female voices enter with (l) in imitation at 151 and the soloist continues her embellishments. Altos, tenors and basses sing (m) in contrary motion at 156–8.

The soloist starts (n) at 158, which is taken up by the whole chorus at 162, and six bars of unaccompanied singing follow. Figure (m) is heard at 166, and when the orchestra re-enters at 168 the quavers from (l) are sung and played in all parts. The oboe takes them over again at 172, and this leads to (m) sung *ppp* in the choir against a new figure (*o*), which is heard first in the oboe at 177 and then by the soprano soloist at 179. Figure (*m*) continues in the sopranos, altos and tenors at 182, while the basses sing (*i*) to 'bless ye the Lord'.

These three figures continue in this way until a new figure, (*p*), enters in the basses at 191. This is used by all the four voice parts in turn until they all sing (*i*) at 199. They continue repeating (*i*) at intervals until 214, though a new figure, (*q*), appears in the solo part at 202 and 205 and is taken up by the sopranos at 208,[4] the tenors at 209,[4] the sopranos at 210,[4] and the soloist again at 211.[4]

At the end of this section the female choir sings the quaver part of (*l*) at 215 against (*b*) in the tenors at 216, while the soloist again sings (*q*) at 219.

The third section is *moderato* and, like the second section, starts with the soprano soloist. She now sings the words of Jane Austin, starting with 'Hark my soul' to (*r*) at 224. She is answered by the choir singing (*s*) unaccompanied at 228. The soloist continues with (*r*) at 231, again answered by the choir singing (*s*) at 235. Then, at 238, the soloist sings a new figure, (*t*), but the choir again answers with (*s*) at 241. The soloist takes over (*s*) at 248 while the choir switches over to (*r*) at 252. The soloist joins in with (*r*) at 255, and choir and soloist continue it until the end of the section at 296.

The final section starts at 297 with a return to the original speed and to compound time. The soloist sings 'Bless ye the Lord' to (*k*), which is taken up by the whole choir at 300, by the tenors at 303, the sopranos at 306, the basses and altos at 307, and the tenors at 310. During this time (*e*) is sung by the altos at 304, the tenors at 306, the altos again at 309 and sopranos and basses at 310.

Then the sopranos sing (*k*) in augmentation at 313 against its original form in altos and tenors and (*e*) in the basses.

At 317 the soloist sings (*b*) answered by the choir singing (*d*) at 320, and the two continue to alternate up to 330, while (*e*) is heard in the orchestra at 328. Finally (*f*) is heard augmented and varied at 331, sung by the whole choir.

44 Ireland

Phantasie Trio in A minor

This work, written in 1906, was dedicated to Ireland's teacher, Sir Charles Stanford, and was the earliest of his chamber works to be published. He later wrote two other piano trios: all his published chamber works contain a piano part, as Ireland himself was a pianist.

The trio was entered for a Cobbett chamber music competition, and won a prize. Cobbett was a wealthy amateur who did much to stimulate English composers at the beginning of this century, by instituting chamber music competitions; and he particularly favoured the free form of a one-movement phantasy which, he thought, derived from the Elizabethan fancy. Cobbett also compiled a *Cyclopedic Survey of Chamber Music* which contains a few comments on this work.

The trio is one of Ireland's earliest works and is therefore more traditional than his later, more individual works. It is in a very free kind of sonata form. As Cobbett says 'The feeling is classic-romantic and, though themes occur in derivative form, unity is effected more by their psychological than by their textual affinity.

The work is tonal, in that one can feel a key centre most of the time; and the main key-changes bear some resemblance to classical usage and are clearly defined. But the key is constantly shifting, in a Wagnerian kind of way. The piano writing is thick and luscious—one can feel that Ireland is revelling in the pianistic sounds. The work is certainly enjoyable to play for all three instruments, the string parts being very melodic, in spite of the swift changes of key.

Although the main outlines of sonata form are clearly heard the work is nevertheless largely built up of contrasting rhythmical figures, and it will be clearer to label these, as one would in an Elizabethan fancy or a Scarlatti sonata.

The first subject, then, contains two rhythmic figures in the opening 'cello melody: (*a*) in bars 1 and 2 and (*b*) in bars 3 and 4, against a thick, chordal accompaniment in the piano. The violin takes them up at 5, imitated by the 'cello at 6, so that bar 6 contains (*b*) in the violin and (*a*) in the 'cello. Then both play (*b*) together for the next few bars, and end in C major at 10.

Bar 11 begins a modified repetition, two octaves higher, starting with the melody in the violin instead of the 'cello, but differently harmonised. The two instruments, changed round, continue as before and again reach a cadence in C major, at 18.

Then the piano enters with (*a*) in the bass in C minor and uses the figure continuously for some time. The 'cello enters in imitation, but goes on at 20 to another rhythmic figure, a beat of semiquavers, (*c*). The violin takes up (*a*) and (*c*), starting at 21, and by 23 violin and 'cello are alternately using (*c*).

This works up to a *ff* climax at 25, where the transition starts in E major with imitative entries of another new figure, (*d*), between strings and piano. This figure, (*d*), is more complex, containing a triplet and semiquaver rhythms. As it continues (*b*) is heard in the piano at 29, followed by a recitative-like passage which leads to A flat major, and ends with a pause over a held C at 37–8.

Over this there is a quiet reference to (*a*) and (*b*) in 39–42. But now a new figure, (*e*), enters unobtrusively in the violin which, in reality, presages the second subject. A new, more flowing accompaniment figure starts in the piano a bar later. The 'cello again refers to (*a*) at 44, but the violin continues with (*e*) and by 48 the 'cello is joining in with it, too, in imitation. Two more references to (*a*) occur in the 'cello at 55 and 57, and bars 54–60 are built over a dominant pedal of key C, which leads to the second subject in that key at 61.

This *grazioso* second subject grows out of (*e*), first heard at 42, and is given to the piano alone in the first ten bars. Then the violin enters with the melody at 71, imitated half-a-bar later by the piano and two bars later by the 'cello. The violin and 'cello continue with the figure up to 81, accompanied by rhapsodic broken chords in the piano.

Then the second half of bar 61 is developed as a new figure, (f). It is played ff by violin and 'cello at 82–5. The piano interrupts, *animando*, for two bars; and a development of (f) continues, first in the violin and then, at 91, in the 'cello. The two instruments continue together up to the climax at 95.

Then a variant of the first half of bar 61, the beginning of the second subject, appears at 96 in the piano, followed at 97 by the strings. This works up to ff at 100, where the codetta starts in A major. The piano has (a) while the strings have (e), and gradually the music quietens down until it merges into the development section at 108.

The development starts in A flat major with a *meno mosso* version of (a) in the violin. But, although references to (a) occur quite frequently, the development section consists mostly of new matter. Bar 111 contains a descending crotchet scale in the 'cello, (g), which is imitated by inversion a bar later in the piano. In this bar a new figure, (h), appears in the violin, which is imitated by 'cello and piano two bars later. Then, at 116, violin and piano, take it up.

At 118 another new figure, (i), appears in the piano, against light trill-like figures in the strings. This continues up to 122, when (a) reappears in the 'cello against (g) in the piano. At 124 (a) is heard in the violin against (g) in the piano. This quietens down to a cadence in E flat at 128.

At 132 (a) appears in the violin in A flat major, imitated by the 'cello two bars later against (g) in the piano. The violin goes on to (h) at 135, imitated by the 'cello two bars later. The violin has a bar of (a) at 138 and goes on to (h) while the 'cello has (a).

Then the violin plays (i) at 141 against (h) in the 'cello, and this continues against broken chords in the piano up to 145, when (a) reappears in the piano against (g) in the strings, producing a climax in A flat major. The strings go on to (h) at 147 against (g) in the piano. Then 145–6 are repeated, with piano and strings changed round; and 151–2 are a repetition of 147–8. This is followed by an extended cadence, which dies away on an indeterminate diminished triad at 157. The prevailing key of the development section has been A flat, which is quite unrelated to A minor.

The recapitulation starts at 158 with very mysterious harmonies, high in the piano. Figure (*a*), but not (*b*) of the first subject appears in the violin at 160, starting in a kind of no-man's-land, as far as key is concerned, but reaching F sharp minor at 162 and B minor at 163. Bar 166 is the equivalent of the repetition which occurred at 11, but now the 'cello starts the theme instead of the violin and it is in G major. The violin enters a bar later, but both instruments use (*a*) and (*c*) ignoring (*b*). Figure (*c*) is developed in imitation between the strings at 170–3, and this leads to the transition at 174. The first subject has been sixteen bars, instead of twenty-four bars as in the exposition, and it has been considerably modified.

The transition, beginning at 174, starts the same as at 25 but changes four bars later. It only lasts up to 185, so it is very much shorter than in the exposition, and it contains no hint of the second subject.

The second subject appears in the tonic major at 185 but it, too, changes almost immediately, and the theme is not reserved to the piano for ten bars, as it was in the exposition. The 'cello enters with it at 190 and the violin imitates a bar later; then all three instruments play with it for a while.

Bars 201–21 correspond to 77–97, and the variant of (*e*) used in the last few bars continues, reaching a climax at 225 and the *vivace* coda at 227.

In the coda figures (*a*), (*b*) and (*c*) of the first subject are used by the string instruments in varied imitations against an excited accompaniment in the piano, until (*c*) takes over completely at 238–42. Against this the piano enters with (*a*) at 240 and 242. Then, at 243, it too changes to semiquavers, against *pizzicato* chords in the strings at 245–6.

A *vivacissimo* starts at 247, in which all the instruments play semiquavers, though rhythm (a) reappears at times in the piano. The phantasie ends *fortissimo* in A major.

45 Ireland

Two of 'Three London Pieces'

Although Ireland (1897–1962) was born near Manchester he settled in London after being trained there at the Royal College of Music, and he developed a great affection for that city. This is shown in his *Three London Pieces* for the piano, written in 1917 and 1920, and also in his *London Overture* written in 1936.

'Ragamuffin', the second of his *Three London Pieces* was analysed in Book 2 of this series. The other two are analysed below.

Chelsea Reach

This picture of the Thames at Chelsea has been compared to Whistler's pictures of London river. It is marked *tempo di Barcarolle*, and has the swinging 6/8 rhythm of a barcarolle, though there is nothing Venetian about it. Its shifting atmospheric effects make one think of the changes produced by mists on the Thames.

Although it contains the clumps of chromatic chords beloved of Ireland in his piano writing and is often so full of accidentals that it is very difficult to read, the piece is tonal in its conception, though perhaps it is stretching tonality as far as it will go.

The piece is largely based on one haunting phrase that appears in various keys and different textures in different parts of the keyboard. It starts quietly in A flat, simply and diatonically. The figure is repeated in B flat minor in bar 5 with an added melodic part above it, and reaches E flat at 8, with fuller harmonies in a higher register.

A dominant pedal of C flat appears at 14, followed by a dominant pedal of A flat, the tonic key, at 18, resolving on to the tonic at 20.

I

Bar 24 reverts to the dominant pedal again, but this time it leads to D flat at 26. Yet another pedal of the tonic key at 31, *poco piu moto*, followed by a few bars of *crescendo*, leads to a return of the opening theme, *ff*, with a wide-ranging texture at 39. This time, however, instead of moving to the dominant, as at 8, it reverts to the tonic at 47, and then gradually quietens down over a tonic pedal at 54.

A few link bars, 60–7, lead to the middle section which starts in B major. There is, however, no change of theme, though the melody is now in the middle of the texture. The music modulates freely: to G (74), A (76), D flat (78), F (84), G (86); and finally reaches B major again at 88, *ff appassionato*.

A dominant pedal of the tonic key starts at 93 and the music gradually quietens down until the opening theme reappears in the tonic key at 103. This time the tune is in the alto part, and it corresponds to the version starting at 39 rather than at bar 1, thus staying in the tonic key at 111.

Chromatic dominant harmony at 118–20 leads to a coda at 121 which is built over a tonic pedal until the piece finally dies away, *ppp* at 132.

Soho Forenoons

This was written in 1920 and gives Ireland's impression of Soho's foreign quarter in the mornings. It is marked *quasi tambourine*; and as the music progresses tambourine rhythms certainly appear. But although the piece is attractive there is nothing particularly distinctive or foreign about it.

It begins in A minor with an inner dominant pedal. Figure (*a*) appears in bar 2, and a decorated version of it is heard in 7. At 11 figure (*b*) appears in the alto, as the music moves to G major. There is another appearance of (*a*) at 16, over a dominant and tonic pedal in A minor; and (*b*) reappears in G major at 20 and 24. This section ends with a double dominant and tonic pedal in E minor at 26–30, and the tambourine rhythm becomes more pronounced.

The middle section begins at 32 with a change of both time and key signature. The time signature changes frequently in the next few bars, and the key reaches A flat at 35 and E flat at 41. Bars 32–45 can be thought of as (*c*), while (*d*) starts in E flat at 45, and has a resemblance to the tambourine rhythm of 30–1.

The first section returns with figure (*a*) at 58 but in A flat minor instead of the expected A minor. However (*b*) reappears in G major, the same key as before, at 67, though in a fuller version. Figure (*a*) reappears in the tonic key at 74 (compare 16), with the tambourine rhythm now more pronounced; and (*b*) reappears in G major at 78 (compare 24).

The music then merges into a coda, with cadenza–like passages in which the tambourine rhythm is much in evidence. A dominant pedal of B flat minor at 88–92 leads to a tonic pedal in the same key at 93–4, over which the tambourine rhythm is softly heard, shadowing figure (*a*). However, the music returns to A minor from 98 to the end, still shadowing figure (*a*). It starts with a double dominant and tonic pedal and ends with a *fff* plagal cadence.

46 Bartok

Music for Strings, Percussion and Celesta

This work was written in 1936, at the end of Bartók's second period and the beginning of his third, and is one of his greatest works. It was written for Paul Sacher, of Basle.

It is, in effect, a symphony for an unusual combination of instruments, in cyclic form, with one leading theme running throughout the work, and thus owing something to his compatriot, Liszt. Nevertheless, the four movements are quite different, each bearing a resemblance to a different contemporary style and yet hanging together because of Bartók's great genius. He said himself, 'I do not wish to subscribe to any of the accepted musical tendencies. My ideal is a measured balance of these elements.' And this he achieves in this work.

The combination of instruments used is most unusual: a string orchestra divided into two groups, to be seated at the far right and far left, with the percussion in the middle. One player plays side drums, with and without snares, cymbals, tam-tam and bass drum. Another player has a set of modern timpani, the pitch of which can be changed mechanically and instantaneously. There is also a xylophone, a celesta, two pianos and a harp. Precise instructions are given as to how the instruments are to be played, and some quite new effects are obtained, both by the strings alone and in combination with the percussion.

First Movement, *Andante tranquillo*

A is the tonal centre of the whole work, and the first movement begins and ends on A. It is a fugue based on a most unusual chromatic and atonal, irregular four-phrased theme, with no interval larger than a third, and contained within the range of a fifth.

This theme starts on A in the violas; the answer starts a fifth higher on E in the third and fourth violins; then the 'cellos enter, starting on D; then the second violins, starting on B; then the basses, starting on G; and finally, after a longish interval, the first violins enter at 27, starting on F sharp.

This completes a six-part texture, and might be thought of as an exposition though, of course, there is no question of tonic and dominant keys. All the entries, so far, have been *con sordini*, as is also the extra entry, starting on C, in stretto in 'cellos and basses in bar 27. Notice the continual changes of time-signature: the impression is of waves of melodic lines with no accents.

At 34 the mutes are taken off and, to the accompaniment of a *pp* timpani roll, partial entries appear in stretto, starting on C sharp (second violins, 34); F (third and fourth violins, 34); G sharp (violas, 35); and B flat ('cellos and basses, 37).

The violins have a modified entry starting on E flat at the end of 44, and all the string parts continue together, with cymbals and timpani joining in softly, until 56, when the bass drum strikes and all the strings converge on E flat, *fff*.

This is the climax; and now Bartók embarks on the homeward journey back to the unison *ppp* A. He begins by inverting the subject, and starts on E flat in the third and fourth violins, 'cellos and basses at the end of 56, continuing with partial entries of all the strings in stretto starting on C or F sharp, a tritone away from each other, at 65-7. Then the mutes are put on again and the string parts re-enter gradually with the inverted theme until all six are playing again.

On the last quaver of bar 77 the first violins enter with the inversion, while the fourth violins have the original theme, both starting on A, but three octaves apart. This could be thought of as the beginning of the coda. Notice also the colourful addition of the celesta, playing against the *pp* strings. When the celesta ceases at 82 the strings are left to themselves, with partial entries all starting on A, in both original and inverted form, until finally the violins converge, *ppp*, on the unison A.

This movement bears traces of the influence of Schönberg, both in its atonal, chromatic fugue subject and in its mathematical conception of the fugal entries. Some students may have noticed that, after the first entry starting on A, the alternative entries rise a fifth—E, B, F sharp etc, while those in between fall a fourth—A, D, G etc, making a sequence of A, E, D, B, G, F sharp, C, C sharp, F, G sharp, B flat, E flat=D sharp. At the point E flat=D sharp the two series meet and produce the climax, a tritone away from the original A, a relationship which Hindemith also considered significant, and which Bartók frequently stresses in this work.

Then the inverted theme returns, though not by such regular steps, until it reaches the unison A again. The beginning and end are *pp*, while the E flat in the middle is *ff* and reiterated several times, thus stressing its importance.

249

Second Movement, *Allegro*

This is completely different from the first movement. It is in neo-classical style, tonally conceived with C major as its key centre, and in sonata form. Its rich orchestral colouring and harmonies at times remind one of Richard Strauss, though part of the development section (187–242) certainly shows the influence of Stravinsky. Yet it is unmistakably Bartókian; and many of its themes bear a resemblance to the fugal theme of the first movement.

Four bars of *pizzicato* introduction in the second orchestra lead to the first subject in the first orchestra. The first two notes of the introduction, a rising anacrusic minor third, have an affinity with the second and third notes of the fugue subject; and they become a motto theme for the movement, their two anacrusic notes, though often becoming a fourth or even larger interval, being frequently interjected into the texture. The first subject itself has an even closer resemblance to the fugue theme, though the intervals between the first three notes are changed round.

The first subject is vigorously tossed from one string orchestra to the other, and ends at 18–19 with an unequivocal dominant tonic in. C major.

The transition starts at 19, with the entry of the piano. There are frequent interjections of the motto, soon producing counter-rhythms between the two orchestras; and a new figure grows out of them at 32, still bearing a resemblance to the fugue subject, which passes from one instrument to another, *scherzando*, over a repeated A flat in the timpani. At 40 the motto begins to be tossed from one instrument to another in close stretto, sometimes alone, at other times as the beginning of a longer phrase. This works up to a climax, ending with a *ff* F sharp C sharp in the timpani at 65–6, and followed by a general pause.

The second subject starts at 69 with a *leggiero* theme in the first violins centred on G, the dominant of the movement. The motto rhythm has now become a major seventh, and the theme is very angular, though it still bears a peculiar resemblance to the fugue subject. It is transferred to the bass at 77.

A second section of the second subject, still bearing this curious resemblance to the fugue theme, starts at 94, and is passed from upper to lower strings and back again in ever-continuing cross-rhythms.

The third section starts at 110, with a *forte* unison figure in the first orchestra at 115 against semiquavers running round E flat (the climax note of the first movement) in the second orchestra, and with a peculiar *pizzicato* effect in the first orchestra's double bass, combined with a roll on the side drum.

The fourth section starts at 128 with a theme in the second orchestra which bears an even closer resemblance to the fugue subject. The first orchestra interjects the motto rhythm from 139 onwards, and continues with this after the second orchestra has practically ceased.

The fifth section starts at 155 with a rhythmic figure in the piano, again with peculiar *pizzicato* effects, this time in the second orchestra. The motto rhythm is heard, starting at 167, soon alternating between *arco* and *pizzicato*, and with the celesta joining in, ending at 175 in vigorous syncopation. Syncopated *ff* chords of G major (the dominant) at 180–2 bring the exposition to an end.

The development section starts with repeated Gs in the timpani, getting softer until they end with a glissando on to B flat, an effect which only a mechanical drum can produce. This G–B flat is the motto figure, which is then passed to the 'cellos, played *portamento*, and it starts a peculiar arpeggio of ten *pizzicato* quavers, divided into two sets of five, and based on the introduction to the movement. These move continuously from one instrument to another; and as the time is 2/4, they cut across the metric rhythm and thus start on a different part of the bar at the later entries. The harp joins in with the same figure at 196.

Then, at 199, the piano, playing *f staccato* chords, and the first orchestra playing the same chords *pizzicato* in such a way that the strings hit the fingerboard, add to the texture a variant of the fugue subject, treated inversely. Notice that they again emphasise E flat, the climax note of the first movement. They play in a syncopated cross-rhythm, and the side drum and bass drum add occasional notes while, at 220, the xylophone effectively joins in with the inverted fugue subject variant.

This extraordinary combination of the two cross-rhythms, with its wonderfully piquant orchestration continues up to 242; and this is the passage that bears evidence of Stravinsky's colourful influence.

The climax is reached at 220 and then the music gradually dies down to 242, where the next section starts. This consists of a quieter version of the continuous quavers, the other theme having vanished; and now they play *pizzicato* in the ordinary way, with imitative entries. Soon there are continuous changes of time-signature, and everyone is playing quavers, rising and falling independently. The harp enters effectively at 287 with the two-note motto figure, now descending a fourth, high up above the continuous quavers and, by 298, the figure is being taken up, portamento, by the lower strings.

Then, at 302, the timpani plays a repeated F, while hints of the first subject appear in the lower strings. The timpani F continues in various rhythms as a pedal up to 338, where it ends with another glissando third. During this time *pp* muted semiquaver variants of the first subject appear imitatively in the lower strings, gradually building up to the violins, with continually changing time-signatures.

By 339, where the F pedal point ends, imitative entries of the first subject appear, combined with frequent interpolations of the motto figure, in which the timpani join at 359. The violins of the second orchestra play a theme which grows out of these two notes at 366, and this leads, *allargando*, to the recapitulation at 373.

The recapitulation is condensed, and the themes are often rhythmically transformed, there being even more rhythmic irregularities. But it follows roughly the same plan as the exposition: first subject, 373; transition, starting over a dominant pedal at 385, but now 3/8 instead of 4/8; second subject, now centred on C, the tonic, still in 3/8, with its first section starting at 413, its second section 429, third section 450, fourth section 458 and fifth section 480.

The coda starts at 490 with a variant of the first subject in the tonic key. Each orchestra has it in turn, *allegro molto*, until they combine at 506; and a very discordant passage starts at 510, which is 'brought to heel' with reiterations of dominant tonic in timpani and piano to finish the movement.

Third Movement, *Adagio*

The third movement is in quite a different style again; and yet it is still unmistakably by Bartók. It bears frequent references to the fugal theme.

It is an example of modern expressionism, full of the most extraordinary effects, often three, four or five combined at the same time. It is on the plan **A B C B A**, with the fugue theme acting as a link between each section.

It opens with a single, high, repeated F on the xylophone, joined three bars later by the mechanical timpani, glissandoing from B down to F sharp. The extremes of pitch are noticeable, as are also the contrasted tonalities of F and F sharp, which begin and end the movement. But notice, also, that against the F sharp the timpani and double bass play C, producing the tritone once more. The timpani C lasts for twelve bars, with occasional digressions to F sharp, and the very last note of the movement is C. So: is the beginning and end bi-tonal, with F and F sharp as keynotes, or is it really C, with the tritone taking the place of the more usual tonic chord?

At bar 6 the viola starts a plaintive, arabesque-like melody, beginning with a falling minor third. This is the first theme, **A**, and it continues in the strings against the extreme sounds of the xylophone and timpani.

At 18 the violas and 'cellos have a brief reference to the fugue theme, as a link to the next section, **B**, which consists of *five* different, unusual sound effects. It starts with *pp* discordant muted trills on four different notes in the violins of the second orchestra. Then the violins of the first orchestra enter with muted glissando sevenths, while the piano has the same sevenths as *staccato* chords. Then the celesta and two solo violins from the first orchestra enter with a chromatic, tortuous melody, which is reminiscent of the fugue theme, while the 'cellos play *pp tremolos* on the same sevenths that are being played by the piano and the glissando violins. The violin and celesta melody, the *staccato* piano chords, the violin glissandos, the 'cello *tremolos*, and the muted violin trills are all five unusual impressionistic effects, and they are combined to produce the most extraordinary colour. The glissando timpani and the high notes on the xylophone join in at 31, and E flat once more becomes the prominent note, as it was in the first two movements.

Another brief reference to the fugal theme in the strings at 33–4 again acts as a link to the next section, **C**, which consists of harp and piano glissandos, with fast runs in the celesta, and *flautando tremolos* in the strings playing a variant of the fugue subject and producing a flute-like tone by drawing the bow lightly over the strings near the bridge. All these four strange effects are combined to produce yet another weird effect. They build up to a climax at 45.

Now a variant of the fugue theme appears in a much longer link passage, starting *forte* in celesta, harp and piano, then transferring to the strings, *ff*. At 48 the figure is heard backwards and at 50 in diminution. It builds up to a *crescendo* tutti, but then gradually quietens down until only the strings are left.

Now Bartók returns on his tracks. The next section is a combination of **B** and **C** in yet a new guise. The theme that was played by the two solo violins and the celesta in **B** is now played by all the strings, while the celesta runs from **C** accompany it, and the harp and piano have a peculiar trill effect which is new but is reminiscent of the string trills in **B**.

The fugue theme appears briefly as a link once more at 73–4; and finally **A** reappears at 76, with the first violins starting the arabesque theme, answered by second violins and then sinking down to the violas, where it was at the beginning of the movement, while the timpani has its glissandos from D down to A. Finally the viola sinks to rest on F sharp while the xylophone plays the high F with which it began. At the end the timpani quietly adds the C to bring the movement home to rest.

Fourth Movement, *Allegro molto*

The fourth movement is an exciting vigorous movement, using a number of Hungarian-style melodies, and at times some barbaric rhythmic effects which again remind one of Stravinsky. But there are several reminders of the fugal theme, and it appears near the end in a *molto espressivo* version.

The movement returns to A for its key centre, and it starts with exciting *pizzicato* chords in A major, over which a Hungarian-style melody, **A**, soon appears. But even this has a resemblance to the fugue theme, though it now falls before it rises, and it is more diatonic and straightforward rhythmically. The melody moves from the second string orchestra to the first, while the other orchestra continues the *pizzicato* chords. A second phrase starts at 15, which is freely imitated between various string instruments, in ever closer stretto.

An ostinato on D flat and A flat in the timpani starts at 26 and continues up to 44. Over this a new theme, **B**, appears in the piano which, after the first few repeated notes, moves chromatically like the fugue theme. Against it there are striding *pizzicato* fourths in both string orchestras, producing linear harmony. The piano theme transfers to the strings at 36, and leads into a return of **A** in the second orchestra at 44, answered by the first orchestra as before.

But the last note is omitted and the theme ends with a pause at the end of 51. This is followed by a strongly reiterated syncopated B flat, over which a new theme, **C**, appears, *ff* in the first orchestra. It is interrupted by the tritone in the timpani at 62–3, reaching E flat which is strongly reiterated, as it has been so often before, in this work. The theme, **C**, continues in the second orchestra, while the first orchestra holds or repeats the E flat.

The E flat changes to A flat at 70 and this leads to another repetition of **A**, which starts in the piano but changes to tutti strings at 78.

So far, the shape has been rondo-like, as befits a folk-style. But now a series of new themes appear, one after another. They start with an ostinato effect of the chord of E flat (stressed yet again), played by harp and two pianos, the cellos playing it *con legno* and the basses *pizzicato*, the whole producing a novel and unusual effect. Over this the violas play a theme, **D**, which is, in effect, a scale of E flat. It is transferred to the violins at 90, while more of the strings play *con legno*. This builds up to another climax at 103, again on E flat, after which the theme, **D**, continues more quietly, now sometimes descending as well as ascending the scale.

At 114 a new section, **E**, starts in which a contrasted bar of melody in the piano, reminiscent of the fugal theme, is contrasted with the ascending and descending scales of **D**.

At 124, *tempo primo*, a new variant of the melodic bar from **E** appears in close canon in various string instruments, **F**. It is based on fourths and therefore reminds one of the *pizzicato* fourths which accompanied the melody, **B**, at 28. It is also combined with the scales, so the texture is very complicated here. A new melody grows out of this at 130, which is also developed in close canon. Bars 123–35, **F**, are really therefore entirely development of previous material.

Bar 136 starts yet another section, **G**. It is another ostinato, starting over alternating chords of C and C flat (B), which begins quietly and builds up a tremendous *crescendo*, *stringendo* up to 180. During its course the ostinato semitonal chords gradually rise in pitch, the orchestras alternate, the piano adds *martellato* discords, the harp adds glissandos at 171, and at 174 the xylophone adds a crotchet theme reminiscent of the fugue subject.

This merges into another section, **H**, in which the xylophone chromatic melody emerges clearly as a variant of the fugal theme, *vivacissimo*. It is also played by the harp, and soon the two string orchestras are playing it antiphonally. The time has now become as irregular as it was in the first movement. The piano interrupts four times with E A, played *ff*, as if trying to bring order out of chaos, and re-establishing the main tonality of A.

This leads to a clear statement of a variant of the fugal theme at 204. It is played *molto espressivo* by both orchestras, the original and the inverted forms being combined at 210. It also appears in close imitations at 215. At 219 there are rising stretti, at 221 falling stretti. Gradually the theme dies down, with continuing imitations, until a 'cello solo interrupts with a cadenza at 232–4.

After this the fugue theme continues in stretto until it leads to a *calmo* version of **A** in even crotchets. But four bars later **A** returns in its original form and speed, as a recapitulation to the whole movement. Imitations of it continue, and it reaches a climax at 262–4, after which it gradually sinks, with continuing imitations.

At 276 **A** is transformed into a high *cantabile* melody over a series of sevenths. But, after reaching its climax at 282, *largo*, it ends very abruptly *in tempo*, on a chord of A major.

47 Stravinsky

The Soldier's Tale

Students will presumably study this work with the aid of the Chester miniature score and the gramophone record. But the teacher should also obtain the libretto (with the English translation by Michael Flanders and Kitty Black), also published by Chester. The score alone gives little indication of the story; and the libretto is required to see the stage directions and also to discover how the record and the score fit together. A piano arrangement is also available.

Stravinsky, born near Leningrad in 1882, was the son of a famous opera singer. He studied law until he was twenty-three, but then came under the influence of Rimsky-Korsakov, who helped and encouraged him as a composer. And in a surprisingly short time he had become famous.

He first made his name in collaboration with his fellow Russian, Diaghileff, who produced a wonderful series of Russian ballets in Paris before the 1914 war. Stravinsky wrote *The Fire Bird*, *Petroushka* and *The Rite of Spring* for his Russian ballet company. These works used a large orchestra, were very discordant, but also very vivid and full of colour.

During this period Stravinsky had acquired the habit of living in Switzerland every winter, returning to his country home in Russia in the summer. When the 1914 war broke out he stayed in Switzerland, and soon found himself in straitened circumstances, because no money could reach him from Russia.

So, together with a few friends in equal pecuniary difficulties, he thought of producing works for a small travelling theatre which could pay its way in Switzerland. *The Soldier's Tale* was the first result.

It was planned for a stage divided into three. On one side was a narrator, sitting on a stool in front of a small table on which was a jug of white wine; on the other, the small orchestra, consisting of a violin, a double bass, a clarinet, a bassoon, a cornet, a trombone, and one percussion player who had to be prepared to play a whole battery of percussion instruments. This was a most unusual combination, but very well thought out, because it gives a surprising range of pitch and tone quality for its size.

Stravinsky intended the narrator and the small orchestra to be seen, just as much as the play that was being enacted in the middle of the stage, thinking that this would facilitate auditory perception. He wanted the same set-up when his choreographic cantata *The Wedding* was produced by Diaghileff in Paris after World War I, but Diaghileff would not agree.

The story of *The Soldier's Tale* is based on a Russian folk tale, as were so many of Stravinsky's early works. His friend, Ramuz, took one of Afanassiov's collection and made a libretto from it. It concerns a soldier who deserted, as frequently happened in the cruel period of enforced recruitment under Nicholas I, and who sold his soul to the devil. It has something in common with Rip van Winkle and with Faust, for the soldier sells his soul in return for all kinds of worldly power; but he also teaches the devil to play the violin, and when he returns from his visit to the devil ten years have elapsed, and everyone in his village shuns him.

The soldier has a speaking part, the devil speaks and dances, and the Princess, whom the soldier eventually marries, dances only. The rest of the story is carried on by the narrator.

The first performance took place in Lausanne on 28 September 1918. Stravinsky's friend, Ansermet, conducted. It was a fine performance, but then the 'Spanish 'flu', that swept through Europe, hit performers and audience alike, and no more performances were possible in the immediate future. Stravinsky later arranged the work for piano, violin and clarinet, as a suite.

Part I

Before the curtain rises, the orchestra plays a soldier's march during which the narrator speaks through the music, describing the soldier tramping home for his ten days' leave. The martial element is obtained by giving the theme to the cornet and the trombone, with the double bass providing the tramping effect at first. By figure 8 all the instruments have entered; and at 10, the climax, the clarinet plays the melody, very high and shrill. But at 13 the dynamics drop suddenly, as the narrator tells how the soldier is nearing home; and the tune is given to the bassoon with string accompaniment. Just after 14 the curtain rises, showing the soldier tramping now to the accompaniment of the percussion only. He stops as the music stops.

Notice the frequent changes of time-signature in this introductory number, in spite of its being called a march. Stravinsky may be

259

attempting to show that the soldier is marching erratically, as he is tired and by himself. Or it may be that the irregular rhythms and the discordant effects are no more than Stravinsky's natural way of expressing himself.

The soldier is by the bank of a stream. He acts the part as the narrator tells how he throws off his pack and rummages through it, eventually finding his old fiddle.

The soldier speaks for the first time, saying that the fiddle did not cost much. But he tunes it up and begins to play to the music of 'Airs by the Stream' (p. 7 of the Chester score, called 'Music to Scene I'). All the first part of this number is played by violin and bass alone, and sounds like someone improvising badly on a bad fiddle.

Between 5 and 6 the curtain is supposed to fall, and when it rises again the devil appears, unseen by the soldier. He is represented by the clarinet, just as the soldier is represented by the fiddle. When, at the end of the number, the devil steps up to the soldier he stops playing suddenly, running the bow across the open strings.

Then follows a dialogue in which the devil bargains with the soldier, exchanging his fiddle for a mysterious book that can foretell the future. But the devil cannot play the fiddle and eventually persuades the soldier to come to his home and teach him how to play it.

The curtain falls and the narrator tells of the journey, of the time spent with the devil and of the journey back to the side of the stream again. To show this return the introductory march is played again as far as 6, with the narrator speaking the same words through it as before, and ending as at 15.

The narrator then continues the story, with the curtain still down, telling of the soldier's return to the village, where everyone shuns him. According to the libretto he has been away for three years instead of three days, but the gramophone record says ten years instead of ten days. This is the Rip van Winkle element in the story. The soldier despairingly wonders what he is going to do.

When the curtain rises again the village is seen, with the devil disguised as a cattle merchant, leaning on his cane in the middle of the stage. The 'Pastorale' (p. 11 of the Chester score, called 'Music to Scene II') is played, and gives an impression of waiting—the devil silently watching for the soldier who is in despair. Plaintive phrases are played on the clarinet, bassoon and cornet, with occasional subdued chords underlying them on the fiddle.

The music stops just before 6. The soldier enters, sees the devil, rushes at him and calls him a dirty cheat. Eventually the devil persuades him to take the book 'worth a fortune' out of his pack and leads him away. The stage is empty and the plaintive music continues (6 at the bottom of p. 12). The curtain falls.

The narrator takes up the story, telling how the soldier became rich. But soon he realises that the things he can buy are valueless. At this point the music on p. 13 of the score comes in as a background. It is similar to 'Airs by the stream' on p. 7, and the narrator speaks through it, describing the joys of the simple life. As the music ends the narrator tells how the soldier realises he has nothing—'What can I do to be as I used to be?'

The curtain rises, showing the soldier sitting at his desk, and looking at his book. He says he is dead inside to the world outside, and throws the book to the ground. The devil, dressed as an old clothes woman, first peeps in and then enters, and in a falsetto voice offers the soldier various things which he refuses. Then he offers the fiddle. The soldier siezes it, but discovers he cannot play it. He hurls it away, the devil disappears, and p. 13 of the score is played once again, as the soldier returns to his desk. He picks up the book, tears it to pieces, the curtain falls and the music ends.

Part II

Part II starts with the music on p. 14 of the score, which is the same as the opening of Part I as far as 3, and then goes on to the equivalent of 8–9 of the opening march. The narrator then starts speaking through the music—a varied form of the original 4–6—as before.

The music stops and the narrator explains (on p. 23 of the libretto) that the soldier is running away. The music starts again, continuing the first 'Soldier's March' from 10–12, on pp. 17 and 18 of the score.

The music stops again and the narrator tells how the soldier has reached another land, where a princess lies ill. Whoever cures the princess will be able to marry her, and the soldier decides to try his luck.

The 'Royal March' on p. 19 of the score starts. It has a certain rhythmic resemblance to the 'Soldier's March' at the beginning of part I, but is much grander and noiser, with the trombone and the cornet having the tune most of the time; though, in the quieter parts, the bassoon has a turn.

At 14 the curtain rises to the rat-a-tat of the side drum, and a room in the palace is seen. The devil is there, dressed as a virtuoso violinist, but the curtain falls again at 19, just before the end of the March.

All the lights in the theatre go out. The narrator has lit two candles on his table, and he shuffles a pack of cards as he tells how the soldier asks to see the princess. When the curtain rises the soldier too, is sitting at a table with two candles and a similar pack of cards, with the dimly-lit room of the palace in the background. He shuffles the cards, wondering if he will have any luck. But the devil appears once more and taunts him, and the soldier hangs his head in silence.

Suddenly the narrator turns round and speaks directly to the soldier, telling him to allow the devil to win at cards, until he has nothing left belonging to the devil: in this way he will be free. The soldier takes his advice, making the stakes higher and higher and losing all the time. He forces the devil to drink the wine, the devil sways and then slowly sinks to the ground. The narrator tells the soldier to take back his own again. The soldier takes the fiddle and begins to play as the curtain falls.

Now follows the 'Little Concert', p. 30 in the score, using the rhythmic figure that has been associated with the soldier in the past in 'Airs by the Stream'. The cornet has the theme at first, but the fiddle is being tuned-up on its open strings, and at Fig. 2 the violin takes over the theme. The violin plays throughout the number, though the other instruments often play little descants over it. At 22 the narrator begins to talk through the music and the lights go up, as he tells how the soldier is going to bring the princess back to life.

The curtain rises, showing the princess's bedroom, brilliantly lit. The soldier plays his fiddle and she turns towards him. According to the libretto the curtain falls again and the following three dances are danced by a ballet in front of the curtain, after which it rises again, showing the princess and the soldier in each other's arms. But according to the score the curtain remains up, the princess rises from her couch and begins to dance at 4 on p. 40, presumably continuing to dance until the end of 'Ragtime', when the curtain falls.

But, whichever is the case, the violin comes into its own in these three dances; and now it no longer sounds like a badly played, second-rate fiddle but produces a virtuosic performance. One can see the point of Stravinsky's wish for the instrumentalists to be seen, for it certainly helps the story to see the violinist fiddling away during the dances.

In the Tango the violin has a wayward, low and languid theme, to the accompaniment of peculiar percussion effects described in French at the bottom of p. 39 of the score; in the Waltz the violin has a higher and more tuneful theme, with the bass providing the main accompaniment; and in the Ragtime percussion effects again come to the fore, use being made of the triangle, tambourine and side drums without snares. But all the other instruments take turns in accompanying the violin, too, producing strange effects. The violin sounds very improvisatory, in the style of ragtime.

Then the devil enters, this time dressed as a devil and crawling on all-fours. He circles round the soldier, trying to snatch his violin, and the princess hides behind the soldier.

But then the soldier begins to play his violin to the music of p. 51 of the score, 'The Devil's Dance'. The devil is forced to dance, bewitched, until he falls, exhausted. This is a very noisy dance, using all the instruments, with all kinds of special effects, including muted cornet and trombone playing loudly, and various strange percussion effects. The violin playing is mostly hard and brilliant, and the time is very irregular.

The princess has lost her fear. She dances round the devil, and eventually she and the soldier drag him, by his paws, into the wings.

The lovers fall into each other's arms, and the 'Little Chorale' on p. 56 is played, the cornet having the melody. This, and the melody in the following Great Chorale have a resemblance to 'A safe Stronghold our God is still'.

But the devil suddenly pops his head round the door, and speaks through the music of 'The Devil's Song', pp. 56–8, saying that if once they should pass the frontier they will be in his power again. Trombone and cornet, the devil's instruments, play little counter-themes, but the devil is mostly accompanied by *pizzicato* strings, with some percussion towards the end. The curtain falls.

Then the 'Great Chorale' on p. 59 is played, and the narrator speaks through the pauses at the ends of the lines, telling the soldier he must not seek for more. But the princess says she would like to see the soldier's home, and they decide to travel there. The devil passes in front of the curtain, wearing a magnificent scarlet costume, while the narrator is speaking.

Then the curtain rises, showing the village and the frontier post. The soldier crosses the frontier as the devil appears, playing the violin once more. 'The triumphant March of the Devil' is played (p. 61 of the score) as the soldier slowly follows him without resisting. Cornet, trombone and percussion are much in evidence as the violin plays the familiar, irregular march theme. Gradually the music dies down until little is left but percussion and the violin. The princess is heard calling the soldier in the distance, but the soldier slowly follows the devil off the stage, to the sound of the percussion alone, as the curtain falls.

48 Stravinsky

Petroushka

Diaghileff, the creator of the Russian Ballet that toured Europe in the five years before the 1914 war, quickly realised that Stravinsky was an ideal composer for his ballet. The first Stravinsky ballet produced by Diaghileff was *The Fire Bird* in 1910 and this was followed by *Petroushka* in 1911 and *The Rite of Spring* in 1913. All three were first produced in Paris. *The Rite of Spring* nearly caused a riot because of its subject, involving the sacrifice of a young girl in pagan rites, and its harsh musical idioms. But *Petroushka* was immediately successful and has frequently been played as a ballet ever since. Stravinsky chose to be buried near Diaghileff when he died in 1971.

These three ballets were the first works that brought Stravinsky fame in Western Europe and were all scored for a large orchestra. *Petroushka* was originally written for quadruple wood-wind, but the 1947 version, which is usually played today, is written for a slightly smaller orchestra, requiring triple wood-wind; and various instruments receive more individual attention.

During and after the 1914–18 war Stravinsky began to write for smaller groups of instruments, often in unusual combinations and in concertante style; but these first ballets remain as examples of exciting and unusual uses of a large orchestra.

Grove states that *Petroushka* grew out of a work originally intended for piano and orchestra, the piano representing a mischievous puppet playing tricks to provoke the orchestra to suitable retaliation. It was Diaghileff who suggested turning it into a ballet in which puppets performed in a fair ground in Admiralty Square, St Petersburg, during Carnival week. Admiralty Square is surely one of the most enormous squares in the world, and it requires little imagination to see the crowds milling around it, with the little puppet theatre in the centre.

It has been said that *Petroushka* is the first of Stravinsky's works to reveal true originality, with the burlesque sections being the most original. Certainly it is full of striking scoring, and the music makes the most effective background for a ballet. The piano is still a very important part of the scoring, as was the original intention.

The Columbia record issued for Stravinsky's eightieth birthday, conducted by himself, has an account of the circumstances surrounding the writing and the first performance of *Petroushka*, written by the composer. The work was composed in Switzerland and the French Riviera, with a visit to St Petersburg in the middle to study the setting with Benois, who designed the décor. Then all the collaborators met in Rome for final decisions, and the work was produced at the Châtelet Theatre in Paris on 13 June 1911.

Scene I The Shrove-tide Fair: Day Time

There are places in this score where the intentions with regard to the choreography are obvious. Otherwise a good deal of variation is possible; and we know that Stravinsky was not very happy about the original choreography by Fokine, so it seems unwise to attempt to interpret the music in too much detail. It is easy to imagine the crowd at the Shrove-tide Fair in this first scene, and there seem endless possibilities for choreographic interpretation.

The main theme at the opening is played by the flutes in an irregular rhythm, accompanied at first by *tremolos* in clarinets and horns and then by a semiquaver figure in strings, piano and harp. The flutes, accompanied by the piccolo and the piano, are soon playing in septuplets and quintuplets, in 3/4 time. Stravinsky, at eighty, said he was still pleased with this opening.

The second main theme appears at figure 7. It is a heavy, tutti, chordal theme, doubtless intended to portray the organ grinder, with the peasants dancing and stamping to it.

It is interrupted three bars before 13 by a chord on the horns and trombones, followed by a downward run in the piano and the timpani drumming out an augmented fourth; and then by a figure in the strings, in a mixture of 3/8 and 5/8 rhythm, not unlike the figure between 3 and 6. These rhythmic irregularities are a feature of much of Stravinsky's music.

The first theme returns at 16 but is again interrupted at 17; and at 18 there is a hint of the third main theme in the clarinets, which is based on a Russian folk song and is probably meant to be played by the itinerant musician. But the interruption occurs again at 19.

Then, at 22, more of the Russian folk song appears in the clarinets, but it is interrupted at 23 by the fourth main theme, a simple, dance-like rhythm played by flutes and clarinets with a triangle accompaniment, probably meant to be danced by the street ballerina.

The Russian folk song theme reappears at 26, and the ballerina's theme at 28, but the interruption occurs again at 30, 31 and 32, finally leading to a recurrence of the first main theme at 33 and the second theme at 36. This feels recapitulatory. Stravinsky quite often uses recapitulations, but we know that he had little use for development sections.

The interruptive figure occurs four times more, at 42, 46, 48 and 50, with the first theme recurring at 45 and 53; and the latter works up to a climax which is interrupted at 56 by a noisy, drumming figure, as the two drummers emerge from the puppet theatre and the showman comes from behind the curtain.

Extraordinary chromatic chords appear in the bassoons at 58, taking one into another world. The Showman plays a cadenza on the flute at 60 and, to more chromaticisms in the strings at 61, opens the curtains, showing the three compartments containing the lifeless puppets. Stravinsky calls this the sleight-of-hand trick. The Showman animates each puppet in turn, to the sound of two notes on the flute and piccolo at 63.

Then follows the 'Danse Russe' at 64, in which the three puppets dance. After all the previous rhythmic irregularity this has a simple and regular 2/4 rhythm. One might have thought that each of the puppets would have its own theme, to be identified with them later in the ballet, but this is not so. They dance together; and, although

Stravinsky tells us that Petroushka attempts to express his love for the Ballerina, it looks as if the choreographic interpretation is free until Petroushka unmistakably attacks his rival, the Moor, at 88, and they are all ordered back to their cells.

There are two main themes in the Russian Dance. The first one appears at 64. The second one, appearing at 66, is divided between flutes, trumpets, clarinets and oboes, each taking a few notes in snatches. The first theme returns at 80, rather more lightly scored, and quietens down to a solo clarinet and a cor anglais at 81, presumably providing an opportunity for love making.

But the piano noisily returns to the first theme at 82, and soon the whole orchestra takes it up until the harsh chords, representing the rivals attacking each other, occur at 88, and all are ordered back to their cells. The two drummers appear again as the curtains close.

Scene II Petroushka's Cell

This starts with Petroushka being kicked into his cell, followed by the Showman's chromatic harmonies just before 94. There is a pause as Petroushka lies on the floor. The clarinets then play in two keys at 95, which Stravinsky intended as Petroushka's insults to the public; and this is followed by a piano cadenza representing Petroushka's convulsive movements as he lies on the floor.

The second theme occurs at 100 in muted, *fff* trumpets. It is an inversion of the first theme at 95, and represents Petroushka beating the walls with his fists, as he tries to escape from his cell. This again ends with a pause.

The third theme occurs at 102, as the Ballerina enters. It is a delicate theme, played by flutes, clarinets and piano, with many acciaccaturas. She daintily flutters about at 103.

The fourth theme appears at 104 in the cor anglais, as Petroushka clumsily attempts to make love to the Ballerina. The fifth theme, at 105, is the Ballerina's reply in the flute. This section ends with some plaintive, discordant chords in the solo piano, two bars before 108.

But an *allegro* starts at 108 in which the Ballerina is represented by the wood-wind, piano and harp, while the pathetic Petroushka is heard in the brass. This section builds up rapidly, until a *ff* chromatic variant of Petroushka's arpeggio theme is heard in the clarinet at 112, accompanied by syncopated brass.

In the next few bars Petroushka pleads in the cor anglais against the Ballerina's petulant arpeggios in the piano. She runs back into her cell, and we hear Petroushka's angry arpeggios in the trumpets at 116. At 118 the bi-tonal effect is heard again in the clarinets and the curtain falls as the drummers reappear.

Scene III The Moor's Cell

Stravinsky states that the Moor lazily tries to cut a coconut in half and, being unable to do so, bows before it.

Then his main theme appears at 125 in clarinet and bass clarinet, a most peculiar effect. Notice also the low, hollow effect of 'cellos and basses playing *sul ponticello* at 127. His main theme returns at 132 and continues until the Ballerina enters at 134 to a side-drum roll. She carries a toy trumpet which she plays at 135.

She begins to dance to the 'Valse' theme starting at 140 and this is followed by a second theme at 143. The Moor clumsily attempts to join in at 144, his theme appearing in the cor anglais and double bassoon. They continue together up to 148, when a few link bars lead to the recapitulation of the first valse theme, with the Moor having little interjections in the cor anglais and horn.

This is interrupted at 151 by Petroushka bursting in, his arpeggio theme being heard in trombones and trumpets. An *agitato* section starts at 153, during which the Ballerina faints, and Petroushka and the Moor fight, Petroushka's theme being heard in two keys, as before (156). He is kicked out at 156 and 158, and the triumphant Moor takes the Ballerina on his knee, as the curtain falls to the sound of the drum roll. Stravinsky, at eighty, said he was particularly pleased with the end of this scene.

Scene IV The Shrove-tide Fair: Evening

This last scene is divided into sections, thus indicating what is happening on the stage more than in the other scenes.

The first part has no particular themes, but gives an impression of crowds and bustling excitement. This is produced by *tremolo* effects and sudden arpeggios in harp and piano, with trumpet calls and xylophone glissandos soon added to the texture.

At 164 a quintuplet figure appears in piccolo and piano and is clearly heard above the rest of the orchestra. At 165 it is transferred to horns and at 166 to oboes and then to trumpets. Stravinsky, at eighty, expressed his pleasure at the effect of these quintuplets.

At 167 triplets in the strings and horns, slurred in twos, are heard against sextolets in the wood-wind, thus producing even more excitement, but by 169 only the triplets are left, and they lead into the first dance.

WET NURSE'S DANCE This starts with a chattering effect produced by *staccato* wind figures, *pizzicato* lower strings, and *marcato* quavers in the violins. The Nannies' first theme appears at 171 in the oboe and is taken up by the horns one bar after 173; and, a bar before 175, the violins join in.

At 178 the slurred quavers and *pizzicato* strings return, as a preliminary to the second theme, which starts at 181 in the clarinets, transferring to the trumpet at 183 and to the violins and wood-wind at 184.

Slurred quavers again at 185 lead to the return of the second theme in the horns, soon joined by the first theme in the strings. Then, at 187, the first theme is played by the trombones, while strings and wood-wind play the first theme.

PEASANT WITH BEAR The peasant plays a quick irregular figure in the clarinet while the bear, walking along on his hind legs, is indicated by lumbering minims in the bassoon and double bassoon with an occasional grunt on the tuba.

By 191 the general bustle from the beginning of the scene has returned, and leads to the next dance.

GYPSIES AND A RAKE VENDOR A Merchant is on the spree with two gypsy girls. He distributes bank notes to the crowd, and then, taking an accordion from a street player, begins to play it while the gypsies dance.

The Merchant's swaggering theme is heard immediately, in unison strings. The gypsies' theme appears at 199 in oboe and cor anglais, against an accordion-like effect in piano and harp. Soon the gypsies are playing a tambourine. The Merchant's theme returns at 206, followed by the gypsies again at 209.

DANCE OF THE COACHMEN This is a heavy, lumbering dance, with stampings. The theme appears in the trumpets just after 216; and after four notes it is transferred to *pizzicato* strings. From there it moves to the trombones, then to the horns, and then back to the strings again at 218. A few bars of syncopation at 219 lead to the return of the theme at 220, in the brass.

At 223 the Nannies re-enter in the clarinets with their first theme, which is transferred to unison strings at 225.

A *ff* tutti at 228 leads to the Coachmen's theme again at 229 in the brass. From 228 to the end of this dance there is a continuous pedal on E.

MASQUERADERS This starts quietly with discords in piano and harp, followed by chromatic sextolets in the violins, creating the effect of masked figures fluttering about. But soon the brass start a stamping effect again, which is followed by repeated quaver chords in the strings at 239.

A hint of the Masqueraders' theme appears at 240 and again at 241. Then preparatory trills at 242 lead to their theme at 243, in piccolo, flutes and piano, in syncopated 5/8 time.

The music changes to 2/4 at 246, when a theme in the horn is heard against quiet *pizzicato* chords. The latter build up to *ff* at 250 and are interrupted at 251 when the puppets rush in.

THE SCUFFLE Petroushka is heard first on the trumpets, answered by the Moor on the cor anglais. Then Petroushka again appears in two keys in the violins, while the little runs in the wind perhaps represent the Ballerina trying to hold the Moor back. A scuffle breaks out at 256, with Petroushka in the trumpets and the Moor in the cor anglais.

At 257 the strings play *sul ponticello* and then glissando up an octave, while a *ff* octave leap down in piccolo and flutes coincides with the Moor striking Petroushka with his sword. This is followed by a little whimper in piccolo and flute against a cymbal roll; and Petroushka falls, his head broken.

DEATH OF PETROUSHKA This is *lento lamentoso* and consists of *pp tremolo* strings against a pathetic theme in clarinet, solo violin and bassoon.

POLICE AND THE JUGGLER The Police summon the Showman (*staccato* quavers in bassoon), and the Showman appears with his magical chords at 261 in the horns. Divisi strings perhaps signify his reassurance that Petroushka was only a puppet; and, to muted horns, the crowd gradually disperses. The Showman begins to drag the body of the puppet back to the theatre.

APPARITION OF PETROUSHKA'S DOUBLE At 265 the trumpets, in two keys, herald the appearance of Petroushka's ghost, still defying the public in his bi-tonal way. Terrified, the Showman drops the body of the puppet and runs from the scene. The music ends with quiet *pizzicato* single notes, quite unrelated to the preceding key. Stravinsky, at eighty, said he was prouder of this ending than of any part of the score.

There is, however, another ending, marked 'for Concert Performance', in which quiet *tremolos* make a rapid crescendo to a *fff* ending; but it is rarely played, even in a concert performance.

49 Lennox Berkeley

Four Poems of Saint Teresa of Avila

Lennox Berkeley was born in Oxford in 1903 and went to Oxford University. But he only took up music seriously after leaving Oxford, when he studied with Nadia Boulanger in Paris. Much of his early work shows a Parisian influence, whether it be that of French composers, such as Poulenc, or composers of other countries working in Paris, such as Stravinsky.

However, he returned to London before the war, and worked for the BBC during the war, afterwards becoming a professor of composition at the Royal Academy of Music.

He has written music in almost all media, though his best-known works are perhaps those written for the voice, and for piano solo. His form and texture is always transparently lucid, and most of his work has a lovely, lyrical quality, in spite of frequently being very discordant.

St Teresa (1515–82) belonged to a noble family of Avila and joined a Carmelite convent. She was a woman of great ability as well as sanctity and reformed the Carmelite order, opening fourteen new religious houses in Spain. She was canonised in 1622. Her spiritual writings are thought of very highly.

Arthur Symons was a poet who translated many foreign works, such as the sonnets of Michelangelo. He translated the four poems by St Teresa that Lennox Berkeley chose to set for contralto and string orchestra in 1947.

1 'If, Lord, thy love for me is strong'

This poem expresses the passionate longing of the soul for God, and also speaks of the heart-searching which expresses its doubts and fears. It is a dialogue between the two sides of the human personality. There is a stark harshness in the music that seems in keeping with the Spanish temperament; and yet, in spite of all the discords, there is a lucid clarity of texture with no unnecessary notes added. Every melodic part goes its own way, without relation to the other parts; and the singer must surely possess absolute pitch and, in particular, a clear awareness of the difference between tones and semitones, in order to hold her part against the clashes in the orchestra. There are many semitones where tones are expected, and vice versa. But the general effect of the song is most moving.

It begins and ends on B and has a key signature of B minor, though there is little or no feeling for tonality. The first five bars are based on a *ff* B, with semitonal movement above and below it, producing a feeling of passionate discordance. The strings start bar 5 in unison but then move outwards in two-part contrary motion in whole tones until they finally come to rest on B again at 9, as the voice enters.

The singer expresses her love for God in tortured discordance—notice the diminished fourth in 10 and the semitonal return to B at 15–16. The strings join in with syncopated chords, and move in two-part contrary motion again at 16, as the singer cries out 'What holds thee, Lord, so long from me?', reaching a climax at 22 on top F sharp, followed by E flat and then a leap downwards of a minor ninth. The strings in this passage reach a height of intensity, in support of the voice.

As she finishes the phrase the strings reach a unison A, sounding empty after all the intense dissonance, and the questioning heart quietly sings on C natural and then C sharp 'O soul·what then desirest thou?'

The orchestra becomes *più vivo*, making use of a little stepwise descending figure, as the soul answers 'Lord, I would see thee', and the orchestra ends with a harsh discord at 33.

The low, quiet questioning continues 'What fears can yet assail thee now?', on B and C natural, the notes heard in the first bar.

The orchestra takes up the *più vivo* figure again at 37, starting a semitone lower than at 29, as the contralto sings 'All that I fear is but to lose thee'. As she finishes the orchestra builds up a passionate discordant texture, starting over a double pedal, there soon being four independent moving parts. They come together rhythmically, in syncopated chords at 45, and then revert to the *ff* two-part texture at 48.

The singer enters again at 50, over held discords; and the stepwise descending figure she sings at 54 to the words 'And I will build' are taken up by the orchestra in a series of imitations, the orchestral quavers carrying on after she has finished.

Bar 62, marked *tempo primo*, reverts to the semitonal movement round B in the bass, heard at the beginning, but now with chords above it. Then the contralto enters with the final answer in the dialogue: notice the lovely haunting phrase at 'What more desires for thee remain' and the effective triplets at 'All on flame with love within', the whole accompanied by harsh crotchet chords. Then, at 71, the strings rush outwards in semiquavers and she reaches a climax at the words 'Love on'. Her part then gradually sinks down, unaccompanied, to end with the semitone C natural B, as the orchestra takes up the movement round B with which it started the song. Notice the lovely effect of the unexpected concord at the end.

2 'Shepherd, shepherd, hark that calling'

This is a dialogue between a simple shepherd and the poet, and is like a very free rondo in form. The main theme, **A**, is musette-like, with a dance-like decorative double pedal on G and D, over which the poet sings a phrase which sometimes contains the major third, B natural, and at other times the minor third, B flat. She is speaking to the shepherd, telling him that angels are calling. Notice that no 'cellos are playing at this stage.

B starts at 18 with stepwise quavers in the 'cellos and basses under chromatic crotchets in the viola. As the music builds up the shepherd asks 'What is this ding-dong?' The poet answers with **C** at 34, singing 'Come now the day is dawning' *ff* against dancing quavers in the orchestra. Then she reverts to **A**, now in the key of F instead of G, and with violins imitating the voice. By 50 the texture is becoming more elaborate, though *pp*; and it ends with the major third followed by the perfect fourth above the tonic, instead of the minor and major third as before.

The crotchet figure of **B** returns at 62 and the shepherd asks whether it is the Alcalde's (sheriff's) daughter that he is hearing. The poet answers with **D** at 75 'She is daughter of God', and the orchestral part becomes even more ecstatic, with imitative entries at 85–8.

Then **A** returns at 89 in G major again, but with the 'cellos now included in the texture and no basses. A solo violin runs up to top G, *pp*, at the end, as the musette rhythm fades away.

3 'Let mine eyes see Thee'

This is a love song to Jesus with a haunting refrain, consisting of the first two bars of music. It is in a gently-moving triple time, and is more chordal than the other three songs.

The orchestra starts, *pp*, with four bars of the refrain figure. Notice the F natural in bar 1 and the F flat at 2. This pathetic device frequently occurs: see also the C natural and C flat in bars 5–7 and 11–12. The voice enters at 5 with the same refrain figure.

At 13 the refrain figure passes to the violin while the voice sings a contrasting theme over it. Notice the melody at 'Roses and jasmine', which the singer uses again three bars later, after which it is imitated by the violin.

A new section starts at 23, and there are four bars without the refrain figure; but it returns again in the violins at 27, though not in the voice.

The refrain passes to a solo violin and 'cello at 35, while the voice sings an independent melody over it.

Then, at 47, there is a return to bars 4–12. After the singer finishes the first bar of the refrain passes to the 'cellos and basses in the form of a pedal, while the upper strings quietly rise, in a series of discords, until they reach concordance.

4 'Today a shepherd and our kin'

This poem, like No 2, is another dialogue between a shepherd and the poet. The shepherd speaks of God, saying that he is omnipotent and yet of their kin. He asks (44–58) why, if he is omnipotent, he has been crucified. The poet answers (59–69) that, with his dying, sin also died. The shepherd asks two further questions (70–4 and 85–101) which the poet answers (76–83 and 102–30) saying that they should both serve him and die with him, the omnipotent God.

The song reverts to the independent contrapuntal movement of the two earlier songs, again with no unnecessary clumps of notes. It has an affinity with the style of Bach, in that the orchestral part is based on a number of small figures which each appear in turn in different parts of the orchestra, while the voice has a slower-moving independent part, almost in the style of a chorale.

Figure (a) consists of a steady crotchet movement which is heard in the bass from bars 1–40, transferring to the violas at 41–57, to the violins at 58–63, back to the bass at 64–9, to the first violins at 70–3, and to the violas again at 74–5. After a temporary cessation it reappears in the bass at 102–14 and again at 122–7. In other words, it is present almost throughout the song.

The first skipping fragments of figure (b) appear in the violin at 5 and 9, and are heard more fully at 12–15. Figure (c), a quaver stepwise run, appears with imitations at 16–18, followed by (d), a mixture of slurred and *staccato* quavers in second violin and violas at 18–21. Figure (c) reappears in the first violins at 20, followed by (b) at 21 and by (c) inverted at 22, with imitations.

Figure (d) reappears in the upper strings at 26, though now it is entirely *staccato*; (c) and (b) are combined at 33; and (d) enters in the second violins and violas at 35.

As the music becomes more ecstatic, figure (b) with its dance-like rhythm comes more and more to the fore. It appears *marcato* at 39 and then leaps about from 41 onwards in the upper strings, transferring to the lower strings at 59, back to the upper strings again at 64, and to the bass again at 70.

K

All this time the voice has been moving at a slower pace, independently of the strings, though the first two phrases were doubled by viola and second violin. Now (75–101), as the orchestral figures temporarily subside, the instruments begin to double or imitate the voice.

But figures (*a*) and (*b*) return again at 102, as the music reverts to the opening bars. The voice and the accompaniment gradually become more forceful, until the climax is reached in the voice at 122–30, 'For he is God omnipotent', while (*b*) skips about vigorously in the strings.

Then, as a coda, figure (*b*) is heard twice *ff*, followed by a powerful chord. After this, (*b*) gradually quietens down, and the music ends with a softly held discord.

50 Britten

Rejoice in the Lamb

This work, Op 30, was written for a church in Northampton in 1943. It is scored for choir, the usual four vocal soloists and organ.

The words are most unusual for a church cantata. They were written by an eighteenth century poet, Christopher Smart, who was in a mental asylum when he wrote them. The poem is called *Jubilate Agno*, and is in praise of all living creatures from the lamb, the tiger, the cat, the mouse to the flower, and ends with a list of instruments upon which to praise God. Britten has taken extracts from the poem, unifying them with a Hallelujah in the middle and at the end.

The first section starts with a chorus, asking every creature to praise God. It is marked *andante misterioso*, and starts *ppp* with everyone singing a unison C, which does not change until four bars after figure 1 and then, after rising no further than E flat, falls again to the *ppp* C three bars later. Throughout this section the organ holds a pedal C, but also has occasional interjecting discords, at first between the lines of poetry and then gradually building up, starting at one bar after figure 1 to a *forte* discord two bars later, but ending *ppp* with a chord of C major.

The next section, marked *con brio*, has a variety of 4, 5, 6, 7, 8, 9, and even 11 quavers in a bar, and links various old testament heroes with an appropriate animal, asking them all to praise or bless the Lord. The same sort of springy chords accompany them all: Nimrod with the leopard; Ishmael with the tiger; Balaam with his ass; Daniel with the lion; Ithamar with a chamois; Jakim with the satyr; and finally David with a bear. The singers remain in unison until figure 6 when they change to two parts. But they return to unison singing three bars after 7 and only reach four-part harmony at their climax at 8. The whole texture is built over a bass part in the organ, which is either stationary or moves in *staccato* quavers. At first, figure 2, it is built round F; one bar after 4 it changes to C; 5 to A; 6 to B flat; 7 to E flat; and at 8 it returns again to the original F. These notes become the tonic of a key for the time being, and are frequently preceded by their dominant. *Staccato* chords are frequently played above.

This section has frequently had semiquavers running from the tonic by step up to the dominant as, for example, two bars before 3 and five bars after 3 in the voice parts; and after 7, when they 'dance' in the voices and then appear in the organ part, continuing at intervals in the organ until the end of the section.

Now the same figure starts the next section at 9 in dotted notes in the vocal parts to the word 'Hallelujah'. All the four voices have the figure in imitation, while the organ accompanies with the same stepwise movement, more sedately, in even crotchets.

The next section is sung in praise of Smart's cat, Jeoffry, who worships God in her own way. It is a treble solo and is an *andante tranquillo* in A major. The quietly accompanying organ part, mostly on the manuals, makes much use of a stepwise triplet figure; while the treble solo is a development of the stepwise figure previously heard in the last two sections, combined with occasional chordal leaps. But it sounds very different, because A major is so far removed from the keys of C and F that have been predominant so far; and it modulates beautifully to C sharp major at 12. At the end the treble sings in *parlante* style on one note, 'For I am possessed of a cat, surpassing in beauty'; and the music ends in A major, with a final high quiet triplet on the organ.

The next section is an alto solo about the mouse. It starts in D flat major (the remotest possible key from the previous A major), changes to D flat minor at 14 at 'Cat takes female mouse', to E flat major at 15 and returns to D flat major for the last seven bars.

The left hand manual plays a unison melody, doubling that of the singer, while the right hand plays a quick, light, mouse-like accompanying figure in the same rhythm throughout. The main melody is yet another variant of the stepwise movement between the tonic and dominant, but always beginning and ending with a lower dominant, making an anacrusis or a feminine ending.

Next follows a tenor solo about the flowers, in a mixture of 3/4, 4/4 and 5/4 time. It begins and ends in B minor with a modulation to C sharp minor six bars before 17 and to C major one bar before 17. This time the right-hand manual follows the voice, but in broken double thirds, while the pedals play occasional low notes that seem to have very little connection with the rest of the texture, though they help to establish the two modulations by playing their tonics at the beginning each time.

The first phrase of the melody consists of the usual stepwise movement, but lies only between the tonic and mediant; the next phrase rises to the subdominant, and the third to the dominant, so that, by this stage, a variant of the main melody has been established. Notice the melisma on the word 'poetry' near the end.

Now follows a chorus dealing with the poet's own hardships in the asylum. It is *grave ed appassionato* and starts with bare unaccompanied fifths in the chorus, which move to a discordant and unrelated 6/4 chord in the third bar. A disjointed, syncopated melody appears in the organ before the voices continue in discords, ending with the bare fifths *pp* again on 'beside himself'.

The same syncopated melody then reappears in the organ before the voices re-enter at 19, again in bare fifths moving to an unrelated 6/4 chord. Next comes the same organ interruption, followed by the chorus again moving in discords, but this time making a *crescendo* to *forte* on the first inversion of E flat minor.

After an even more discordant interruption on the organ the choir enters *forte* in unison at 20, singing high notes to the words 'For silly fellow'; but they change to discordant harmony again at 'And belongeth neither to me nor to my family', ending in a pathetic unison.

At 21 the four voice parts enter imitatively, accompanied by organ chords following the voice parts over a pedal B. They reach a climax on 'shall deliver me', when the pedal changes to E, but fall again to a bare fourth *ppp* at the end; and the organ finishes the section with its heartbreaking syncopated figure. The use of bare fifths and fourths and 6/4 chords and other discords, and the disjointed organ interruptions all combine to give an effect of unhappiness and derangement.

A short bass recitative comes next. It speaks of four letters and what they stand for, saying that they all represent God. The chorus enters in a *ff* unison at the end.

Now follows a long *vivace* chorus in F major, the same key as the chorus starting at 4, the prevailing key of the contata. It names a number of instruments and says what words they 'rhime' with, though the rhymes are so disconnected as to betray a deranged mind.

A new figure of *soh₁ soh₁ doh me doh soh* is introduced. It is played first by the organ, then in unison by the chorus in F major, followed by the men alone and then by the women alone, in the same key. The organ frequently has gay triplets; and it starts an F pedal at 24 which continues until just before 28. Over this the voices continue with the chordal figure in G major five bars before 25, A flat major five bars before 26, B flat minor one bar before 26, and D major in the basses three bars after 26.

After some stepwise entries the voices enter in unison with the chordal figure again in A major, four bars after 27, and the F pedal ends as the choir repeats long and high Ds and Fs.

At 28 the chordal figure appears *fff* on a chord of B flat major at 'for the trumpet of God', and later soars upwards on a chord of F major at 'and so are all the instruments'. During this time the chordal figure continually appears in the bass in the organ, rising by step in each bar until it reaches a chord of B flat.

Starting at 29 the organ bass part repeats a major triad on B flat up to 30, while the singers imitatively repeat a triad of D minor, accompanied by the right hand manual of the organ, to the words 'For God the Father Almighty plays upon the harp.'

This chorus ends *molto meno mosso*, starting at 30 on a chord of F major, over a pedal F, as 'malignity ceases and the devils themselves are at peace'.

The cantata ends with a Hallelujah which is an exact repetition of 9–11. This means that, although the prevailing key is F major, it ends on a chord of the dominant.

51 Britten

Saint Nicolas

This work was composed in 1948 for the centenary celebrations of Lancing College, Sussex, and is written for tenor, chorus, string orchestra, piano duet, percussion and organ. The words are by Eric Crozier.

St Nicolas, the patron saint of children, would naturally appeal to Britten, who is famous for his love and understanding of children, and for the many works he has written for them.

A mixed chorus, easy enough to be sung by a boys' school, a female chorus which can be sung by a girls' school, string and percussion parts which can be played by school children with a little professional stiffening, are cleverly written so that they can be performed by young people, though the tenor part of St Nicholas requires a professional singer. As with other of Britten's works he also brings in the audience, to sing two hymns.

It is hoped that many schools will muster the forces, either singly or in combination with other schools, and afford to hire a professional tenor and string quartet, so as to let their students learn this work by performing it.

It was first performed at the Aldeburgh Festival; then a month later at Lancing College, with the choirs of three boys' schools and one girls' school.

St Nicolas was the Bishop of Myra in Asia Minor in the fourth century, and was present at the famous Council of Nicaea. His life is surrounded by many miraculous legends. He is the patron saint of children, seamen and travellers, the original of Santa Claus, and the patron saint of Russia and Greece.

I Introduction

This begins in E minor with hollow, slow-moving *pizzicato* chords over which the solo violinist (a professional) plays a very discordant though expressive melody, which seems to have little harmonic connection with the underlying chords, except at the cadences. There are many fourths in the melody, interspersed with sevenths, which are really two fourths added together. (Notice particularly bars 8–12.) The music is held together by a pedal on E which continues until the middle section starts at figure 3.

Notice the melodic line in the bass from bars 20 to 25, which starts by rising and ends by falling by step, beginning and ending on the prevailing E.

The S A T B chorus enters at figure 1. Their parts are easy, though the harmonies are discordant and modern. The pedal

283

continues and the harmonies are a repetition of bars 1–29. But, surprisingly, the violin melody is repeated in its entirety a fifth higher than before—there is so little connection between melody and harmony that it works equally well. The bass part previously noted at bars 20–5 is now sung by the chorus in unison at 'obscure the simple man within the saint'.

Then the chorus objures St Nicolas to 'strip off your glory, Nicolas, and speak'; and this leads to the middle section at figure 3.

The middle section begins and ends in C major and consists of a solo sung by St Nicolas, mostly to the accompaniment of the two pianos, percussion and *tremolo* strings. The striding fourths are heard again in the voice part, aptly illustrating 'Across the tremendous bridge of sixteen hundred years'. The harmonies mainly consist of a series of root position triads, over which occur frequent rising scales in the piano. The voice part, like the violin part in the first section, consists of difficult, discordant intervals, which move independently of the harmonies.

Within this middle section there is a *con moto*, *cantabile* section, preceded by 'Yet still their shining seed of faith survives in you', in which the strings play repeated crotchet chords. But the piano and percussion accompaniment and the leaping vocal fourths return again at 'Preserve the living faith'.

The final section, starting at figure 6, is in A major with a tonic pedal thoughout. The chorus returns and is the same as in the first section except that it is a fourth higher and has two extra bars at 'Strengthen us O Lord'. The harmonies are also the same except that they are a fourth higher. But this time the violin part is a ninth lower than at first, which produces yet a third relationship with the harmonies.

As the chorus comes to an end with its haunting rising and falling stepwise phrase the solo violin is left alone over the tonic pedal, and its rising fourths end on a high A as the pedal dies away.

II The Birth of Nicolas

This tells the story of Nicolas from birth to maturity. It starts with a hesitant introduction of *pizzicato* string chords and speeds up into an *allegretto* at bar 7, which is a mixture of 6/8 and 2/4 time. At first it is in 6/8 with a conventional waltz piano accompaniment based on I and V in A major, with the *pizzicato* chords changing once a bar until the time-signature becomes 2/4, when they occur every beat.

Over this accompaniment the sopranos of a choir of young boys sing a simple little tune in unison. The first note of each bar rises: *d r m fe*; then, after two bars of 2/4 time, when they sing in quavers, which has a *stringendo* effect, they reach *fe* again and this leads to the *soh* on which a boy soloist, representing the boy Nicolas, sings 'God be glorified', to the accompaniment of *pp* organ chords.

Then the altos repeat the sopranos' tune a fourth lower in E major, while the strings add slurred pairs of falling quavers to the accompaniment. The two bars of 2/4 undergo an enharmonic change into A flat major, but they again end on *fe* (D natural in key A flat) which again leads to the cry 'God be glorified' on E, the same note as before.

The sopranos return to their tune in A major, as they continue the story. Now the strings add *arco* dotted minim chords to the waltz accompaniment. And again *fe* leads to the boy Nicolas's 'God be glorified' on E.

Once more the altos take up the story in E major. But this time everyone is playing, though the texture is light, the piano playing little runs representing the gurgling and splashing of the bath water, and the percussion giving a *giocoso* effect.

When the sopranos return in A major a cross-rhythm descending scale of sixths is heard, dividing the beats into two against the waltz rhythm.

When the altos return in A major at figure 8 the speed has become *più lento*, and arpeggio triplet sixths are heard against a new descending scalic bass in dotted crotchets. And the boy Nicolas follows with 'God be glorified' for the last time.

The final return to the waltz tune starts in the tonic key, *tempo primo*, with the original accompaniment. But the tune is taken up by the altos at figure 9 in the subdominant key, with the sopranos singing a descending scale of dotted crotchets above it. Four bars later they reach C major and sing in quavers, mostly in sixths, reaching E flat major and the climax in 3/4 time four bars later again.

Now the *man* Nicolas sings 'God be glorified' in E. Then the waltz rhythm returns as a short coda, *molto animato*, with the tune *d r m fe* rising every half bar instead of every bar, and ending with a precipitate run down the scale.

The little tune is haunting in its simplicity and is eminently suited to the voices of small boys, while the accompaniment consists of a series of variations on the chord scheme in tonic and dominant keys alternately, ending with the subdominant key; and every repetition ends with 'God be glorified' on E.

III Nicolas devotes himself to God

There is a great contrast between the simplicity of the children's singing in the previous number and this difficult and discordant recitative and aria for the tenor soloist sung by Nicolas, as he describes his journey from riches and dissatisfaction into the harbour of humility and acceptance of God.

The first part is a recitative sung against slow-moving discordant string chords, moving outwards by semitones until they reach a *ppp* discord at bar 7 which is held for six bars making a gradual *crescendo*. As the soloist sings 'defying God' the accompaniment reaches *ff* and then descends in a series of first inversions into the aria at *andante molto lento*.

The string accompaniment to this consists of slurred pairs of despairing quavers, with much semitonal movement. The soloist starts a haunting phrase 'heartsick' on high F. After describing how he sold his lands he reaches 'heartsick' again, but this time a tone higher, starting on G. He thrust away all distractions but again reaches 'heartsick', this time starting on A flat. Now he begs for humility, and the semitonal heartsearchings end on a quiet minor concord. Strings alone have accompanied this number throughout, a contrast to the orchestration of the numbers on either side of it.

IV He journeys to Palestine

This tells the story of Nicolas's journey to Palestine and of the storm at sea. It gives an opportunity for the older boys to tell the story, tenors and basses singing separately or in combination, usually in unison; and for the older girls, singing as a semichorus in the gallery, to describe the storm.

The tenors and basses start in unison in lilting 12/8 time against the sound of the waves in piano and percussion and a low, deep tonic pedal on F. They sing a simple tune in F minor, which starts by rising by step and makes use of a falling sequence in its second phrase. This sentence could be called **A**.

The next sentence, **B**, changes to C minor, with another low pedal chord of C, and the melody starts by falling instead of rising, though the sequence now rises instead of falls.

The next sentence, 'The sailors jeered at Nicolas', returns to the first sentence, **A**, in the tonic key. But the sequence now rises at 'Up he stood and stopped their game'.

Then the tenors sing a modified version of **A** in F minor, but with a high, *tremolo pp* accompaniment, as Nicolas prophesies a storm. There is an enharmonic change at ' "Nonsense" they all said', but this leads to a return of the low pedal in F minor. Now the basses sing the **B** version of the tune in F minor, descending till it ends on low F, as the captain goes below to sleep.

Tenors and basses return to the opening theme, **A**, in its original form and key at 'Nicolas swore he'd punish them', and the strings are now added. The theme rises over a pedal G at 'waterspouts rose in majesty', and this sentence ends with the voices in harmony at 'and all aboard cried "lost" '. They end on a high 6/4 chord on F sharp and their voices portamento downwards at 'lost'.

Now the semichorus of girls in the gallery dramatically describe the lightning in *staccato* semitonal movement, singing in consecutive thirds at 'ah!'.

A *presto* starts at figure 15 with high, *staccato* notes in percussion and piano as the tenors and basses sing antiphonally 'Spare us, man the pumps'.

The altos in the gallery continue with semitonal movements describing the tempest, ending with antiphonal 'ah's. The tenors and basses again sing antiphonally at figure 17, followed by the gallery choir continuing to describe the tempest. They end on a discordant 'ah', which sounds much harder to sing than it is. The sopranos sing an arpeggio of a minor ninth while the altos sing a whole-tone scale!

At figure 19 tenors and basses sing antiphonally against glissandos in the pianos. The gallery choir answers again with semitonal movement. The sailors sing 'Pray to God' at figure 21 over a drum roll, followed by the gallery choir also in harmony over string arpeggios.

Figure 22 brings a return to *tempo prima*, now in E; the tune is now in the strings while the tenors and basses sing in quiet chords.

Then Nicolas prays in recitative over a drum roll and the tenors and basses add 'Amen' at figure 23. Finally he describes the ensuing calm using first **A** and then **B** over a high tonic pedal in F major, with limpid, slow, *staccatissimo* arpeggios in the piano.

V Nicolas comes to Myra and is chosen Bishop

This number starts with the organ playing two short themes, which are much heard throughout. The treble has minims rising by step, a theme which is later heard to the word 'Amen', and then as the fugue subject. The bass has a crotchet theme which is later to become the counter-subject of the fugue.

The full S A T B choir then call on Nicolas in simple harmonies to become Bishop of Myra, the two motto themes occurring again in the organ at the end of each phrase.

Nicolas then takes up the 'Amen' theme, which immediately merges into a recitative, as he accepts his calling. He ends with coloratura to the words 'blessed church'.

Now the full chorus takes up the 'Amen' theme. They sing it twice and then the gallery choir describes the investiture of Nicolas as Bishop, sopranos and altos alternating. In between each phrase the full chorus sings 'Amen'.

At 'set the ring upon your hand' the sopranos and altos sing in imitation in contrary motion; and they end with coloratura imitations on the word 'wedlock'.

The full chorus sings 'Amen' twice more and then they start the fugue. The minim 'Amen' theme becomes the subject, to the words 'Serve the Faith', while the crotchet theme heard in the organ at the beginning becomes the counter-subject to the words 'and spurn his enemies'.

The keys of the entries are, however, not the tonic and dominant that one associates with Bach. It is made easy for the singers by having each voice part start on the last note of the previous entry, and the result is that the keys rise in fourths: A, D G, C.

This is followed by another set of entries, starting in D major, in which each voice part stands a third above the last note of the previous part. They are now no longer always *s l t d'*, but start on different parts of the scale. And all the time the counter-subject continues, so that every voice is singing either subject or counter-subject, which is again easy for young singers.

At length this reaches a climax at the bar before figure 28, when the orchestra plays an inversion of 'Amen', *ff*, while the singers give it a rest and confine themselves to the counter-subject.

Seven bars later the choir, singing the counter-subject, alternates with the orchestra playing the subject at a *ff* climax; and then they change over.

Figure 29 starts what could be considered as the final section of the fugue. The subject and counter-subject are again heard together, starting in A major as at the beginning of the fugue, but now the

289

subject is in stretto, the imitations occurring at two minim's distance. It reaches a climax on a *ff* IVb in D major.

Then Britten brings in everybody, including the congregation, to sing 'All people that on earth do dwell'. This device of audience participation has been used effectively by Britten on several occasions, notably in *The little Sweep* and *Noye's Fludde*.

But though the congregation sings in unison the harmonies played by the organ are not the usual hymn-book harmonies; and this causes frequent surprises.

At verse 2 the gallery choir enters with a kind of double descant over the tune.

Verse 3 reverts to the unison again, with pianos and organ playing the chords *ff*. In between each line the orchestra interjects a crotchet figure which has a resemblance to the counter-subject. It is used for the final 'Amen', when it is played in crotchets by the orchestra and sung in augmentation in semibreves by the choir. This produces a wonderful climax as an end to the first half of the work.

VI Nicolas from Prison

This is another solo for Nicolas, in which he tells of his years in prison. And again it starts with a recitative, but this time it is accompanied by restless, discordant arpeggios in piano and strings. A plaintive held B appears in the viola at the words 'and I lay bound', but the discordant arpeggios soon return, and the recitative ends with coloratura on the word 'loose' at 'wolves ran loose among my flock'.

The aria is very restless and discordant, the wolves appearing to run loose most of the time. It divides into three sections. In the first part the violin has a restless, almost continuous quaver obbligato above a staccato bass, while the voice sings passionately over it.

In the second part, starting at 'Yet Christ is yours', the obbligato quaver part is transferred to the piano and is played over a pedal D. At the word 'crucified' the strings interrupt harshly with *staccato* quavers, but the piano takes over again in the next bar.

In the third section, starting at 'Turn away from sin', the singer takes over the quavers that were played by the violin in the first part while a solo 'cello plays a slower-moving obbligato part. And it is the 'cello that brings the aria to an end.

VII Nicolas and the pickled Boys

Britten is very fond of using various kinds of pedals and ostinatos. This number is largely based on an ostinato of a repeated rising fourth. It is F sharp and B up to one bar before 39, B and E up to one bar before 41, E and A up to one bar before 43, and then it returns to the original F sharp and B until the words 'The mother's cry'. It ceases until 44 and then starts again on E and A. When the three small boys enter their 'alleluias' are based on a descending scale; and then, after the voices cease, the original F sharp and B are heard again in the orchestra as a coda. This is the chief architectural feature in the number, so it is advisable to look at it first.

The orchestra starts *alla marcia*, *pp*, in strings and timpani; then the choir enters, telling the story of the famine and of the marching, starving beggars: the sopranos and altos singing in consecutive thirds or sixths, and the tenors and basses singing an octave lower, a device which again makes things easy for young singers.

Then, after a harsh discord at 38, the sopranos in the gallery sing of the missing three boys in a *parlando* style in free rhythm over string *tremolos* and timpani. The full chorus returns at 39, still in thirds and sixths, as they continue the story; and again they are interrupted, this time by the altos in the gallery, still crying for the missing boys. And so it goes on, alternating in the same styles, the full choir singing at 41, the sopranos and altos in the gallery at 42, and the full choir again at 43.

But this is interrupted when Nicolas cries out 'O do not taste!', *più mosso ed agitato*. When he gets to 'The mother's cry' the ostinato ceases; and Nicolas calls for the three pickled boys to appear.

The S A T B choir returns at 44, in the same style over the ostinato, but *più lento*. They start *pp* and increase to a *f* 'alleluia'. The three small boys appear at *poco meno mosso*, and sing an 'alleluia' accompanied by the organ over a descending bass. This is taken up by the gallery choir at 46 and then by everyone, singing in unison at 47. The final ostinato is *ff* tutti.

VIII His Piety and marvellous Works

This number summarise the life of Nicolas, bishop for forty years, telling of some of his good works and of the legends which surround them. It is based on three contrasting ideas: (a) a gently swaying one-bar figure in strings and piano which usually has a falling seventh as a melody; (b) anthem-like passages in four-part unaccompanied vocal harmony which seem like a mixture of old and new, as they are full of modern discords; and (c) a stepwise descending melodic vocal phrase which is eventually treated in seven-part canon.

The swaying accompaniment (a) is heard for four bars followed by the unaccompanied choir (b) for twelve bars. Then four bars of (a) are heard, now in E major instead of G major as at first, and the unaccompanied choir (b) continues to tell the story, ending in B minor, in which key (a) appears again for four bars. Then the choir (b) appears again at 49, opening out into lovely harmonies at 'pleasant hills of grace', but ending discordantly at 'mortal sin'. The four bars of (a) appear again, over C in the bass.

At 50 the choir sings only three bars before (a) interrupts for two bars. It interrupts again five bars later; and then the choir returns to its opening figure, though it soon reaches a pedal on C and ends the first half of the number in G major, the tonic, two bars before 51.

The second half starts with (a), as did the first half, but now the figure is continuous, though with ever shifting harmonies, up to 59, when the unaccompanied choral theme (a) returns. Between 51 and 59 a new melodic vocal figure, (c), appears over (a). The semi-chorus are first heard by themselves, singing in unison with figures similar to (c), as they tell their story. But, (c) returns in its original form, and is then heard in canon in all seven parts, a bar's distance from each other.

Then, at 59, the anthem-like unaccompanied chorus returns, exactly repeating the eleven bars with which the first part ended. The swaying figure (*a*) is heard for four bars at the end.

IX The Death of Nicolas

The final number starts majestically, in full orchestra, with the gong sounding at the beginning of every phrase. The orchestra plays the plain-song 'Nunc dimittis' that the choir is to sing later, in block chords, with unrelated bass notes underneath it; and it continues in the same style, becoming ever more discordant until Nicolas enters. He welcomes death, singing in an ecstatic style, with many broadly-flowing quavers over string *tremolos*.

At 61 the chorus enters singing 'Nunc dimittis' in unison plain-song over *pp* piano arpeggios which slide about from chord to chord with many semitonal changes. Over all this Nicolas continues to sing in the same style. The choir and the orchestra continue after he finishes until one bar after 63, when the choir finishes with a *ff* 'Amen' and the orchestra returns to the majestic style of the opening.

Gradually it quietens down to *pp*, ending with a pause; and the organ, heard softly by itself, plays the opening four notes of the hymn 'God moves in a mysterious way', twice. This is the signal for the congregation to start singing the hymn. Everyone sings the first verse in unison, softly. The congregation continues in unison with the second verse, while the tenors and basses of the choir sing a firm, crotchet counter-melody against it. But all sing in unison again for the last verse, now *ff*, which ends with an *allargando* 'Amen'.

ANALYSES OF MUSICAL CLASSICS

52 Britten

Noye's Fludde

Britten set this Chester miracle play to music in 1957; and it had its first performance in Orford Parish Church at the Aldeburgh Festival in June 1958.

Like his cantata *St Nicolas* written for Lancing College in 1948 and *Let's Make an Opera*, containing *The Little Sweep*, written for the Aldeburgh Festival in 1949, this work can be performed largely by children. All three works require a little professional stiffening, and all bring in the audience or congregation as an integral part of the performance. But they offer great scope for children of all ages to make an essential contribution. *Noye's Fludde* is a most moving and powerful work, making remarkable uses of the limited material available; and the best way for students to study it is to take part in a performance themselves.

The voice of God requires a mature, commanding personality; Noye's part is written for a bass–baritone and Mrs Noye for a contralto. These parts really require professionals; but the parts of Noye's sons and their wives can well be taken by older children, as also the gossip's parts, though they are quite difficult. The parts of the animals and birds can be taken by children of all ages, including the very young, and there can be as many as the producer wishes. This work therefore lends itself to a performance given by several schools, combining children of both sexes and all ages in a corporate effort.

Similarly there is great scope in the orchestral accompaniment. Some professional stiffening in the form of a string quintet is advisable. But the orchestra makes provision for string players of all stages of ability. Some schools will have pianists, an organist and a timpanist good enough to play these parts though the timpani part, in particular, is difficult. Recorders, bugles and hand bells are frequently found in schools; and many children will enjoy playing the other percussion parts under the guidance of a good teacher.

Noye's Fludde was first performed in a church, and lends itself very well to this. But imaginative settings in all kinds of buildings, such as school halls, are possible; and again there is much scope for the producer.

Introductory Scene

The work starts with a majestic introduction based on the hymn soon to be sung by the congregation. Perhaps its most noticeable colouring is caused by repeated drum rolls on E, B and F natural (the F natural sounding peculiarly menacing), the cymbal rolls at the end of each phrase, and the powerful short chords in piano and strings.

Then the congregation sings four verses of the solemn old hymn-tune 'Southwell' from *Damon's Psalter*. At first the harmonies are comparatively simple, with the three-note drum roll and the short piano chords still in evidence, but with the organ now added. Verse three introduces a discordant, syncopated rising bass, and verse four is a tutti, with violins playing an octave higher than the melody.

During the hymn Noye solemnly walks from the back to the front of the congregation (or audience) and on to the back of the stage.

Then, through the continued timpani rolls on the same three notes and the cymbal crashes, the voice of God (marked 'tremendous') is heard speaking in four-line verses, every fourth line in solemn crotchet rhythm. He says he will destroy all creatures on earth, because of their sin, except Noye and his family, and the creatures Noye is to bring into the ark God tells him to build.

At figure 5 Noye joins in, repeating the instructions in the same measured tones, over a timpani pedal on E, first in crotchets, then in quavers and finally in triplets. At 6 he starts to sing, instead of speak, as God's voice dies away and the strings enter again—but still over a pedal E. At 7 he calls his sons in recitative, telling them to start building the Ark.

Sem appears first, running in with an axe, to the accompaniment of *staccato* quaver chords played by the piano. The opening notes, *s l s d'*, form a figure which is repeatedly used in this section. When he starts to sing his part is doubled by the viola; and each singer in turn is doubled by an appropriate string instrument or recorder, thus supporting his or her voice, and making the part easier to sing. Sem sings a theme in A major, and ends with the figure *l s d' s l*, now in crotchets.

Then Ham appears with a hatchet, the pedal E is left at last and a moving *pizzicato* bass takes its place. He sings the same theme as Sem but a tone higher, in B major, and Sem joins in at the end with *l s d' s l* at the end, in canon after Ham.

When Jaffet comes in with a hammer he sings almost the same theme as the other two boys but in A flat major; and if his voice is 'broken' he sings an octave lower. At the end all three boys sing *l s d' s l* in canon.

Mrs Sem then comes in to a descending chromatic scale in double third quavers in the piano. She sings a new descending theme, starting in crotchets, which is very similar to the boys' theme, and which contains the same syncopation in the second bar. She is accompanied by a recorder, and sings in the key of B flat, with the boys' theme in the lower strings. The three boys make comments at the end of every phrase, either on a repeated F or with their usual *l s d' s l* figure.

As the activities become more exciting the other two wives run in and make appropriate comments. There are four independent voice parts in this section; but they are either in imitation with each other or just interjections of one or two notes, so they present no difficulties. Britten is very clever in writing voice parts which are free and modern and sound difficult and yet which are quite easy for youthful singers. Here there is a mixture of the boys' theme, the girls' theme and the refrain, which, at later stages, changes to *l s d' t d'*.

All this excitement is interrupted at 15 by the entrance of Mrs

Noye and her gossips. She is accompanied by a slow 'cello theme, and she starts by singing the boys' theme slower, in mock solemnity. The gossips laugh at this at 16, but are rebuked by Noye, who tells his wife in recitative to stop making such a noise. He ends with the usual *l s d' s l*, which is imitated quietly in the orchestra; and Mrs Noye and her gossips settle at the side of the stage, drinking and watching the building of the ark.

The building of the Ark

Most of this scene is accompanied by a string ostinato in dotted minims, which rise a fifth and are then repeated a tone lower. Noye announces he will begin to build and, as they work, his children make appropriate comments, based on the opening hymn, at the end of every stanza he sings. At 19 more percussive effects are heard, and at 20 the recorders enter with another, higher quaver ostinato, combining with the one in the bass. Semiquavers are introduced at 21 and the children begin to imitate Noye at the end of every phrase.

Figure 23 is marked 'lively'; and the dotted minim ostinato now changes to heavy quavers starting with rising fourths, with another crotchet ostinato above it, rising in sevenths. All these ostinatos give the effect of continuous work, getting more energetic as it continues. The singers are in unison in this section; but at 25, when the music reaches a climax as the children sing 'At the cominge of the fludde', they start to sing in three parts, which are discordant but are again easy to sing. At 26 we hear the first splashes of rain.

The Entrance to the Ark

Now a wrangle takes place between Mrs Noye and her husband. Against a slowly rising bass Noye tells his wife to enter the ark but she refuses to do so. She swears 'by Christ', the kind of anachronism that is often heard in medieval plays, and husband and wife interrupt each other on *l s d'*. At the end of the quarrel, five bars before 30, we hear the original ostinato of E B F natural on the timpani and the cymbal crashes again, and then God's voice is heard speaking in

297

the same measured way as before, with the fourth line in regular crotchet rhythm. He tells Noye to take a male and female of every kind of beast and fowl into the ark.

A tramping march rhythm starts as Noye calls the animals; and the first waves appear. A bugle call is heard from the back of the church at 32, and gradually the animals march through the congregation into the ark. The children comment on each group as they appear, and the animals sing 'Kyrie Eleison' at a pitch appropriate to their kind, sounding louder as they approach the ark. The steady crotchet tramp continues, and each new group of animals is heralded by a bugle call. This is contrasted with a flowing violin melody which accompanies the voices of the children. Percussion is gradually added too. Soon after 43 the children are singing in three parts in canon; and by 45 there is an orchestral tutti, with bugles, strings and percussion playing the last of the animals into the ark. They sing 'Kyrie Eleison' in three octaves, followed by a final *ff* bugle call.

At 48 Noye and the children go into the ark, singing a rising 'Kyrie Eleison' in a gradual *diminuendo*, and ending in quite an elaborate coloratura.

But still Noye's wife refuses to leave her gossips, singing 'I will not out of this towne'. Noye calls her and Sem pleads with her but Mrs Noye just laughs and sings that the gossips shall not drown.

At 56 the gossips sing in *staccato* style of the rising flood in a 'slow and lumpy' 6/8 time, with a heaving bass in strings and piano. Noye again calls his wife but she and her gossips continue to sing and drink. Her sons come down from the ark in an attempt to get her in; but the gossips continue, often making use of scraps of canon or imitation, until they end on a drunken *portamento* just before 62.

Then the three sons passionately urge her in, singing either in unison or in chords of the first inversion. Finally the boys carry her into the ark, just in time; and the gossips run away screaming. Mrs Noye shouts to Noye to get him a new wife and boxes his ears. But all are safely in.

The Storm

The storm is built over an ostinato that is heard no fewer than twenty-nine times, but with very varied treatments. The first hymn and also the hymn 'Eternal Father' are combined with it. It consists of a one-bar figure ending on G, repeated a note higher on each of the next two bars though it still returns to G, with the fourth bar reaching a climax before falling back to the beginning. Each G has a timpani roll. Its continuity, and the way it rises to a climax, most effectively convey the rising storm.

At its first appearance, at 67, it is in unison in the strings; at 68 Noye sings that the boat is moving; at 69 mugs and piano give the impression of rain; at 70 the Noye family sing a rhythmic variant of the first hymn in unison over the ostinato, while the piano plays repeated quaver chords; at 71 the piano and percussion give the impression of more rain, and at 72 the recorders, playing quaver scales, give the effect of wind, while Noye sings that he will shut the window of the ark.

From 73 to 82 (the seventh to the fifteenth repetitions) the orchestra has the field to itself, and it is surprising how many varied sound effects can be got with the limited orchestral material available. At 73 the added percussion give the impression of thunder and lightning; at 74 recorder trills sound like the wind; at 75 string triplet arpeggios (starting with open strings that even beginners can play) give the impression of waves; at 76 recorders, playing in high, bare consecutive fifths, give yet another impression of wind; at 77 *staccato* strings and percussion, including the whip, portray the flapping rigging; at 78 a powerful tutti, with the piano and cymbals much in evidence, indicates great waves; quaver violin scales at 79 indicate the rocking of the ship; while 80 and 81, with their slowly rising scale in the treble and the use of the wind machine, express the panic of the animals.

Then, at 82, the Noye family begin to sing the hymn 'Eternal Father' in unison, to the tune 'Melita' by Dykes. The first verse coincides with repetitions 16–18 of the ostinato. The congregation join in with the second verse at 85, while the ostinato is played from the nineteenth to the twenty-first time; and frequent use of cymbals make it obvious that this is the climax.

There are two temporary cessations from the use of the ostinato. The first one occurs at 86, when the third verse of the hymn is sung. This reverts to Dykes's original harmonies, played by the organ, with the congregation singing in unison and with a descant sung by the trebles in the cast.

But the ostinato returns at 87. The storm slowly subsides and the creatures in the ark go to sleep. Repetitions 22–7 quieten down, while fragments of 'Eternal Father' on muted strings glide in and out of the texture, combined with hints of previously-heard effects.

Repetition 28, which starts four bars after figure 92, allows the one-bar figure to fall instead of rise; and at 93 the ostinato ceases for five bars while mugs play quiet scales over a descending bass. One bar after 94 the ostinato starts for the twenty-ninth and last time (during the storm), now in augmentation, as Noye looks out of the window of the ark.

After the Storm

Noye sings that forty days are gone and he sends out a raven. But we have not heard the last of the ostinato, even though the storm is over. Noye sings it himself at 95, against a slowly rising bass; but now the timpani are silent, and the figure falls instead of rises.

The raven is indicated by a 'cello obbligato. It starts hesitantly at 96, but at 97 begins to 'flutter this way and that', accompanied by the piano. First it has four bars of fluttering (with rests in between) followed by two bars of flying (continuous quavers). Then, six bars after 97, this is repeated a semitone lower. The next repetition starts a tone higher and consists of two bars of fluttering and three of flying. Then it occurs a major third higher, with two bars of fluttering and four of flying; then two bars of fluttering a tone

BRITTEN · NOYE'S FLUDDE

higher, followed by a pause. This brings us to 98, when the raven flies off. The 'cello now plays a waltz-like tune, gradually rising by semitones.

At 99 the ostinato reappears, now played by the viola, but again falling rather than rising, indicating the continued subsiding of the waters, and again without the timpani. As Noye quietly soliloquises over it the fluttering voice of the dove is heard on a solo recorder. So Noye decides to send it out, too.

A 'graceful waltz' starts at 101 with arpeggiando chords on the piano and the solo recorder fluttering in between. First we have I V I in A flat major, repeated in sequence in B flat major and C major, a tone higher each time. This is followed by V I in D minor (a shortened rising sequence) and then by single chords rising a semitone, on E flat and E. A dominant seventh on D, ending with a pause, leads to 102.

Now the dove, too, begins to fly, indicated by continuous recorder quavers over alternating chords of D and C for ten bars. Then, as it gradually rises, there are two bars on E, one on F, one on F sharp, and one bar rising from G to A, ending on B flat, as the dove flies away.

At 103 the ostinato reappears, now in the violin. The one-bar figure is still falling but the G at the end of each bar now rises instead of falls; and Noye again soliloquises over it.

At 104 the fluttering of the dove is heard again, as it returns with an olive branch in its beak; and again the quaver dance is heard, with the piano accompaniment now falling instead of rising, as the dove descends. A triangle adds colour. The dove hesitates, looking for the ark, and we hear the semitonal chordal movement at 105 that was heard at 102.

As it alights at 106 the ostinato reappears, now played strongly by all the strings, with timpani again playing the G. The third note of the figure powerfully rises a fourth instead of a second in each bar, and the ostinato reaches a *ff* climax over a pedal F, five bars after 106. Throughout this section Noye is singing his thanks. Nine bars after 106 the ostinato figure is heard for the last time, the first bar being played three times starting on D with the bass falling E, D, C.

The C starts a *pp* pedal, over which God's voice is heard telling them to leave the ark.

They leave the Ark

The pedal C continues until two bars after 109, but over it the bugle calls are heard in B flat, at first softly but gradually gaining in power; and as the animals leave the ark they sing an alleluia in B flat which also gains in strength, as more and more appear. By 109 they are singing in canon; and two bars later Noye and his family join in, at first with chordal hymn-like phrases, but by 110 joining in the alleluias with the animals, accompanied *ff* by full orchestra. It is heard in augmentation six bars after 110, and further augmentation two bars later again.

Then, to the accompaniment of quietly clanging handbells, God's voice is heard promising that there shall not be another flood; and, in token of his promise, a rainbow appears in the sky. The bells ring out in chimes, at first at the end of each stanza, then at two bar's distance, until they finally become continuous. They play by themselves from 112 to 113, after God's voice has ceased.

Final Thanksgiving

The final thanksgiving is based on *Tallis's Canon* which, by its very nature, is able to build up to a wonderful climax. It starts quietly, with Noye's children singing in unison in key G over a pedal D, accompanied by strings and an occasional clang of bells. As they reach the end of the first verse the bells ring out, the sun appears, and the pedal slips down to C and then B.

Over this B Noye and his family sing the second verse, still in unison in key G, and still with occasional clangs of bells. At the end of this verse the pedal slips down to A, the bugles enter and the moon appears.

The third verse is sung by all the animals in unison in F major with the recorders now added to the texture, and the bass slowly moving from G to A and back. At the end the bugles are heard again and the stars appear. The bass moves down from G to F.

Then the animals and the children sing the fourth verse in two-part canon in key F. At the end the full organ enters, which is the signal for the congregation to stand.

The fifth verse returns to G major and is sung very slowly, with the cast singing the four-part hymn-tune version (which means that it is in canon but everyone is singing the same words at the same time). Noye leads the congregation in singing the tune. Bugles and bells sound out at the end.

The final verse is sung in eight-part canon, accompanied by full orchestra, with bugles, bells and percussion. Noye starts with the congregation, and the other seven parts enter at one bar's distance, each group being led by one of the children or Mrs Noye. As they sing they walk slowly out in procession, and each group finishes singing as it gets to the end of the verse, so the effect is of a gradual and awe-inspiring *diminuendo*.

Mrs Noye and her group sing the last 'Amen', and Noye is left standing alone, whilst the bells softly chime. God's voice is heard for the last time, against the sound of bells. As Noye moves down the aisle the bells ring softly, then the strings are added, then recorders. The music broadens to its end, the bugles are added, then the cymbals, leading to a *ff* climax, after which the final chord of G major is heard three times. The soft, discordant bells answer the first two chords, but the last chord is left to die away in a long concordance.

53 Britten

Psalm 150

This work was written in 1962 for the centenary celebrations of Britten's own preparatory school in Lowestoft. The work is for two treble voice parts and an orchestra. The latter can consist of any available collection of treble instruments, bass instruments, percussion and keyboards. But many students or schools will probably buy the recording of the boys of Downside school, conducted by Britten himself. In this they will recognise the sound of violins and 'cellos, recorders and trumpet, timpani (a very efficient player) cymbals, tambourine, castanets, triangle and piano. A school ambitious enough to attempt a performance of it should hire the full score and make use of whatever instruments are available, Britten being very tolerant in this respect. But the work should certainly never be performed with the piano alone. When instruments are referred to in what follows they are those which are heard on the record.

The work begins and ends with a lively march in C major, and has a trio section in the middle in F major. But the phrasing is very irregular throughout, even in the march section, which is in 2/4 time. The tune in the first part of the orchestral introduction is played by the recorders, and its phrases are 5+7+2+2+8 bars long. They are accompanied by the other instruments with the percussion much to the fore, the timpani separating each of the phrases by a solo bar and having four bars to itself after the eight-bar phrase (29–32).

The next part of the introduction (33–56) starts with a low five-bar phrase in 'cello, piano and timpani, answered by a four-bar phrase in recorders and triangle. These two phrases are repeated at 42–50, and are followed by a six-bar phrase based on 33–7.

A codetta to the introduction (57–67), based on an upper dominant pedal in the recorders, and using the rhythm of bar 1 leads to the entry of the voices at 68.

Bars 68–86 are an exact repetition of 1–19 with the voices added. They begin on a unison C; and the first trebles move between this note and the third above, while the second trebles move between the A below the C and the D above it. They move in tones and semi-tones and at times are very discordant with each other; but each part is easy to sing in itself. Bars 87–9 end this part with another timpani roll.

Bars 90–107 are similar to the second part of the introduction, 33–57, with the two treble voice parts having a phrase in turn, and being doubled by the orchestra.

Bars 108–31 are similar to 57–67 in that they form a codetta, and that the rhythm from bar 1 continues, though it is not always shown in the vocal score. But the music is built over a tonic pedal in the bass instead of under an upper dominant pedal. At first the verses alternate, but they come together for the climax; and the section ends with five bars of timpani roll.

The middle section begins at 132 in 7/8 time. The piano starts alone with a chordal bass which is used continuously up to 159; but interjections occur at 134 by the trumpet after it is mentioned; at 136 by *pizzicato* open strings on the violin, after the lute and harp are mentioned; and at 140 by recorders after strings and pipe are mentioned. The singers are in unison; and bars 142–50 repeat 133–41 with the same words and orchestration but with variations in the tune.

Bars 151–9 continue with the same idea but with a variation in the order of the instruments. Then, at 160, the music begins to build up to a climax as the singers mention cymbals and divide into three parts, with cymbal crashes at 161 and again at 163, after the singers have *shouted* the word 'cymbals'.

The next part starts *ppp* as the singers sing 'Praise Him' in unison. At 168 the tempo changes to slow (getting faster) and the time to 6/4, at the words 'Let everything that hath breath', until the music reaches a lively 6/8 at 172, and percussion and recorders are gradually added to the texture. The climax is reached at 184 with a five-bar canon, which is repeated *ad lib* until the last time when the voices reach a four-part discord at 193. Two further tutti discords in the orchestra lead to a return to the first section.

Bars 199–218 correspond to 68–87. Bar 219 starts a coda which, though continuing with the same idea, builds up to a climax until the final *ff* 'Amen' is reached at 230–1.